Tender Care and

Early Learning

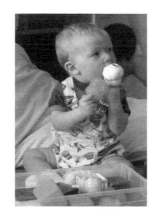

Tender Care and Early Learning

Supporting Infants and Toddlers in Child Care Settings

Jacalyn Post and Mary Hohmann

HIGH/SCOPE® PRESS

Ypsilanti, Michigan

Published by

High/Scope® Press

A division of the High/Scope® Educational Research Foundation
600 North River Street
Ypsilanti, Michigan 48198-2898
(313) 485-2000, FAX (313) 485-0704
press@highscope.org, www.highscope.org

High/Scope Press Editor: Marge Senninger

Cover design, text design, and production: Judy Seling of Seling Design

Photos: Gregory Fox Photography, Ann Arbor, MI, with the following exceptions—
Photos on pp. 107, 115, 125 (top), 129 (bottom), 130, 142 (top left), 146 (top), 147 used with permission from Torelli/Durrett, Inc. & Spaces for Children. (These include Infant/Toddler Furniture by Torelli/Durrett, Inc., (800) 895-3121, and Childcare Facility Design by SPACES FOR CHILDREN, Berkeley, CA, Louis Torelli, M.S. Ed., Charles Durrett, Architect, 1250 Addison St., Suite 113, Berkeley, CA 94702.)
Photos on pp. 28, 48, 61, 72, 79, 85, 95, 111 (both), 120, 124, 137 (top), 140, 142 (top right, middle), 152, 156, 162 (top), 165, 242 (left), 247, 248, 256, 265 (top), 267, and 275 by Jacalyn Post.
Photos on pp. 2, 24, 76, 134 (top left, middle right), 221, 238, 326, 343 from the High/Scope Home Visit Project.
Photos on pp. 32, 58 by Gary Easter.
Photos on pp. 116, 149 (top), 244, 246 by Beth Marshall.
Photos on pp. 134 (top right, bottom left), 159 (bottom), 203, 271, 294 by Rachael Underwood.
Photos on pp. 293, 355 by Shannon Lockhart.
Photo on p. 188 by Bonnie Czekanski.

Quotations on pp. 21, 63, 118, 145, 148, 161, 223, 226 from *People Under Three: Young Children in Day Care* by Elinor Goldschmied and Sonia Jackson (London: Routledge, 1994) are reprinted by permission of the publisher.

Library of Congress Cataloging-in-Publication Data
Post, Jackie, 1951-
    Tender care and early learning : supporting infants and toddlers in child care settings / Jackie Post and Mary Hohmann.
      p. cm.
    Includes bibliographical references and index.
    ISBN 1-57379-090-7
    1. Day care centers--Handbooks, manuals, etc. 2. Infants--Care--Handbooks, manuals, etc. 3. Toddlers--Care--Handbooks, manuals, etc. 4. Early childhood education--Handbooks, manuals, etc. 5. Child development. I. Hohmann, Mary. II. Title.

HQ778.5 .P67 2000
362.71'2--dc21

                                   99-057942

Printed in the United States of America

10 9 8 7 6 5 4 3

To our very youngest

children and their parents,

families, and caregivers

Contents

Acknowledgments

We appreciate all the dedicated early childhood professionals who responded to our initial questionnaire, invited us to their sites, allowed us to take photographs, or shared their ideas with us during training:

Kay Albrecht, HeartsHome Early Learning Centers, Inc., Houston, Texas
Cathy Albro, The Creative Learning Center, Grand Rapids, Michigan
Beth Apley, Ravenswood Hospital Child Care Center, Chicago, Illinois
Donna Barrett, The Boys and Girls Club Day Care Center, Yarmouth, Nova Scotia
Frances Beck, Debbie School, Miami, Florida
Ann Brown and Therese Armstead, Kalamazoo Learning Village, Kalamazoo, Michigan
Jill Claridge, Child Study Center, Fort Worth, Texas
Cyndi Conard, Educational Service Unit 3, Omaha, Nebraska
Sophie Cordoba and Irene Desverguna, Easter Seal Society, Miami, Florida
Nanette Elrod, Corner Cottage Child Care Center, Ann Arbor, Michigan
Debra Dennisuk, Webster School Detroit Even Start Program, Detroit, Michigan
Daniel DeVito, ARC, Miami, Florida
Carole Fox Abbott, FDLRS/South, Miami, Florida
Pepper Goodrich, Parents and Toddlers Program of the Cherry Creek School System,
  Aurora, Colorado
Marian Houk, ACCA Child Development Center, Annandale, Virginia
George Kelley, Peabody Child and Family Center of Georgia College, Milledgeville, Georgia
Carrie Keys and June Spriggs, COPE North, Miami, Florida
David Langley, First Step Day Care, Ann Arbor, Michigan
Betty Lisowski, Point Park Children's School, Pittsburgh, Pennsylvania
Char Longino and Patricia Travis, Washtenaw Community College Children's Center,
  Ann Arbor, Michigan
Constance Melville, Oberlin Child Development Center, Oberlin, Ohio
Ann Murphy, Kennebec Valley Community Action Program, The Madison Baby Bulldog Center,
  Waterville, Maine
Jenny Orth, South Madison Day Care Child Development, Inc., Madison, Wisconsin
Angela Passador, St. Clair College Child Care Center, Windsor, Ontario
Linda Peavy, Belleville Playland, Belleville, Florida
Mary Pettygrue, private child care home, Inkster, Michigan
Kathy Spitzley, Good Times Family Day Care Center, Holland, Michigan
Terri Strong, Creative Learning Preschool and Child Care Center, Madison, Wisconsin
Maryann Swann, Maryland School for the Deaf, Columbia, Maryland
Joy Vickers, Project TIPP #2, Miami, Florida
Thanks to you, your staff, your children, and their parents!

We also appreciate the ongoing support and feedback we received from our early childhood colleagues at High/Scope and in the field: Lorna Aaronson, Cathy Calamari, Bonnie Czekanski, Linda Dubay, Ann Epstein, Betsy Evans, Michelle Graves, Philip Hawkins, Julie Hoelscher, Charles Hohmann, Shannon Lockhart, Beth Marshall, Jeanne Montie, Polly Neill, Pat Olmsted, Larry Schweinhart, Rosemary Waldron, Sue Terdan, Rachael Underwood, David Weikart, Julie Wigton, Connie Williams, and Diane Williams. Thanks to you all!

Finally, we thank the High/Scope editorial staff—Lynn Taylor, Marge Senninger, Nancy Brickman, Holly Barton, and Pattie McDonald—for carefully reviewing, editing, and preparing the manuscript of Tender Care and Early Learning *for publication.*

Tender Care and
Early Learning

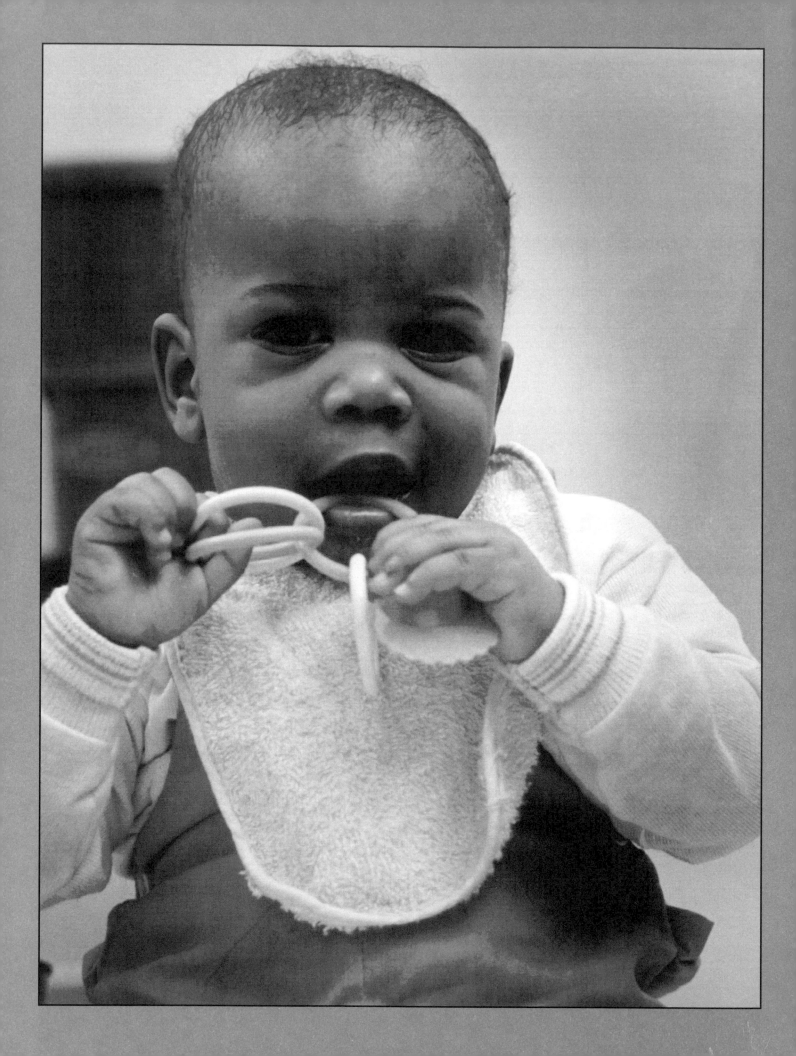

Introduction: The High/Scope Approach to Caring for Infants and Toddlers in Group Settings

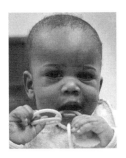

In the High/Scope approach, children construct their understanding of the world from their active involvement with people, materials, and ideas. This principle is based on the constructivist theories of development of Jean Piaget and other developmental psychologists. It suggests that all children—whether they are infants, preschoolers, or second-graders; children with . . . learning disabilities, or above-average intelligence— are active learners. They acquire knowledge by actively experiencing the world around them—choosing, exploring, manipulating, practicing, transforming, experimenting. The range and depth of children's understanding of the world is continually changing and expanding as a result of their day-to-day transactions . . .

—Amy Powell (1991)

round the nation, early childhood professionals using the High/
Scope approach with 3- and 4-year-olds have asked, "How does the
High/Scope approach work for very young children? What does it
mean to 'support active learning' for infants and toddlers?" Searching for and
finding answers to these questions resulted in the writing of this book. *Tender
Care and Early Learning: Supporting Infants and Toddlers in Child Care Settings* represents what we know to date about implementing the High/Scope
educational approach with infants and toddlers (children up to about age 3)
in group-care settings. This knowledge is based on child development theory
and research, the experiences and data collected over the years by High/
Scope home visitors, and the current practices of High/Scope practitioners
who are effectively nurturing and educating infants and toddlers in centers
and family child care homes.

History of the High/Scope Infant and Toddler Approach

High/Scope has a long history of curriculum development, training, and research in the area of infant and toddler development, especially as it relates to
parenting in the early years and community support for families. Members of
the High/Scope infant division, acting under the direction of Dolores Lambie
and David Weikart, began their work in parent-infant education with the
1968–1971 **Ypsilanti-Carnegie Infant Education Project** (Lambie, Bond, and
Weikart, 1974; Epstein and Weikart, 1979). Funded by Carnegie Corporation of
New York, this project trained professional staff to work as home visitors with
mothers of infants between 3 months and 11 months old. The home visitor
would meet with a mother and her infant in their home once each week for
16 weeks to play infant-centered games and to discuss child development.
The parent-visitor discussions focused specifically on what the infant was
doing and communicating during and between visits. Lambie and her
colleagues described the home visitor and parent as working together in a
give-and-take manner, "as equals in determining the goals and practices of
effective child rearing. Expert knowledge . . . [helped home visitors to] be responsive to and supportive of the individual needs of parents and children"
(p. 20). Lambie and colleagues went on to say "A mother's particular realization of the teaching role, although facilitated by home teaching, is directed by
her *own* needs and interests. Ultimately, the mother is the decision-maker, the
teacher of her child" (p. 26). Research findings from this project revealed that
as a result of these visits, mothers who participated in the home visits showed
more verbal interaction with their infants than did mothers in the project's
randomly assigned contrast and control groups; the mothers' increased verbal
interaction in turn facilitated their children's cognitive development (Lambie,
Bond, and Weikart, 1974, p. 122).

Following the Infant Education Project, Carnegie funded the **High/Scope Infant Videotaping Project** (1971–1973), which resulted in 270 hours of video footage of home visitors, parents, and infants engaging in informal interactions. High/Scope staff used this footage to produce videotapes on home visitor training, child development, and strategies for supporting early learning. These videotapes, and the processes they documented, became the basis for High/Scope's entry into the early phases of training and dissemination in the parent-infant arena.

By 1974, High/Scope staff had developed the core of what was called the Parent-to-Parent Model (Reschly, 1979). Between 1975 and 1978, with funds from Lilly Endowment Incorporated and the National Institute for Mental Health, they implemented the **Parent-to-Parent Home Visit Project**. Four women who had participated as parents in one of the earlier High/Scope home visit projects became home visitors themselves. This shift from using professionals to using paraprofessionals as the vehicle for service delivery reflected a then-current trend in the family-service sector. Researchers and practitioners had begun to recognize that members of the community, with some training and with supervision by trained professionals, could establish rapport with families and effectively share child development information with parents. The evolution of four program recipients into program providers enabled the process that began with the Infant Education Project to grow within the community, creating a framework for community service by and for the parents. The four parents who had become paraprofessionals were peers, not outside experts, sharing child development information with parents. By focusing on how to best support children's development, both the peer home visitors and the parents grew in their understanding of how children learn. (See "Home Teaching With Mothers and Infants: Research Results" on p. 6.)

High/Scope's fourth project relating to parents and infants, the **Adolescent Parents and Infants Project**, began in 1977 with funding from the Administration for Children, Youth and Families. High/Scope research staff interviewed 98 teenagers from diverse socioeconomic backgrounds twice—once during pregnancy and once 6 months after giving birth. They also videotaped these young parents interacting with their infants. The project's goals, as stated in one report (Epstein, 1980a, p. 1), were to answer these questions: "(1) How much do teenagers know, and need to know, about infant development? (2) What are teenagers' expectations and attitudes regarding the role of parenthood? (3) What support systems within the family do teenagers have for coping with pregnancy and parenthood? (4) What support systems outside the family do teenagers have for coping with pregnancy and parenthood? (5) How do these four factors . . . influence teenagers' actual parenting ability in interactions with their babies?" The research documented that adolescent parents' expectations for their infants' development were "too little, too late" and emphasized the need for programs to help young parents become better observers and supporters of their babies' growth. Moreover, family and com-

Home Teaching With Mothers and Infants: Research Results

In a 1979 report of the findings of the Ypsilanti-Carnegie Infant Education Project, "Parent-Child Interaction and Children's Learning," Ann Epstein and Judith Evans relate dimensions of mother-child interaction to children's cognitive and linguistic abilities:

1. "At age two, and again at age seven, ways in which mothers and children interact during the observed teaching activities are significantly related to measures of children's learning. A positive interaction style . . . predicts high performance by children on learning measures . . .

2. "Mother-child interaction styles at age two significantly predict children's academic success five years later. Specifically, when mothers and two-year-olds are observed to have positive verbal interactions, children perform well on school measures five years later. Conversely, negative verbal interactions at age two are associated with poor academic performance at age seven.

3. "Mother-child interaction styles at age two are only somewhat predictive of interaction styles at age seven. Children's linguistic development at age two, however, is highly predictive of their academic success five years later.

4. "At both ages, two and seven, interaction style is a more crucial correlate of children's learning abilities than is socioeconomic status." (p. 41)

munity support was vital to allow the young mother to continue her own development so that she in turn could facilitate the development of her child. (For further details on the research results, see "The Adolescent Parents and Infants Project," p. 7.)

The fifth and largest initiative, the **Parent-to-Parent Dissemination Project** (*Community Self Help*, n.d.), was supported by a grant from the Bernard van Leer Foundation and ran from 1978 to 1984. Members of High/Scope's family programs division, working under the direction of Judith Evans, trained people in seven diverse communities across the United States to set up their own local parent-to-parent programs. By 1981 three communities had each developed a Regional Parent-to-Parent Training and Dissemination Center. Staff at these centers provided parent-to-parent training for their regions, helped other communities start parent-to-parent programs, and acted as community resources for other programs serving families and infants. "This is the first time in my life I've ever been treated like a person and not like a case," a parent receiving home visits reported (*Community Self-Help*, p. 30). A case-study follow-up of participants in the Parent-to-Parent Dissemination Project at four of the project sites was conducted in 1997–99.

The original project and this follow-up are the subjects of a qualitative research report scheduled to be published in the year 2000 by High/Scope Press: *Supporting Families With Young Children: The High/Scope Parent-to-Parent Dissemination Project* (Epstein, Montie, Schweinhart, and Weikart, in press).

A sixth parent-infant project occurred during the 1980s, when High/Scope received funding to evaluate the Ford Foundation's multisite **Child Survival/Fair Start Project**. This project worked with low-income parents and their infants in diverse agency settings and communities around the United States (Larner, Halpern, and Harkavy, 1992). In addition to funding High/Scope's evaluation of its project, the Ford Foundation provided funding that enabled High/Scope to consolidate the lessons learned in the Parent-to-Parent Dissemination Project and Child Survival/Fair Start. This subsequent multisite analysis resulted in publication of *A Guide to Developing Community-Based*

Family Support Programs (Epstein, Larner, and Halpern, 1995), which contains guidelines for all the steps of designing, implementing, and evaluating comprehensive child development programs for families with very young children. As Epstein and her colleagues pointed out in this guide, partnerships with parents are vital: "The sustained personal relationship that develops between the family worker and the family is the key to achieving the objectives of home visiting programs" (p. 76).

The collective experiences of working with infants, parents, and community support agencies and the knowledge of child development gained through these several parent-infant projects also culminated in three High/Scope curriculum-focused publications: *Supporting the Changing Family: A Guide to the Parent-to-Parent Model* (1979) by Barbara Reschly, *Good Beginnings: Parenting in the Early Years* (1982) by Judith Evans and Ellen Ilfeld, and *Activities for Parent-Child Interaction, Supplement to Good Beginnings* (1982). These publications in turn have shaped and influenced this book, *Tender Care and Early Learning: Supporting Infants and Toddlers in Child Care Settings*.

All four books are grounded in a profound respect for parents and families, for the primacy of parents' bond with their children, and for parents' role as teachers. The books reflect the constructivist child development theories of psychologist Jean Piaget (1952) as well as current research and the observations and experiences of parents, home visitors, practitioners, and child care providers working on a daily basis in the field and "on the floor" with infants and toddlers. This combination of respect for parents, theory, and practice has led to a terminology that is both theory- and observation-based and is accessible to parents, infant-toddler caregivers, college educators, researchers, and theorists. Both *Supporting the Changing Family* and *Good Beginnings* use everyday language to identify seven successive stages that infants and toddlers negotiate, at varying rates, between

The Adolescent Parents and Infants Project

Findings Regarding Teenage Parenthood

1. "Pregnant teenagers expect too little, too late from newborn babies.

2. "Teenagers' babies, while physically well cared for, are often neither played with nor talked to by their mothers.

3. "On the brighter side, teenagers recognize their need for more information about the mental growth of their infants."

Findings Regarding Support Services for Teenage Parents

4. "A recurrent theme among those teenagers who are coping relatively well with parenthood is that they had someone who taught them how to 'negotiate the system.'

5. "We find that the teenage mothers who are most supportive in their interactions with their infants are those who receive part-time child care help from their families while they finish school and/or go to work. Teenage mothers who receive no child care assistance become very controlling and directive. But those whose families assume almost full-time infant care never have the opportunity to develop a comfortable interaction pattern with their infants; consequently, they play least with their babies.

6. "Teenagers like services in which providers are caring and sensitive; information is offered spontaneously as well as in response to questions; there is a chance to share with other pregnant teenagers and teenage parents; and there is consistency and follow-through on the part of the staff."

—Ann Epstein (1980b, pp. 6–7)

birth and 36 months of age: the heads up, the looker, the creeper-crawler, the cruiser, the walker, the doer, and the tester stages. The first six of these seven stages correspond to Piaget's substages of cognitive growth within his *sensory-motor* stage, while the last one, the tester stage, corresponds to the early part of Piaget's *preoperational* stage. Within each of their seven stages, author Reschly and authors Evans and Ilfeld (p. 7) identify "five elements of children's mental and physical responses to the world. These elements work together to determine the quality and nature of the child's growth. They are (1) the child's physical abilities; (2) the child's understanding of the physical world; (3) the child's sense of self; (4) the child's relationships with other people; and (5) the child's ability to communicate thoughts, wishes, needs, and feelings." In *Tender Care and Early Learning* these five elements have been translated into nine key experience categories—*movement, exploring objects, creative representation, early quantity and number, space, time, sense of self, social relations,* and *communication and language.* Each of these categories contains a series of experiences describing the social, emotional, physical, and cognitive development of infants and toddlers.

The Impetus Behind This Book

Throughout the 1980s, as High/Scope evaluated multisite parent-infant program initiatives implemented by other agencies, funding for its own parent-to-parent dissemination activity virtually disappeared. Later on, between 1989 and 1992, the Transactional Intervention Program (TRIP) under the direction of Amy Powell merged with High/Scope to become the High/Scope Program for Infants and Toddlers With Special Needs, a 3-year national outreach training project funded by the U.S. Education Department's Handicapped Children's Early Education Program. The purpose of this project was to "provide training and technical assistance to early childhood programs throughout the U.S. in implementing a family-focused intervention model for special needs infants and toddlers and their families" (Powell, 1990, p. 12). The project was based on findings that "children with handicaps are more actively engaged and achieve higher levels of language and cognitive functioning when their parents engage in a responsive, nondirective style of interaction—a style we call child-oriented. Parents with this child-oriented style are highly sensitive to their children's cues and interests, responsive to the activities their children initiate, and relatively nondirective in interactions with their children" (p. 13). (For a summary of High/Scope's infant-toddler work, see "A History of High/Scope Infant and Toddler Activities" on p. 10.)

At the same time, the demand for training in the High/Scope *preschool* approach for 3- to 5-year-olds accelerated, resulting in a network of High/Scope certified trainers working in early childhood settings across the nation. Over time, many of these preschool trainers assumed positions that required them to train and support staff working in group settings that served infants and toddlers. Some of these trainers, on their own, adapted the High/Scope active learning, constructivist approach to the infant-toddler programs they were working with. By the early 1990s, there was a clear need for High/Scope to provide new infant-toddler materials directed toward center-based programs and family child care homes. In 1993, therefore, the authors of *Tender Care and Early Learning* initiated a project to (1) gather the most accurate, up-to-date information about supporting infants and toddlers in High/Scope-inspired settings and other active learning group-care settings and (2) relate these findings to the earlier High/Scope work represented in *Supporting the Changing Family* and *Good Beginnings*.

Altogether, caregivers and directors from 21 infant-toddler programs across the country completed surveys about their current practices and collected anecdotes and child observations for this book. These programs ranged from small (6 children) to large (10 rooms of 12 children each); and from serving mixed-age groups (infants and toddlers together) to serving groups separated by age (for example, young infants together, older infants together, young toddlers together, older toddlers together[1]). They included center-based programs, family child care homes, and a college-based drop-in child care center. In some programs, parents attended with their children for all or part of each session. Collectively, these programs served the needs of families with a wide spectrum of income levels.

Eight of the 21 programs were visited by one of the books' authors; the remaining 13 programs submitted their survey information in writing and through telephone conversations. Staff at all 21 sites answered questions about their program routines, interactions, adult teamwork, and child observation. In addition, staff at each site received a working list of the key experiences for infants and toddlers (see "High/Scope Key Experiences for Infants and Toddlers" on p. 38) along with anecdote-collection sheets and guidelines for collecting anecdotes through child observation. (For a discussion of anecdotes and child observation, see Chapter 5.) The idea was to observe and collect anecdotes about infants and toddlers involved in the key experiences,

---

[1]These infant-toddler descriptors, without exact ages specified, will be used throughout this book. In general, we focus on children's actions and behaviors rather than on their ages, because we realize that human development occurs sequentially but at highly individual rates (for example, babies usually learn to roll over before they learn to sit by themselves, but some begin to sit unaided at 6 months, whereas others do so at 10 or 11 months). In our "shorthand" for children at various developmental stages, "young infants" means babies who are not yet sitting by themselves (they may range in age from birth to 9 or 10 months); "older infants" can sit unaided and are learning to creep, crawl, pull themselves up to stand, and cruise upright from place to place by holding on to props (they may range in age from 5 months to 18 months); "young toddlers" can toddle and walk unaided, with both hands free for exploration; "older toddlers" are more sure on their feet, more skilled with their hands, and more adept at verbal communication ("toddlers," as a group, range in age from 12 months to 3 years, with "younger toddlers" generally ranging from 12 to 24 months, and "older toddlers," from 24 to 36 months).

A History of High/Scope Infant and Toddler Activities

1968–1971	Ypsilanti-Carnegie Infant Education Project: Home Teaching With Mother and Infants
1971–1973	High/Scope Infant Videotaping Project
1974	Publication of *Home Teaching With Mothers and Infants,* by D. Z. Lambie, J. T. Bond, and D. P. Weikart
1975–1978	Parent-to-Parent Home Visit Project
1979	Publication of *Supporting the Changing Family: A Guide to the Parent-to-Parent Model,* by B. Reschly
1979	Publication of *The Ypsilanti-Carnegie Infant Education Project: Longitudinal Follow-Up,* by A. S. Epstein and D. P. Weikart
1977–1980	Adolescent Parents and Infants Project
1978–1984	Bernard van Leer Parent-to-Parent Dissemination Project
1982	Publication of *Good Beginnings: Parenting in the Early Years* and its supplement, *Activities for Parent-Child Interaction,* by J. Evans and E. Ilfeld
n.d.	Publication of *Community Self-Help: The Parent-to-Parent Program*
1982–1989	Evaluation of the Ford Foundation's Child Survival/Fair Start Project
1989–1992	High/Scope Program for Infants and Toddlers With Special Needs
1995	Publication of *A Guide to Community-Based Family Support Programs,* by A. S. Epstein, M. Larner, and R. Halpern
1997–1999	Case-study follow-up of the Parent-to-Parent Dissemination Project
2000	Publication of *Tender Care and Early Learning: Supporting Infants and Toddlers in Child Care Settings,* by J. Post and M. Hohmann
2000 (in press)	Publication of *Supporting Families With Young Children: The High/Scope Parent-to-Parent Dissemination Project,* by A. S. Epstein, J. E. Montie, L. J. Schweinhart, and D. P. Weikart

both to confirm the validity of the key experiences and to try out the High/Scope system of child observation with very young children.

Staff at each site collected observations of their children over 4 to 6 months, then submitted their anecdotal records for possible inclusion in this book. It was gratifying to find that the child observation system worked! Many of the submitted anecdotes now appear throughout *Tender Care and Early Learning* to illustrate the key experiences and to give examples of daily interactions in infant-toddler programs. You can be sure that they are descriptions of what actually takes place with infants, toddlers, and their caregivers in High/Scope settings around the country.

Tender Care and Early Learning, then, draws together the High/Scope Foundation's experiences with infants and mothers over the past 30 years and the current experience of High/Scope trainers and caregivers as they provide active learning settings for groups of infants and toddlers in their care. This book strives to embed the practical experience in a framework based on current theory and research in infant and toddler development. It is our hope that this blend of field-based and academic knowledge proves both friendly and useful to caregivers who provide day-to-day care and education to very young children and their families in group-care settings.

Principles Guiding the High/Scope Infant and Toddler Approach

The High/Scope Infant and Toddler "Wheel of Learning" (see below) graphically represents the major ideas that guide the High/Scope approach to infant-toddler group care and education: active learning for children; warm, supportive adult-child interaction; a welcoming, child-oriented physical environment; schedules and routines that flow with the children; and daily child observation that guides caregivers' interactions with children, caregivers' teamwork, caregiver-parent partnerships, and program planning.

Active learning

Infants and toddlers are active learners from birth. Through their ongoing relationships with people and their explorations of the materials in their immediate world, they figure out how to move at will; how to hold and act on

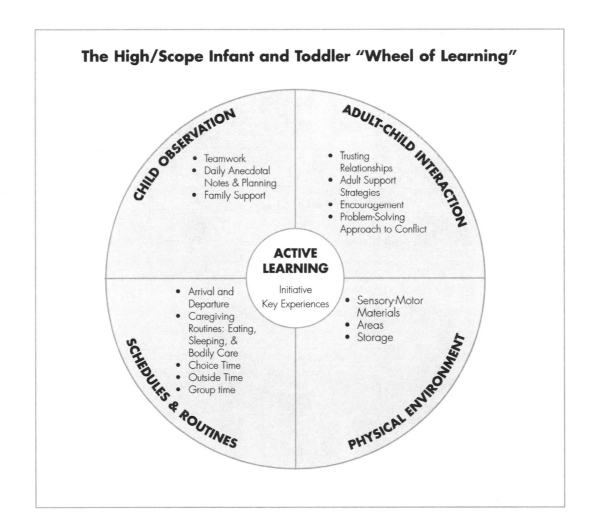

The High/Scope Infant and Toddler "Wheel of Learning"

CHILD OBSERVATION
- Teamwork
- Daily Anecdotal Notes & Planning
- Family Support

ADULT-CHILD INTERACTION
- Trusting Relationships
- Adult Support Strategies
- Encouragement
- Problem-Solving Approach to Conflict

ACTIVE LEARNING
Initiative
Key Experiences

SCHEDULES & ROUTINES
- Arrival and Departure
- Caregiving Routines: Eating, Sleeping, & Bodily Care
- Choice Time
- Outside Time
- Group time

PHYSICAL ENVIRONMENT
- Sensory-Motor Materials
- Areas
- Storage

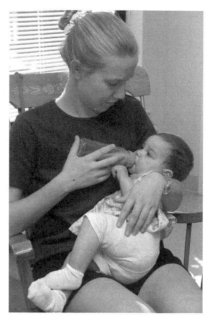

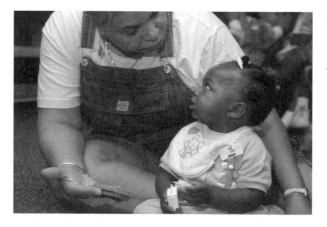

In High/Scope infant-toddler programs, tender care and early learning flow from children's active learning and trusting relationships with caregivers. Support for this is provided by adult teamwork in an engaging environment with child-centered schedules and routines.

objects; and how to communicate and interact with parents, family members, peers, and caregivers. As active learners, infants and toddlers watch, reach for, and grasp people and materials that particularly attract their attention. They choose objects and people to play with and explore, initiate actions that particularly interest them, and respond to various events in their environment. Through their own unique combination of gestures, facial expressions, noises, and (eventually) words, they communicate their feelings and ideas. Throughout their explorations, they rely on parents and caregivers to attend to, support, and build on their actions, choices, and ways of communicating.

When surrounded by adults—parents, family members, caregivers—who understand the very young child's need to explore and thus build understanding, infants and toddlers develop a sense of trust in themselves and others that enables them to become curious, autonomous learners. They *initiate* their own "voyages of discovery" off the blanket and into the next room, driven by the desire to see what interesting people and things might lie around the corner. Even the most adventurous active learners, however, return from time to time to "home base," that trusting and trusted adult, to assure themselves that comfort and safety are well within their reach.

The *key experiences* represent what infants and toddlers discover on their daily active learning adventures. As they explore and play, they gain a **sense of self** (a realization that they are separate individuals)—*This is my hand.* They form significant **social relations**—*This is my mom. This is my friend Sunil.* They engage in **creative representation** by looking at picture books or wearing a saucepan for a hat. They figure out that **movement** serves their purposes—*I can crawl over to that other baby.* They create a **communication and language** system that works for them—*When something pleasant happens, I smile and wiggle, and then something else pleasant happens.* They **explore objects** by mouthing a rattle or dipping a spoon into soup. In the process of their explorations, they construct ideas about **early quantity and number**—pointing to each bird on the window ledge and making a sound with each gesture; **space**—*I can climb into the big soft chair with Darren;* and **time**—crawling to the door whenever Mom puts on her coat.

Active learning is the axle on which the High/Scope wheel of learning turns. In active learning settings, adults support children's initiatives and desire to explore with all their senses. They understand that children's self-motivated explorations lead to key experiences—learning that is fundamental to healthy human growth and development.

Adult-child interaction

Infants and toddlers are explorers. To gather the strength and courage they need to go forth each day, they rely on the support of their parents and caregivers. Their *interactions* with trusted adults at home and away from home provide the emotional fuel infants and toddlers need to puzzle out the mysteries of the social and physical world. Because *trusting relationships* are so important, caregivers strive to ensure that each infant or toddler in a child care center or home has the same primary caregiver throughout enrollment, whether that be for 6 months or 3 years; in settings with multiple caregivers, each one is the "primary" for only a small group of children, and the caregivers form a stable team that provides long-term continuity of care for children and families. Caregivers strive to form positive, reciprocal relationships with children—relationships in which *encouragement* is the key. They cuddle, hold, play, and talk with children in a warm, unhurried, give-and-take manner. They establish a psychologically safe environment, where children's initiatives are regarded as purposeful rather than naughty or bothersome for adults. Guided by practical theories of child development, caregivers attempt to see things from the child's point of view, encourage rather than thwart children's efforts and communications, take cues from children rather than impose their own ideas, and assume a *problem-solving* approach to children's interpersonal conflicts rather than punish children or solve their problems for them.

Very young children are just formulating a sense of themselves and an understanding of what the rest of the world is all about. As they are doing so, interactions with parents and caregivers significantly influence the life-long conclusions children draw from their experiences. For example, if parents' and caregivers' interactions are supportive, this shapes children's perceptions of themselves as capable, trusted, and trustworthy human beings. Therefore, positive, consistent, ongoing adult support of children's need to actively explore and thus construct a personal understanding of the world is critical.

Physical environment

Providing an active learning environment for infants and toddlers encourages their need to look, listen, wiggle, roll, crawl, climb, rock, bounce, rest, eat, make noise, grasp or mouth or drop things, and be messy from time to time. In a High/Scope infant-toddler program, the physical space is safe, flexible, and child-oriented to provide comfort and variety and to accommodate children's changing developmental needs and interests. It includes a wide variety of *materials* infants and toddlers can reach, explore, and play with in their own way at their own pace. The *storage of materials* is consistent, personalized, and accessible so that infants and toddlers can reach or get to the materials they see and want to explore. The space and materials are organized into *play and care areas* that serve the needs of infants and toddlers. The diapering area, for example, may be located next to a window that looks out onto a flower box or a bird feeder. The toddler block area includes a good supply of small and large blocks for satisfying stacking and balancing experiences. The physical environment, in short, is secure and inviting. Within its boundaries, infants and toddlers are free to move about, explore materials, exercise creativity, and solve problems.

Schedules and routines

In an active learning infant-toddler setting, schedules (the daily sequence of events such as *choice time, lunch, outside time*) and routines (caregiving interactions during *eating, napping,* and *bodily care*) are anchored, for each child, around a primary caregiver. Having this caregiver as a "home base" provides the very young child with a sense of security while away from home. Following children's cues and initiatives, caregivers, in partnership with parents, establish center schedules and routines that are consistent in order and interaction style, so children can anticipate what happens next, yet flexible enough to accommodate children's individual rhythms and temperaments. The schedules and routines are repetitive enough to enable children to explore, practice, and gain confidence in their developing skills, yet they allow children to move smoothly, at their own pace, from one interesting experience to another. Caregivers plan flexible, child-centered *group times.* They also work with parents to make *arrival* and *departure* leisurely and comforting. Children make choices about materials and actions throughout the day, and adults support and encourage children's initiatives during each time period and routine interaction. Altogether, caregivers design schedules and routines around children's needs and interests to give children a sense of control and belonging.

Child observation

Child observation is an essential component of the High/Scope infant and toddler approach, since knowledge of individual children shapes not only the interactions caregivers have with children and parents but also the physical environment and the schedules and routines at the center. To observe and learn as much as possible from children, adults in infant-toddler centers rely on *teamwork.* Caregivers work as partners with parents to provide continuity of care between home and center. Primary caregivers work together in teams for mutual support throughout the day; together, they provide *family support;* make decisions about space, materials, schedules, routines, and daily responsibilities; and discuss and plan around their daily observations of children. As they work "on the floor" with children, they collect *daily anecdotal notes.* At *daily team-planning time,* they discuss their observations of what individual children did and said that day, and they use these observations to guide their own behavior in supporting children the next day. They also exchange child observations with parents, both to celebrate children's actions and development and to nurture a partnership with families, so children can be supported consistently at home and at the center.

These guiding principles—active learning, supportive adult-child interaction, a child-oriented physical environment, schedules and routines that flow with the children, and daily child observation to guide teamwork among staff and parents—keep the High/Scope infant and toddler wheel of learning turning. They also serve as a framework for this book, which elaborates on each of these five principles so caregivers in infant and toddler group-care settings can put the High/Scope approach into practice.

How This Book Is Organized

Tender Care and Early Learning starts in the middle of the infant-toddler wheel of learning, with active learning; it then turns to each of the four sections of the wheel:

Chapter 1, "Active Learning and Key Experiences for Infants and Toddlers," describes how infants and toddlers learn through action and social relationships and introduces the key experiences as a way of seeing, understanding, supporting, and building on the broad range of things they learn about.

Chapter 2, "Supportive Adult-Child Interactions," discusses the role of the primary caregiver, continuity of care, and specific adult-child interaction strategies caregivers can use to nurture and support active learners.

Chapter 3, "Arranging and Equipping an Environment for Infants and Toddlers," provides general guidelines for organizing active learning environments and specific strategies for selecting materials and arranging spaces to support the exploration and play of infants and toddlers.

Chapter 4, "Establishing Schedules and Routines for Infants and Toddlers," defines child-centered schedules and caregiving routines and discusses specific caregiver roles during each part of the day.

Chapter 5, "The Caregiver Team and Their Partnership With Parents," focuses on the elements of effective caregiver teams and caregiver-parent partnerships and describes strategies for working together to support infants' and toddlers' growth and development.

Altogether, *Tender Care and Early Learning: Supporting Infants and Toddlers in Child Care Settings* presents High/Scope's body of experience and knowledge about ways to create caring, child-centered communities for our youngest and most vulnerable active learners. Group care for infants and toddlers is a fact of life in today's world, in which increasing numbers of employed parents must find out-of-home care for their children. In this book, we present strategies for out-of-home care that promote a tender approach to early learning. It is an approach that focuses on children's strengths; builds healthy relationships between parent and child, caregiver and child, center and family, and children themselves; and supports the growth and development of very young children, their families, and their caregivers.

References

Activities for Parent-Child Interaction, Supplement to Good Beginnings. 1982. Ypsilanti, MI: High/Scope Educational Research Foundation.

Community Self-Help: The Parent-to-Parent Program. n.d. Ypsilanti, MI: High/Scope Educational Research Foundation.

Epstein, Ann S. 1980a. *Assessing the Child Development Information Needed by Adolescent Parents With Very Young Children.* Final project report for Grant No. 90-C-1341 submitted to the U.S. Department of Health, Education and Welfare. Ypsilanti, MI: High/Scope Educational Research Foundation.

Epstein, Ann S. 1980b. "New Insights Into the Problems of Adolescent Parenthood." In *Bulletin of the High/Scope Foundation,* 6–8. Ypsilanti, MI: High/Scope Press.

Epstein, Ann S., and Judith Evans. 1979. "Parent-Child Interaction and Children's Learning." In *The High/Scope Report,* ed. C. Silverman, 39–43. Ypsilanti, MI: High/Scope Press.

Epstein, Ann S., Mary Larner, and Robert Halpern. 1995. *A Guide to Community-Based Family Support Programs.* Ypsilanti, MI: High/Scope Press.

Epstein, Ann S., Jeanne E. Montie, Lawrence J. Schweinhart, and David P. Weikart. In press. *Supporting Families With Young Children: The High/Scope Parent-to-Parent Dissemination Project.* Ypsilanti, MI: High/Scope Press.

Epstein, Ann S., and David P. Weikart. 1979. *The Ypsilanti-Carnegie Infant Education Project: Longitudinal Follow-Up.* Ypsilanti, MI: High/Scope Press.

Evans, Judith, and Ellen Ilfeld. 1982. *Good Beginnings: Parenting in the Early Years.* Ypsilanti, MI: High/Scope Press.

Lambie, Dolores Z., James T. Bond, and David P. Weikart. 1974. *Home Teaching With Mothers and Infants.* Ypsilanti, MI: High/Scope Press.

Larner, Mary, Robert Halpern, and Oscar Harkavy. 1992. *Fair Start for Children: Lessons Learned From Seven Demonstration Projects.* New Haven, CT: Yale University Press.

Piaget, Jean. 1952. *The Origins of Intelligence in Children.* New York: Norton.

Powell, Amy. 1990. "The High/Scope Program for Infants and Toddlers With Special Needs." *High/Scope ReSource* 9, no. 1 (Winter): 1, 12–16.

Powell, Amy. 1991. "Be Responsive!" In *Supporting Young Learners,* eds. Nancy A. Brickman and Lynn S. Taylor, 26–34. Ypsilanti, MI: High/Scope Press.

Reschly, Barbara. 1979. *Supporting the Changing Family: A Guide to the Parent-to-Parent Model.* Ypsilanti, MI: High/Scope Educational Research Foundation.

Related Reading

Bredekamp, Sue. 1997. "Developmentally Appropriate Practice for Infants and Toddlers." In *Developmentally Appropriate Practice in Early Childhood Programs* rev. ed., eds. Sue Bredekamp and Carol Copple, 55–94. Washington, DC: National Association for the Education of Young Children.

Godwin, Annabelle, and Lorraine Schrag, eds. 1996. *Setting Up for Infant/Toddler Care: Guidelines for Centers and Family Child Care Homes.* Washington, DC: National Association for the Education of Young Children.

Greenman, Jim. 1988. *Caring Spaces, Learning Places: Children's Environments That Work.* Redmond, WA: Exchange Press.

Hohmann, Mary, and David P. Weikart. 1995. *Educating Young Children: Active Learning Practices for Preschool and Child Care Programs.* Ypsilanti, MI: High/Scope Press.

Provence, Sally, Jeree Pawl, and Emily Fenichel, eds. 1992. *The Zero to Three Child Care Anthology 1984–1992.* Arlington, VA: Zero to Three/National Center for Clinical Infant Programs.

White, Burton L. 1975. *The First Three Years of Life.* Englewood Cliffs, NJ: Prentice-Hall.

Zigler, Edward F., and Mary E. Lang. 1991. *Child Care Choices: Balancing the Needs of Children, Families, and Society.* New York: The Free Press, A Division of Macmillan.

Related Videos

The High/Scope Approach for Under Threes, U.S. Edition. 1999. Color videotape, 68 min. London, England: High/Scope Institute U.K. (Available from High/Scope Press, Ypsilanti, MI.)

In this book, we present strategies for out-of-home care that promote a tender approach to early learning.

1
Active Learning and Key Experiences for Infants and Toddlers

A society can be judged by its attitude to its youngest children,

not only . . . what is said about them but how this attitude

is expressed in what is offered to them as they grow up.

—*Elinor Goldschmied and Sonia Jackson (1994)*

J n a High/Scope child care setting, it is important to have caregivers who lovingly, consistently, and creatively support children's natural desire to be active learners. Creating an active learning environment for infants and toddlers means consciously considering all their needs—their social and emotional needs for security and companionship; their physical needs for nourishment, bodily care, rest, movement, and safety; their cognitive needs for opportunities to make choices, explore interesting materials, and try out a range of challenging experiences; and their sociolinguistic needs to communicate their desires and discoveries to responsive caregivers and peers. What caregivers offer to infants and toddlers in group-care settings speaks eloquently of the interactions and experiences they understand to be essential for supporting children as they develop into healthy, secure, creative people.

This sensory-motor learner bends intently over her bucket. At close range, she can smell the sand, see it shift as she stirs, and feel and hear the scraping sound of the spoon.

An understanding of High/Scope's active learning approach guides the decisions infant-toddler caregivers make about every major aspect of their work—interacting with children and families, arranging and equipping the physical environment, establishing schedules and routines, and observing and planning for children. To establish the framework for the High/Scope infant-toddler approach, this chapter examines the meaning of active learning and describes what children learn through key experiences with people and materials.

Very Young Children in Action: How Infants and Toddlers Learn

Based on child development theory and experience with infants and toddlers, High/Scope developed the following propositions[2] that guide our work with very young children and, in broad strokes, describe the ingredients of active learning:

- Infants and toddlers *learn with their whole body and with all their senses.*

---

[2]These propositions, presented here in a slightly altered form, originally appeared in *Home Teaching With Mothers and Infants* by D. Z. Lambie, J. T. Bond, and D. P. Weikart, 1974.

- Infants and toddlers *learn because they* want *to.*
- Infants and toddlers *communicate what they know.*
- Infants and toddlers *learn within the context of trusting relationships.*

Infants and toddlers learn with their whole body and with all their senses

Infants and toddlers gather information with their every action—by gazing at the face of a parent or caregiver, playing with their hands, stroking a bottle, tipping a cup, fingering a caregiver's clothing, chewing on a book or toy, crumbling crackers, splashing water, kicking off a blanket, crying when another child cries, or carrying around a baby doll. By coordinating taste, touch, smell, sight, sound, feelings, and action, they are able to build knowledge. Developmental psychologist Jean Piaget (1952, 1966) used the term *sensory-motor* to characterize this direct, physical approach to learning. *Sensory* refers to the way that infants and toddlers gather information about the world through all their senses; *motor* refers to the way they learn through physical action. Recent brain research summarized by Rima Shore (1997) confirms the appropriateness of Piaget's term. She reported the following:

> The brain's intricate circuitry is not formed at a steady pace; rather, brain development proceeds in waves, with different parts of the brain becoming active "construction sites" at different times and with different degrees of intensity. By studying the PET [positron emission tomography] scans of children who came to his hospital for diagnosis and treatment, Harry Chugani [1997] and his colleagues have quantified the activity levels of different parts of the brain at various stages of development. In this way, they have gained insight into brain plasticity at particular ages. At one month of age, for example, there is intensive activity in the cortical and subcortical regions that control sensory-motor functions. Cortical activity rises sharply between the second and third months of life—a prime time for providing visual and auditory stimulation. By about eight months, the frontal cortex shows increased metabolic activity. This part of the brain is associated with the ability to regulate and express emotion, as well as to think and to plan, and it becomes the site of frenetic activity just at the moment that babies make dramatic leaps in self-regulation and strengthen their attachment to their primary caregivers. (p. 39)

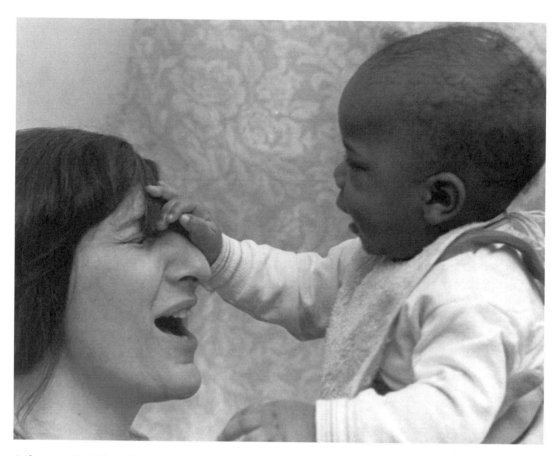

Infants and toddlers like to explore things that are soft, cuddly, or easy to grasp—like a caregiver's hair, eyes, and nose.

Infants and toddlers, then, learn by doing because their young brains are particularly primed for action. In the beginning of their lives, their discoveries about themselves and their immediate environment come through action— through waving their arms, watching their hands, kicking, turning over, reaching out, grasping, poking, smelling, listening, touching, mouthing, tasting, crawling, pulling themselves up. Before they can talk, it is also through action that they express what they discover and feel to attentive adults—by crying, wiggling, stiffening, turning away, making faces, clinging, cuddling, cooing, sucking, and looking. Their active engagement with attentive and responsive adults and with interesting and challenging materials provides them with a base of experience for interpreting their world. Shore (1997) underlined that brain research shows "the brain is uniquely constructed to benefit from experience" (p. 4) and that children's actions "directly affect the way the brain is wired" (p. 18). In fact, their early explorations and interactions with people and materials form, exercise, and strengthen the synapses (brain connections, or neural pathways) they will use for the rest of their lives: "The synapses that have been strengthened by virtue of repeated experience tend to become permanent; the synapses that were not used often enough in the early years tend to be eliminated. In this way the experiences—positive or negative—that young children have in the first years of life influence how their brains will be wired as adults" (p. 21). (See "Brain Development Is Rapid and Extensive" on p. 26.)

Very young children's pressing need to act and learn from experience takes the form of direct contact using the tools at their immediate disposal—eyes, nose, ears, mouth, hands, and feet. They watch people or pets or objects move, closely examine patterns of light and shade, feel the textures and temperatures of things with their hands and feet, still themselves to listen to a voice or song, and put nearly everything they can grasp into their mouths. In fact, they cannot resist touching and exploring anything or anyone with sensory-motor appeal. They are fascinated with everyday household objects—pots, lids, keys, boxes, spoons—and natural materials—stones, sticks, leaves. They especially like to explore soft and

This little girl's caregiver understands that she is powerfully self-motivated to explore and learn about paint with her hands, eyes, nose, mouth, and fly swatter "paintbrush"!

cuddly items, easy-to-grasp objects, squishy or messy materials, things they can set in motion, objects they can pull themselves up onto and climb, materials that make noise, and other people! In their care setting, infants study their caregiver's face, listen for and respond to the sound of her voice, know how she smells, and settle into the comfort of her arms and body.[3] Toddlers use her to lean and relax against or to steady themselves as they maneuver into a sitting or standing position. Her shoelaces, hair, jewelry, glasses, and

---

[3]Because women predominate as infant-toddler caregivers in both center-based and home-based programs, throughout this book we use "she" and "her" to refer to caregivers unless a specific example requires otherwise. We do this with apologies to the small but possibly growing number of men in the field.

Brain Development Is Rapid and Extensive

"A newborn's brain is in a largely subcortical state; its cerebral cortex—the part of the brain responsible for complex cognitive functions like language and spatial orientation—is relatively dormant. By the time the candle is lit on the baby's first birthday cake, the brain has achieved a highly cortical state. But the cortex is not the only region of the brain to mature quickly. PET scans show that by the age of one, a baby's brain qualitatively resembles that of a normal young adult. This transformation corresponds to the dramatic changes that parents and other people who care for babies witness in the first year, as newborns progress with incredible speed from virtually helpless beings to children who are starting to reason, to walk and talk, to form intentions and carry them out, and to enjoy interactions with a variety of people, pets, and objects.

"By the age of two, toddlers' brains are as active as those of adults. The metabolic rate keeps rising, and by the age of three, the brains of children are two and a half times more active than the brains of adults—and they stay that way throughout their first decade of life. Compared with adult brains, children's brains also have higher levels of some neurotransmitters, which play an important role in the formation of synapses. All these factors—synapse density, glucose utilization, and the level of some neurotransmitters—remain high throughout the first decade of life, and begin to decline only with puberty. This suggests that young children—particularly infants and toddlers—are biologically primed for learning."

—Rima Shore (1997, p. 21)

clothes provide a variety of textures and colors they stroke and clutch. To infants and toddlers, she is every bit as interesting as many other items and playthings, and generally more responsive!

Increased mobility brings new learning experiences. When babies learn to sit unaided, they find they have greater freedom to see, turn, twist, reach, bend, and shake or bang objects. Mobile infants, whenever they can manage to do so, crawl, pull themselves up, and climb onto any inviting surface. Toddlers enjoy the balance, uprightness, pace, and freedom of walking, running, and climbing to new heights. They also use their new powers of locomotion to move materials from place to place. They pull and push wagons and wheel toys and drag chairs or large containers to a more desirable spot. They might try to push and tug a large tub of blocks, find it does not move, empty all the blocks out, and try again. Mobile infants and toddlers mean mobile materials and playthings!

As infants and toddlers interact with people and act on materials, they construct a basic store of knowledge about what people and things are like, what they do, and how they respond to certain actions. What may begin as random movement—waving a wooden spoon and accidently hitting it against a cardboard box—leads to a fascinating discovery and is repeated deliberately again and again. Through these repetitions, children gain a sense of purpose and mastery; they enjoy feeling with their whole body the stiffness of the wooden spoon, for example, and the sturdy resistance of the box. Later on, gaining this experiential knowledge will lead them to try even more complex action sequences, like stirring with a spoon and stacking boxes. For infants and toddlers, learning through action involves encountering and solving infant-and-toddler-sized problems—*What made that noise? How can I make it again?*—and, in the process, forming their ideas about what things and people do and how they respond to one's actions.

Caregivers who base their programs on the principles of active learning understand and support infants' and toddlers' sensory, whole-body approach to learning. They respect and accommodate children's ongoing need for space, materials, and exploration time. Because infants and toddlers can be expected to grasp and hold things and put toys and other objects in their mouth, caregivers provide playthings that are safe and too large to swallow and they design play areas that ensure both comfort and safety. Anticipating drool and stickiness, caregivers routinely sanitize the materials children come in contact with. They encourage children's curiosity and mobility; respect their need to crawl, walk, run, and carry or move articles from place to place; and establish safe and spacious environments where these things can happen.

Infants and toddlers learn because they *want* to

Juan, a young infant, grasps his pacifier and puts it in his mouth, then takes it out to look at it and turn it around a bit, and finally puts it back in his mouth.

∾

Marian, a toddler, sorts through the basket of pictures until she finds the one with two puppies and, looking at it, says "Dog, dog."

∾

Deidre, an older infant, pushes her caregiver's hand away, takes off her own bib, and hands it to the caregiver.

∾

Charlie, a toddler, uses the wooden mallet from the play dough shelf to pound the floor.

As young as they are, infants and toddlers are powerfully self-motivated to explore and learn—at their own pace, through their own means. Learning develops from their intrinsically motivated activity. No one has to tell them to learn or prod them into action. Their own choices and desire for autonomy and initiative take care of that! In fact, in extensive home observations of children 12–15 months old and 24–27 months old, psychologist Burton White and his colleagues (1972) found that over 80 percent of the children's experience was self-initiated.

Even the youngest infants make simple choices and decisions all day long—choices about what to look at; whether to reach for the shell, the rattle, or the ribbon; whether to stick with the wooden spoon or go for the ball; when to drink from the bottle or just stop and gaze; whether to watch the shadows on the wall beside the crib, call out for someone's attention, or coo at the stuffed bear; when to stop playing and go to sleep. As the infant grows into toddlerhood, the choices and decisions become increasingly complex— when and how to remove a bib, whether to climb into a lap or settle into the big pillow with a book, where to roll and then retrieve all the balls, what child to play beside, how to flatten the play dough, how to fit all the toy

This young toddler decides to play in *the toy box!*

animals into a purse, how to eat a cracker, what comfort item (stuffed animal, blanket, book) to take to nap time, what to use to wipe up a spill, how to reach out-of-the-way objects. Infants and toddlers indicate the people or materials or experiences they prefer, decide what they will explore, and figure out how to solve problems and accomplish meaningful tasks. By making infant-and-toddler-sized choices and decisions, they gain a sense of self-control and efficacy—*I am somebody who can do things!* (as opposed to somebody to whom things are done).

In a supportive environment with appropriate opportunities and interactions, very young children act with increasing autonomy and independence. They become curious about peers and other adults. In the spirit of adventure and exploration, they roll, crawl, and eventually walk on their own to discover the unknown in the social and physical world beyond Mom and caregiver. They open and close doors; play simple hiding games; hunt for hidden toys, people, or pets; seek out playmates; climb up and down stairs; look at books with peers; fill and empty shelves, boxes, bags, and baskets. Sometimes their daring evokes feelings of delight and mastery—an infant crawls behind the couch and finds a ball, or two toddlers stand at the window watching older children play outside in the yard. Other times their adventures scare them—the ball behind the couch tastes odd; a dog barks at the children outside—and they hurry back to Mom or caregiver for comfort and reassurance. In fact, at the same time that infants and toddlers are independent and curious, they also depend on strong social ties with Mom and caregiver to affirm their autonomy. Psychologist and human development specialist Erik Erikson (1950) observed that in the course of their adventures, toddlers need adult support rather than criticism, restraint, or shaming. "As their environment encourages them to 'stand on their own feet,' it must protect them against meaningless and arbitrary experiences of shame and of early doubt" (p. 252). Curiously enough, autonomous young learners rely on dependable social relationships.

Over time, very young children in active learning environments develop the desire and capacity to act with persistence and to have an impact on people and things involved in their interactions and explorations. A toddler, for example, decides to carry a favorite truck around all day through meal times, naps, and outside time. Three toddlers decide to bang on the mounds of sand that are formed as their caregiver tips out the sand she has packed in some pails. Whatever the caregiver had in mind, she respects the children's initiative as they smash what she might have thought of as sand cakes. "All gone!" she says as the children smash the sand mounds. "More!" they cry, and the mound-making-and-smashing game is on. When children's initiatives are arbitrarily and frequently thwarted—"Don't touch that!" "Take your hands out of your mouth!" "Stop banging!" "Sit still!" "Come away from there!"—children begin to doubt their own capacity to shape and order their day-to-day existence. By contrast, according to developmental psychologist Marion Hyson (1994), "When children feel they can count on important, loved people to provide comfort, they have a strong foundation of confidence that allows them to explore their surroundings" (p. 98). With adult support for their initiatives, infants and toddlers—and children of all ages—enjoy the risks and satisfactions of creative learning and social discourse.

In practical terms, this means that a group-care setting supports young children's development if it is stocked with a variety of safe, appropriate, challenging, and accessible materials for children's exploration. In such a setting, caregivers support children's preferences and attend to their language of action and gesture. For example, when infant Halley crawls away from her caregiver to the tub of balls, her caregiver interprets Halley's actions to mean *I really want to play with the balls right now.* Rather than attempt to direct children to learn specified things at certain times, caregivers support and build on children's *self-motivated* choices and learning initiatives. A caregiver or teacher in an active learning infant-toddler program, according to educational researcher Dolores Lambie and colleagues (1974),

> . . . is not someone who inevitably "knows the right answers," "instills knowledge," or even "motivates the child to learn." Rather, a teacher is someone who responds to the abilities, needs, and interests of the "learner" by providing real opportunities for learner-initiated activities which contribute to development. Put differently, a teacher does not struggle to motivate the child but [attempts] to create a social and physical environment in which the child's intrinsic motivation is not frustrated. Effective teaching depends upon the teacher's having an adequate framework—some view or model of learning processes and the course of development—for interpreting the [child's actions] and for formulating coherent, appropriate responses. (pp. 25–26)

Infants and toddlers communicate what they know

Humans beings are social creatures from birth. Infants and toddlers eagerly seek direct contact with parents, other family members, and caregivers and use a variety of strategies to convey their desires. In the beginning, babies cry—for nourishment, comfort, security, and sleep. As people respond to them, they communicate—for the pleasure of engaging in and prolonging face-to-face exchanges. They gaze and smile at their parents and caregivers. They frown and make funny faces—when the water or juice in their bottle tastes different, when they hear a new noise. They move their hands, arms, and legs in excitement, happiness, or contentment. They coo at favorite people, pets, and playthings. They begin to babble and repeat the vowel and consonant sounds they hear in conversation. Gradually, their babbling takes on the inflections and cadences of human speech as they attempt to join the give-and-take of social conversation with parents, other family members, and caregivers.

When an infant or toddler does begin to talk, early language is streamlined and economical: "Ba" for *I see my bottle,* "Me do" for *I'll do it myself,* "Out" for *Let's go outside,* "Dog-dog" for *This is a picture of a dog.* Young children hear and understand language long before they can produce it themselves in its standard grammatical form. In the meantime, they string together sounds, gestures, and words in a fashion that makes sense to them.

By communicating what they feel and discover to receptive and responsive adults, infants and toddlers enter into the sustaining social life of the community, where they connect with other people, test their ideas, and gain feedback about their actions or feelings or perceptions. Therefore, caregivers in active learning settings pay particular

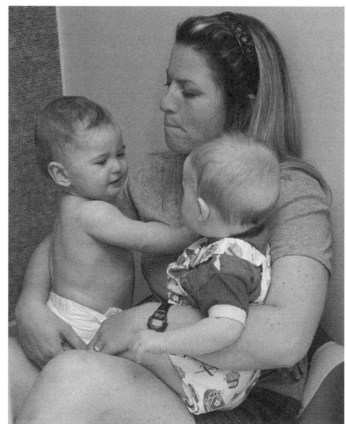

By communicating what they feel and discover, these infants enter into the sustaining social life of the community.

attention to children's actions, sounds, expressions, gestures, and words. They watch and listen carefully to children and give them sufficient "airtime" and room in a conversation to express themselves in their own particular fashion. They enable children both to hear language and to participate as active partners in communication. Infants and toddlers *want* to communicate, connect, and convey meaning. The more they are respectfully supported in these desires, the better communicators they become. Children's later facility with speaking, listening, reading, and writing has its roots in the very early partnerships they form with supportive parents and caregivers who take time to talk and listen to them with care. Such adults understand that infants and toddlers "talk" in their own way and *need* to talk, even before they ever use "proper" words.

Infants and toddlers learn within the context of trusting relationships

To learn and grow, children need the kind of emotionally rich environment that psychoanalyst Erik Erikson (1950) described as supporting *trust* rather than mistrust. The bedrock of healthy human development is "trust born of care," as Erikson puts it (p. 250). "The infant's first social achievement is his willingness, then, to let the mother out of sight without undue anxiety or rage, because she has become an inner certainty as well as an outer predictability" (p. 247). Children who form mutual, affirmative relationships with parents and caregivers draw upon these relationships for the courage they need to explore the world beyond their mother. While infants and toddlers are powerfully self-motivated to learn with their whole body and all their senses and to communicate what they know, they depend on the affirmation and warmth of trusting relationships to be able to do so. Parents and caregivers must "be able to represent to the child a deep, almost somatic [bodily] conviction that there is a meaning to what they are doing" (p. 249). When parents and caregivers, through their actions, convey a deep-seated belief in children's intrinsic worth, children develop an empowering sense of trust, human connection, and eagerness to explore the world.

As self-motivated social creatures, infants play an active role in shaping the trusting relationships they depend on. Observing mothers and infants in Uganda, developmental psychologist Mary Ainsworth (1963) was struck by "the extent to which the infant himself takes the initiative in seeking an interaction. From at least two months of age onwards, and increasingly through the first year of life, these infants were not so much passive and recipient as active in seeking interaction" (p. 203). Psychiatrist Daniel Stern (1985) called this interactive process *attunement*. Through deeply felt, finely tuned reciprocal interactions, the parent or caregiver matches the child's emotions and level of interest to convey her sense of what the child is feeling. For example, the baby coos and smiles at the caring adult, and the caring adult smiles and coos back to the baby and strokes the baby's cheek. This sensitive response to the

This mother's warm, attentive response to her baby son's gaze lets him know that he is understood and loved.

child's bid for attention gives the child the feeling of being known, understood, attended to, and cared for. The child learns to trust that the caring adult will respond. At the same time, the child trusts herself or himself to elicit a satisfactory response from the adult. In this manner, a child gains confidence: *When I cry, someone hears and comforts me. When I feel hungry, I can get someone to feed me, and I feel better.*

Children involved in trusting relationships seem to know at some deep level that parents and caregivers will support them through new challenges and accomplishments—*Look! I can sit up all by myself!*—and provide comfort and contact when the going gets rough—*Help! I hear a scary noise!* They learn, said developmental psychologist Jillian Rodd (1996), "that the world in which they live is a safe and friendly place and that the people who care for them can be trusted to meet their needs promptly, responsively and consistently. If infants learn that they are valued, cared for and respected as significant members of the group, they will have a strong foundation from which to confidently explore and learn about the world" (p. 21).

Without trusting relationships, children can lose the will to live. Psychoanalyst Rene Spitz (1945) and animal-learning theorist Harry Harlow (1958) found that human infants and monkeys raised without close physical contact and loving attention fail to develop normally and may even die, although their needs for food, shelter, and bodily care are adequately supplied. More recently, brain research has documented similar effects on babies of depressed mothers (Shore, 1997) and on infants and toddlers raised in large groups in understaffed eastern European orphanages (Talbot, 1998). Maps of the electrical activity of the brain reveal that emotional stress "can impede healthy brain activity" (Shore, p. 42), and under extreme conditions of prolonged physical or emotional distress, the brain shuts down altogether. Without the fuel of trusting relationships, the child is overwhelmed with fear, sadness, or grief and becomes increasingly passive and unable to signal for help.

Children involved in trusting relationships seem to know at some deep level that caregivers will support them through new challenges and accomplishments.

By contrast, trusting relationships promote physical development and emotional health. Further, one trusting relationship leads to another, as explained by Jillian Rodd (1996):

> An infant who has at least one secure attachment will be more likely to develop secure relationships with other people in the world, such as grandparents, other familiar adults and children, and care and educational professionals. An infant's relationships with other people, such as early childhood professionals, are not considered to threaten the mother-child bond but rather [thought] to contribute to the infant's developing sense of trust in the world and the people in it. (p. 30)

These toddlers know without a doubt that their caregiver shares their interest in the tiny bug they have discovered.

Active learning, then, takes place within an intensely social context in which trusting relationships are key.

Given the absolute necessity of trusting relationships for learning and development, how do caregivers build and sustain such relationships with the children in their care? In a national study of early child care and attachment, psychologist Margaret T. Owen (1996) described the kinds of behaviors shown by caring adults involved in trusting relationships with very young children:

- Sensitivity to the child's nondistress: The caregiver takes interest in the child's play.

- Positive regard: The caregiver enjoys the child's actions and explorations.

- Lack of negativity: The caregiver communicates warmth and respect.

- Shared emotions: The caregiver acknowledges the child's feelings, from delight to frustration.

- Positive physical contact, including cuddling, hugging, holding, stroking, lap-holding.

- Attentive responsiveness: The caregiver responds readily to the child's signals and approaches, communication and talk; gives the child her full attention.

- Stimulation: The caregiver talks with the child; tells the child what will happen next; encourages the child's problem solving; reads to the child.

These trust-building behaviors and lively social exchanges, discussed further in Chapter 2, shape the way caregivers interact with infants and toddlers throughout the day.

The need to form and maintain trusting relationships with the infants and toddlers in her care shapes every aspect of the caregiver's role and guides the decisions a care program makes about staffing. Because trusting relationships are so vital, programs make every effort to ensure that caregivers work in teams, with each team member responsible for a small group of children who remain in her care from one year to the next, as long as they are enrolled in the care setting. The continuity of care that arises from this arrangement supports the growth of trusting relationships between child and caregiver, between caregiver and families, and between caregivers themselves. (See "The Outcomes of a Trusting Relationship" on p. 36. For specific continuity-of-care strategies, see Chapters 2 and 5.)

Key Experiences: What Infants and Toddlers Learn

When all the elements of active learning are in place—materials to explore bodily, with all the senses; opportunities to make choices; opportunities to

The key experiences help caregivers describe what infants and toddlers do.

communicate discoveries and feelings; and the ongoing, responsive support of trusted adults—what do infants and toddlers actually learn? To answer this question, caregivers and parents in High/Scope settings turn to a set of guidelines called *key experiences,* which frame the content of early learning and development (see "High/Scope Key Experiences for Infants and Toddlers" on p. 38).

Based on child observation, the High/Scope key experiences for infants and toddlers provide a composite picture of what very young children do and what knowledge and abilities emerge from their actions. The key experiences are organized under nine broad areas of infant-toddler

The Outcomes of a Trusting Relationship

Confidence

"It is the luck of most babies to be held well most of the time. On this they build confidence in a friendly world, but, more important, because of being held well enough they are able to make the grade in their very rapid emotional growth. The basis of personality is being laid down well if the baby is held well enough. Babies do not remember being held well—what they remember is the traumatic experience of not being held well enough."

—*D. W. Winnicott (1987, pp. 62–63)*

Curiosity

"While emphasizing the infant's need for autonomy, one must keep in mind the utmost importance of the relationship that infants develop with their primary caregiver. An intimate trusting relationship is the prerequisite for children's healthy separation and individuation. Only after they get 'refueled' during the unhurried times spent with their caregiver will they be willing to let go of the caregiver and explore the environment."

—*Magda Gerber (1981, p. 84)*

Resilience

"A young child's experience of an encouraging, supportive and co-operative mother, and a little later father, gives him a sense of worth, a belief in the helpfulness of others, and a favourable model on which to build future relationships. Furthermore, by enabling him to explore his environment with confidence and to deal with it effectively, such experience also promotes his sense of competence. Thenceforward, provided family relationships continue [to be] favourable, not only do these early patterns of thought, feeling and behavior persist, but personality becomes increasingly structured to operate in moderately controlled and resilient ways, and increasingly capable of continuing so despite adverse circumstances."

—*John Bowlby, (1982, p. 378)*

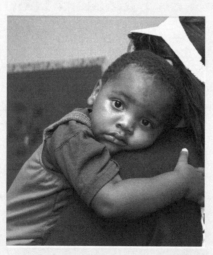

"It is the luck of most babies to be held well most of the time. On this they build confidence in a friendly world."

learning: **sense of self, social relations, creative representation, movement and music, communication and language, exploring objects, early quantity and number, space,** and **time.** The key experiences in these categories[4] provide a basis for the High/Scope Child Observation Record (COR) for Infants and Toddlers, an assessment tool for use in infant-toddler programs (1999). A brief description of the key experiences and how caregivers use them follows.

Developing a *sense of self*

An infant or toddler, through actions with objects and interactions with trusted caregivers, gradually begins to understand that he or she exists as a separate and individual being—*There's me and not me, my hand and Mommy's hand, my skin and the diaper, my foot kicking the squeaker toy, me crying and other babies crying.* With this physical self-awareness comes a child's sense of him- or herself as an independent actor and initiator—*I can do it,* and later, *I can do it myself!* In a supportive active learning setting, infants and toddlers are able to construct an image of themselves as distinct and capable people who can both influence and respond to their immediate world—they are able to develop a sense of self as they engage in the following key experiences:

- *Expressing initiative*—For example, over the course of her development, Makiko turns toward or away from her caregiver or an object; initiates or avoids physical contact with a caregiver or child; selects or rejects a particular toy or object to explore; moves with persistence until reaching a chosen person or object; says "No!" to some choices or proposals from others; expresses her choice or intention in words ("Me, kitty!" "Uppy, uppy!" "Me do it!").

- *Distinguishing "me" from others*—For example, over the course of his development, Alec puts his own fingers, thumb, or toes in his mouth; smiles, coos, babbles at, or touches his image in a mirror; plays with his own hands and feet; claims something or someone as "mine"; spontaneously identifies himself in a photograph or mirror.

- *Solving problems encountered in exploration and play*—For example, over the course of her development, Kelly moves her eyes, head, or hand toward a desired object; repeats an action to make something happen again; moves herself or an object to find someone or something that has disappeared from sight; makes varied attempts to solve a simple problem; verbally identifies a problem before attempting to solve it ("Wagon stuck!").

---

[4] In the COR for Infants and Toddlers, the four key experience categories **exploring objects, early quantity and number, space,** and **time** are combined into one category called **exploration and early logic.**

High/Scope Key Experiences for Infants and Toddlers

Sense of Self
- Expressing initiative
- Distinguishing "me" from others
- Solving problems encountered in exploration and play
- Doing things for themselves

Social Relations
- Forming attachment to a primary caregiver
- Building relationships with other adults
- Building relationships with peers
- Expressing emotions
- Showing empathy toward the feelings and needs of others
- Developing social play

Creative Representation
- Imitating and pretending
- Exploring building and art materials
- Responding to and identifying pictures and photographs

Movement
- Moving parts of the body (head-turning, grasping, kicking)
- Moving the whole body (rolling, crawling, cruising, walking, running, balancing)
- Moving with objects
- Feeling and expressing steady beat

Music
- Listening to music
- Responding to music
- Exploring and imitating sounds
- Exploring vocal pitch sounds

Communication and Language
- Listening and responding
- Communicating nonverbally
- Participating in communication give-and-take
- Communicating verbally
- Exploring picture books and magazines
- Enjoying stories, rhymes, and songs

Exploring Objects
- Exploring objects with the hands, feet, mouth, eyes, ears, and nose
- Discovering object permanence
- Exploring and noticing how things are the same or different

Early Quantity and Number
- Experiencing "more"
- Experiencing one-to-one correspondence
- Exploring the number of things

Space
- Exploring and noticing location of objects
- Observing people and things from various perspectives
- Filling and emptying, putting in and taking out
- Taking things apart and fitting them together

Time
- Anticipating familiar events
- Noticing the beginning and ending of a time interval
- Experiencing "fast" and "slow"
- Repeating an action to make something happen again, experiencing cause and effect

- *Doing things for themselves*—For example, over the course of his development, Dante cries to express a need; holds his bottle or a clean diaper to assist in feeding or diapering; uses his fingers for eating; attempts a simple self-help task, such as drinking from a cup or putting on an article of clothing; does some part or all of such a task as washing his hands, using the toilet or potty, or dressing.

This toddler has a sense of himself as a doer and an experimenter. He expresses initiative when he decides to try waterpainting with the broom!

Learning about *social relations*

Infants and toddlers learn how human beings act and treat one another through their day-to-day interactions with parents, other family members, caregivers, peers, and other adults. When they grow up surrounded by parents and caregivers who care for them in a warm, respectful manner, children learn to trust themselves and others, to be curious, and to explore new learning challenges and adventures. These early social relationships influence their approach to people in later life. Infants and toddlers who are treated well, for example, see themselves and others as "friend-worthy"; they remember and build on their affirming social experiences as they make friends throughout their school years and in adult life—even as they form relationships with their own children. Infants and toddlers learn how social relationships develop as they engage in the following key experiences:

- *Forming attachment to a primary caregiver*—For example, over the course of his development, Ricardo snuggles and cuddles in his caregiver's arms; gazes at the caregiver and exchanges smiles, tongue-clicks, coos, strokes, and pats with her; seeks the comfort of her lap or touch; engages with her in playful give-and-take; summons her by name or tells her what's on his mind ("Mimi! Read book!").

- *Building relationships with other adults*—For example, over the course of her development, Tamara, in the presence of a trusted caregiver, responds to the sounds or gestures of another adult; plays peek-a-boo or simple games with another adult; initiates contact with another adult; brings her toy to or starts a conversation with another adult.

In this child care home, toddlers have the opportunity to make friends with age-mates and older children.

- *Building relationships with peers*—For example, over the course of his development, Nathan watches another child; exchanges sounds or gestures with a peer; physically seeks the company of a peer; pats, hugs, or brings his toy to a peer; addresses a peer by name or talks to a peer.

- *Expressing emotions*—For example, over the course of her development, Emily cries, smiles, frowns, wiggles all over with pleasure; stiffens or turns away from something or someone; laughs at, clings to, pushes away, or hugs someone or something; shows pleasure at being able to make something work or complete an activity or solve a problem; shows frustration with a problem; names her emotion ("I sad!").

- *Showing empathy toward the feelings and needs of others*—For example, over the course of his development, Leon smiles when his caregiver smiles or tenses when the caregiver tenses; cries at hearing another child cry; seeks comforting (by sucking his thumb or seeking a caregiver's attention) when another child is in distress; brings a comfort item (blanket, stuffed animal) to a child who is in distress, hugs

Rochelle who is crying because her mom has left; talks about an emotion displayed by another child ("Baby cry. Sad!").

- *Developing social play*—For example, over the course of her development, Olivia watches another child play; shows pleasure in playing peek-a-boo, This Little Piggy . . . , and other simple social games; seeks the company of a peer and plays alongside; plays hide-and-find the teddy bear; chases or is chased by another person; watches and joins the play of another child by engaging in similar actions or using similar materials.

Learning to hold things in mind through *creative representation*

From their ongoing sensory-motor explorations, infants and toddlers accumulate a critical body of direct experience. They begin to understand, for example, what a blanket is, how it feels, and how to wrap it around themselves for warmth and comfort, and they discover that it continues to exist even when they cannot see it. Gradually, with repeated blanket experiences, they begin to form a mental image of a blanket, that is, to see a blanket in their mind's eye when no actual blanket is in sight. This process of beginning to internalize, or mentally picture, something is the child's first experience with what is called *representation*. Engaging in extensive sensory-motor experience—acting on objects with their whole body and all their senses and repeating these actions at will—enables very young children to experience representation in many forms—to imitate the actions of others, interpret pictures and photographs of actions and objects they have experienced, and begin to use actions and materials to show or represent something they know about their world. Infants and toddlers, building on their direct experiences and experimenting with the beginnings of creative representation, engage in the following key experiences:

- *Imitating and pretending*—For example, over the course of his development, Nicholas watches and listens to another person; imitates the sounds, facial expressions, or gestures of other people; tries to imitate another person who is eating with a spoon or drinking from a cup; repeats the sounds or actions of another person, an animal, or an object; uses one or more objects to stand for something else (uses a basket for a "hat" or some blocks for "pieces of toast").

- *Exploring building and art materials*—For example, over the course of her development, Mai Lee explores her own hands; reaches for and explores blocks, clay, dough, and paper; makes marks and scribbles; stacks several blocks; squeezes clay or dough; labels an object she has built, made, or drawn (paints some blotches and lines on a paper, looks at them, and says "Doggy!").

As they play with baby dolls and in *the baby cradle, these toddlers imitate actions that reflect their own experiences as babies.*

- *Responding to and identifying pictures and photographs*—For example, over the course of his development, Tristan gazes or babbles at a picture or photograph; gestures, points to, or makes the sound of a familiar person, animal, or object in a picture or photograph; selects a picture or photograph to hold or carry; talks about a person, animal, or object in a picture or photograph.

Mastering *movement and music* basics

For sensory-motor infants and toddlers, physical movement plays a major role in all learning. Their emerging sense of themselves as independent actors and doers is strongly connected to their developing ability to control their motions, communicate through the language of gesture and action, handle objects with ease, and move at will from place to place. When children have the space and freedom to move without constraint, they can learn their own physical strengths and limits and can practice movement patterns until mastery propels them to the next physical challenge—*I'm really good at standing up and holding on. Now I'm going to try it without any hands!* Exploring music with their bodies and voices expands children's sensory awareness of sound and steady beat. Here are the movement and music key experiences caregivers will see infants and toddlers mastering:

- *Moving parts of the body*—For example, over the course of his development, Juan lies on his back and turns his head, waves his arms, reaches or grasps or kicks; holds an object with his hands and feet; holds an object and passes it from one hand to another; rolls or throws a ball toward an object or person; kicks a ball; uses small objects with precise coordination (pulls up a zipper, strings large wooden beads, puts pegs into a pegboard).

Learning to crawl means you can find out what's under the "little house"!

- *Moving the whole body*—For example, over the course of her development, Allison wiggles and squirms; rolls over; sits up unassisted; creeps, crawls, scoots, pulls up to a standing position, cruises by holding onto furniture and pulling herself along; balances, walks unassisted; runs, walks down stairs, climbs down a climber by herself.

- *Moving with objects*—For example, over the course of his development, Lukas sets an object in motion by kicking or batting; shakes, bangs, drops, and rolls things; moves an object along while creeping, crawling, scooting, or cruising; carries, pushes, or pulls an object while walking unassisted; propels himself on a wheel toy.

- *Moving, listening, and responding to music, experiencing steady beat, and exploring sounds, pitches, and beginning to sing*—For example, over the course of her development, Tia turns her head toward music; sways or bounces in response to music; imitates sounds; stands unassisted and moves her body to music; moves from one foot to the other; pats, walks, turns, jumps to music; experiments with pitches; joins in singing a simple song.

Learning *communication and language* skills

Social beings from birth, babies want to connect with other human beings to create a context of meaning and belonging. They communicate their feelings and desires through an increasingly complex system of cries, motions, gestures, and sounds and are acutely attuned to the body language and the warm, gentle voices of parents and caregivers. Infants and toddlers listen and respond to the organized sounds of language. They initiate social interaction with trusted caregivers and peers and, in the process, construct a set of useful ideas: that communication is a give-and-take process; that you don't need words to convey and understand safety, acceptance, approval, and respect; that there are lots of ways to make your point; and that trusted people are interested in what you have to communicate and say. In short, infants and toddlers, like all human beings, are "meaning makers" (Wells, 1986). They weave gesturing, making sounds, speaking, watching, and listening into a two-way communication system that draws them into the social community and enables them to participate as contributing members. They learn to communicate by engaging in the following key experiences:

- *Listening and responding* —For example, over the course of his development, Mario turns toward a voice; establishes eye contact and smiles in response to a caregiver's voice; imitates a vocal sound or gesture;

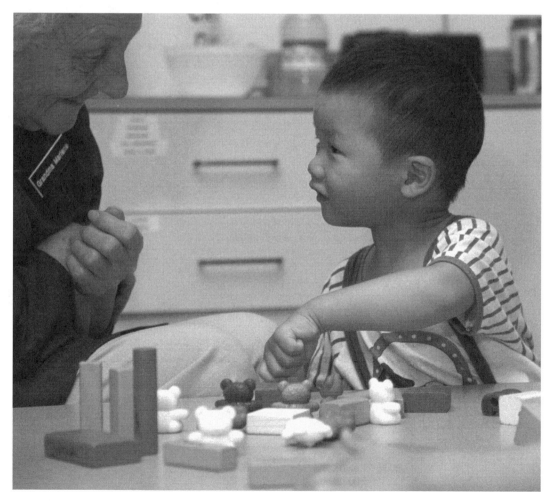

Conversations with infants and toddlers are often nonverbal. This toddler and his caregiver communicate their mutual interest and regard through their closeness, expressions, and gestures.

turns around when his name is spoken; acts on a request or a statement: goes to the coat rack when the caregiver says, "It's outside time!"

- *Communicating nonverbally*—For example, over the course of her development, Katelynn watches, initiates physical contact with, or points to a person, animal, or object; shows an object to a caregiver or child; guides a caregiver to an object, a place, or another person.

- *Participating in communication give-and-take*—For example, over the course of his development, Taylor looks directly at a person's face and coos or smiles; takes turns exchanging sounds or gestures with another person; uses babbling and words to participate in a conversation-like exchange with another person; uses words to make a request or ask a question; sustains a verbal interchange with another person by taking turns talking.

- *Communicating verbally*—For example, over the course of her development, Zongping makes cooing sounds; babbles; uses a word or phrase to refer to a person, animal, object, or action; utters a simple sentence.

- *Exploring picture books and magazines*—For example, over the course of his development, Matthew gazes at a picture book; touches, grasps, or mouths a book; turns the pages of a book; points to or names what is pictured in a book.

- *Enjoying stories, rhymes, and songs*—For example, over the course of her development, Luan becomes still, brightens, vocalizes, bounces, or sways upon hearing a story, rhyme, or song or upon being rocked or patted to the steady beat of a rhyme or song; participates in pat-a-cake or a similar word game, fingerplay, or singing game; asks to hear a story, song, or rhyme; sings or joins in on a story, song, or rhyme.

Learning about the physical world by *exploring objects*

Everything in the world is new for infants and toddlers. Driven by what child psychologist Selma Fraiberg (1959) called an intense hunger for sensory experience, infants and toddlers explore objects to find out what they are and what they do. Beginning with haphazard batting and kicking at things, they gradually expand their exploratory actions and organize their findings into basic working concepts: *That tastes good. This is too cold. That noise scares me. This blanket feels soft. Grass tickles my feet. Spoons make noise. Balls roll away. I can bang with a spoon, and I can bang with a rattle. I can carry stones in a bucket. The wagon moves, and the couch stays still. My blanket feels good in my mouth, and sand feels terrible in my mouth.* As infants and toddlers explore objects to discover their characteristics and how they behave, they engage in the following key experiences:

Reaching, touching, and mouthing are common ways for babies to explore objects.

- *Exploring objects with the hands, feet, mouth, eyes, ears, and nose*—
  For example, over the course of his development, Aidan looks at objects and listens to things that make noise; reaches for and grasps objects; bats at, kicks at, holds, mouths, tastes, pats, waves, turns, drops, and carries objects; uses two objects together, one in each hand; uses an object as a tool to complete a task (shoveling sand into a bucket, pounding dough with a mallet).

- *Discovering object permanence*—For example, over the course of her development, Autumn turns toward a familiar object or person; visually follows an object as it drops, rolls, or moves away; searches for a hidden object; initiates hiding and peek-a-boo games.

- *Exploring and noticing how things are the same or different*—For example, over the course of his development, Marwan shows preference for low rather than high voices, slow rather than fast music, or one pacifier rather than another; repeats a satisfying action or sound; selects like things from a group of toys or materials (all the long-handled objects) to mouth and explore; selects like objects to use for some purpose (filling a bag with just plastic animals or just pine cones); uses the same word to name similar objects (for example, calls all four-legged animals "dogs"); gathers two or more similar objects from a variety of objects.

Learning about *early quantity and number* concepts

As infants and toddlers discover objects through exploration and play, they begin to lay the foundation for an understanding of quantity and number. By holding, mouthing, banging, lifting, carrying, climbing on, and hiding behind things, for example, children begin to see that objects and materials exist separately from them and from their actions on them. Objects come singly or in groups of various sizes; materials come in various quantities. If there is a single object, or a little bit of something, there can also be "more!" As they work with objects and materials, infants and toddlers engage in the following early quantity and number key experiences:

- *Experiencing "more"*—For example, over the course of her development, Tierney prolongs exchanging smiles, coos, or gestures with someone; handles one object after another from a group of objects; selects one object (to put into her mouth or into a container), then another, and another; asks for "more" of something (cereal, juice, blocks); gathers or hoards a number or quantity of something (filling her pockets with several crab apples, pouring more and more sand into a bucket).

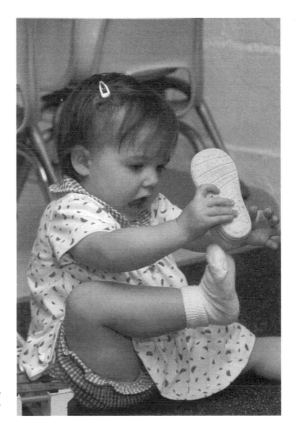

- *Experiencing one-to-one correspondence*—For example, over the course of his development, Daimon puts his thumb or pacifier into his mouth; holds one object in each hand; attempts to put on a hat, or to put a sock or shoe on each foot, or to put a mitten on each hand; puts a toy person in each toy car or in each toy bed.

Trying to put one shoe on one foot is an early experience with one-to-one correspondence!

- *Exploring the number of things*—For example, over the course of her development, Shannon prolongs her gaze at a small collection of objects when the number of objects changes (from one ball to two, or from three wooden spoons to two); anticipates seeing or finding the one, two, or three things that have recently disappeared (continues to search for the other shoe after finding one); says a number name while pointing to each of several objects ("one, two, twee" or "one, two, seben") or in reference to objects ("Two doggies!").

Developing an understanding of *space*

In their active learning journeys, infants and toddlers gain direct bodily awareness of space. Babies inhabit the space immediately around them. With increasing activity and mobility, their sense of space expands as they learn to navigate on their own from one interesting place to another. They experience proximity (nestling in a caregiver's arms), separation (crawling across the room to the steps they want to climb), and enclosure (climbing into a sturdy box). They learn to orient themselves and objects in space so things are easier to see or handle. They attempt to solve the spatial problems they encounter in exploration and play: *I got into this box. Now I have to get out!* Infants and toddlers engage in the following key experiences as, through their own actions, they learn about space:

- *Exploring and noticing location of objects*—For example, over the course of his development, Steen watches a moving object; moves closer to a desired object; moves one object to gain access to another; locates a desired object for exploration or play; retrieves an object he has not seen for a while (remembering and getting a sweater from his tub or personal storage area).

- *Observing people and things from various perspectives*—For example, over the course of her development, Charity observes people and things from a caregiver's arms, from the floor, from the couch, or while lying on her back, front, or side; observes as she sits on the floor or grass, or on a pillow, chair, riser, sturdy

Inside their little cartons, these toddlers experience a sense of coziness and enclosure.

block or carton; observes as she crawls across the floor or grass, under the table, into a carton, up a ramp; watches people and things from an upright position, from perches she has climbed onto, while swinging on a swing, or while bent over to look backward between her legs.

- *Filling and emptying, putting in and taking out*—For example, over the course of his development, Jonathan drinks from a bottle; knocks over a cup of water or a tin of large wooden beads; takes toys off a shelf or out of cupboard; dumps toys out of a can, box, or basket; puts objects into a box, bag, purse, or wagon; fills a cup with water; fills and empties a container of sand, corks, rocks.

- *Taking things apart and fitting them together*—For example, over the course of her development, Latrisha grasps and pulls on objects; waves, shakes, and bangs objects; opens books and doors; takes the tops off boxes; takes off an article of her clothing and attempts to put it back on; fits shapes into shape-sorters, corks into bottles, large pegs into pegboard holes; puts together simple puzzles.

Beginning to learn about *time*

For infants and toddlers, time is now, this moment, the present. In a baby's sensory-motor experience, observed psychologist John Philips (1969), "time is limited to that which encompasses a single event, such as moving a hand from leg to face, feeling the nipple and beginning to suck, or hearing a sound and seeing its source" (p. 20). Babies' internal sensations shape what happens in the present. For example, hunger signals eating, drowsiness signals sleeping. Gradually, children learn to anticipate immediate events from external cues: The sound of running water signals bath time, the sound of Daddy's voice signals play time, the jingling of keys means going somewhere in the car. Some older toddlers can begin to anticipate and express what they are going to do next: "Balls!" (Play with balls.) "Go ducks!" (Go see the ducks.) As infants and toddlers tangle with basic notions of time, they engage in the following key experiences:

- *Anticipating familiar events*—For example, over the course of her development, Leila brightens, becomes still, or turns at hearing a familiar voice or sound; performs a particular action at the sight of a particular person or object (smacking her lips upon seeing food or a spoon, crying upon seeing Mom or a caregiver put on a coat); sees a familiar sight and says what will happen next (saying "Eat, eat!" upon seeing the lunch trays arrive); puts herself in position for the next event (going to the window and looking for Mom at the end of the day); describes her immediate intentions in words ("Wash hands," "Play trucks").

- *Noticing the beginning and ending of a time interval*—For example, over the course of his development, Abdul turns away at the end of a feeding; stops an action to attend to an interesting sound, smell, action, or sensation; uses words to indicate the end of an event ("Down!" "All gone!"); uses a word to indicate a past event (looking out the window, remembering a dog from the day before, and saying "Doggy").

- *Experiencing "fast" and "slow"*—For example, over the course of her development, Lydia rolls, bounces, rocks, bangs, and shakes things at various rates of speed; crawls, cruises, walks, and climbs at various rates of speed.

Here's one sure way to signal the end of your meal—toss your spoon on the floor and look to see what's on the bottom of your plate!

- *Repeating an action to make something happen again, experiencing cause and effect*—For example, over the course of his development, Giles learns to suck; watches an object after accidentally setting it in motion; repeats a simple action to make it happen again; repeats a simple sequence of actions to make something happen again (stacking several blocks, knocking them down, retrieving them, and beginning again).

How Adults Use the Key Experiences to Support Children's Growth and Development

Caregivers can best know, understand, and support each child in their care through close attention, observation, and both physical and verbal interaction. The key experiences guide adults in this effort by broadly defining the actions and learning of sensory-motor children as they build an understanding of their world through direct experiences with people and objects.

The key experiences help caregivers organize, interpret, and act on what they see children doing. When Samantha, a young toddler, unties one of her caregiver's shoes and giggles, her caregiver, Ida, thinks of the **social relations** key experience *forming attachment to a primary caregiver* and thus interprets Samantha's action as a bid for a relationship. Ida knows from her observations of children and from her understanding of child development that playful teasing is one way toddlers typically interact with trusted adults. To let Samantha know that she will play the game Samantha has initiated, and to encourage the **communication and language** key experience *participating in communication give-and-take,* Ida says to Samantha, in mock surprise, "Oh, dear, what happened to my shoe?" Taking this as her cue to continue, Samantha immediately unties Ida's other shoe. "Oh, dear," says Ida, taking her turn in the exchange, "what happened to my other shoe?" After Ida ties her shoes, Samantha starts the game again. In this fashion, Samantha learns both to trust herself to initiate interactions with her caregiver and to trust her caregiver to respond to her actions as though they are playful rather than naughty.

The key experiences help caregivers to understand children's development and thus make decisions about what to do the next day, based on what they observed children doing today: "At lunch time, I noticed Elron exploring and mushing his mashed potatoes with his hands," Ida says to Marta, her teammate. Ida is thinking about the **exploring objects** key experience *exploring objects with the hands, feet, mouth, eyes, ears, and nose.* "So, to extend Elron's mushing of gooey things with his hands, what do you think about using clay tomorrow at group time?" The key experiences help caregivers to select materials and equipment to add to the play space and to think of interactions and experiences that might support and build on children's actions, interests, and need for repetition during each part of the day.

Finally, the key experiences help caregivers to track children's growth and development, to share and interpret children's actions to parents, and to work together with parents to devise common strategies for supporting children's development—in sense of self, social relations, creative representation, movement, communication and language, exploration and early logic—at home and in their care setting. For more about using the key experiences in this manner, see Chapter 5.

As this caregiver reads a story to the children in her lap, she learns about their understanding of the words and pictures.

Active Learning and the Key Experiences: A Summary

Active learning: How infants and toddlers learn

❑ Infants and toddlers learn with their whole body and all their senses.

 ❑ Children explore and play with objects or materials rich in sensory appeal: people, household objects, natural materials, soft and cuddly items, easy-to-grasp objects, squishy or messy materials, things they can set in motion, things they can pull themselves up on and climb, things that make noise.

 ❑ Children engage in direct physical action: reaching, grasping, rolling, sitting, crawling, walking, climbing, carrying.

 ❑ Children return to favorite materials, repeat satisfying actions, and experiment with materials to find out what else they do.

 ❑ Children have access to materials and plenty of space and time for exploration and movement.

❑ Infants and toddlers learn because they *want* to.

 ❑ Children make choices and decisions all day long.

 ❑ Children express preferences for people, materials, and experiences.

 ❑ Children act with autonomy, independence, and curiosity.

 ❑ Children persist in actions they initiate.

❑ Infants and toddlers communicate what they know.

 ❑ Children initiate contact with caregivers.

 ❑ Children express feelings and discoveries to receptive and responsive caregivers.

 ❑ Children string together sounds, gestures, and words in a way that makes sense to them.

❑ Infants and toddlers learn within the context of trusting relationships.

 ❑ Caregivers take interest in the child's play.

 ❑ Caregivers enjoy the child's actions and explorations.

 ❑ Caregivers communicate warmth and respect.

 ❑ Caregivers acknowledge the child's feelings, from delight to frustration.

 ❑ Caregivers provide positive physical contact, including cuddling, hugging, holding, rocking, stroking, and lap-holding.

 ❑ Caregivers give the child their full attention and respond readily to the child's signals and approaches, communication and talk.

 ❑ Caregivers talk with the child, tell the child what will happen next, encourage the child's problem solving, and read to the child.

Key experiences: What infants and toddlers learn

❑ Caregivers are familiar with the key experiences related to sense of self, social relations, creative representation, movement and music, communication and language, exploring objects, early quantity and number, space, and time.

❑ Caregivers observe children and interpret their actions in light of the key experiences.

❑ Caregivers use the key experiences to guide their interactions with children, to plan for activities that support children's learning and development, and to guide their selection of materials for children.

❑ Caregivers use the key experiences to track children's growth and development, to share and interpret children's actions to parents.

References

Ainsworth, Mary. 1963. "The Development of Infant-Mother Interaction Among the Ganda." In *Determinants of Infant Behavior,* vol. 2., ed. B.M. Foss. New York: Wiley.

Bowlby, John. 1982. *Attachment. Attachment and Loss,* vol. 1., 2nd ed. New York: Basic Books.

Chugani, Harry T. 1997. "Neuroimaging of Developmental Non-linearity and Developmental Pathologies." In *Developmental Neuroimaging: Mapping the Development of Brain and Behavior,* eds. Thatcher, Lyon, Rumsey, and Krasnegor, 187–95. San Diego: Academic Press.

Erikson, Erik H. 1950. *Childhood and Society.* New York: Norton.

Fraiberg, Selma. 1959. *The Magic Years.* New York: Scribner's.

Gerber, Magda. 1981. "What Is Appropriate Curriculum for Infants and Toddlers?" In *Infants: Their Social Environments,* eds. Bernice Weissbourd and Judith Musick, 77–85. Washington, DC: National Association for the Education of Young Children.

Goldschmied, Elinor, and Sonia Jackson. 1994. *People Under Three: Young Children in Day Care.* London: Routledge.

Harlow, Harry. 1958. "The Nature of Love." *American Psychologist* 13: 673–85.

High/Scope Child Observation Record (COR) for Infants and Toddlers, field test ed. 1999. Ypsilanti, MI: High/Scope Educational Research Foundation.

Hyson, Marion C. 1994. *The Emotional Development of Young Children: Building an Emotion-Centered Curriculum.* New York: Teachers College Press.

Lambie, Dolores Z., James T. Bond, and David P. Weikart. 1974. *Home Teaching With Mothers and Infants.* Ypsilanti, MI: High/Scope Press.

Owen, Margaret T. 1996. "Symposium on Early Child Care and Attachment: Findings From the National Institute of Child Health and Human Development Study of Early Child Care. Report on the Attachment Task Force." National Association for the Education of Young Children Conference, Dallas, TX, November 22.

Philips, John. 1969. *The Origins of Intellect: Piaget's Theory.* San Francisco: Freeman.

Piaget, Jean. 1952. *The Origins of Intelligence in Children.* New York: Norton.

Piaget, Jean. 1966. *The Psychology of Intelligence.* Totowa, NJ: Littlefield, Adams.

Rodd, Jillian. 1996. *Understanding Young Children's Behavior.* New York: Teachers College Press.

Shore, Rima. 1997. *Rethinking the Brain: New Insights into Early Development.* New York: Families and Work Institute.

Spitz, Rene. 1945. "Hospitalism: An Inquiry into the Genesis of Psychiatric Conditions in Early Childhood." *Psychoanalytic Study of the Child* 1: 53–74.

Stern, Daniel. 1985. *The Interpersonal World of the Infant: A View from Psychoanalysis and Developmental Psychology.* New York: Basic Books.

Talbot, Margaret. 1998. "Attachment Theory: The Ultimate Experiment." *The New York Times Magazine,* May 24, pp. 24–30, 38, 46, 50, 54.

Wells, Gordon. 1986. *The Meaning Makers: Children Learning Language and Using Language to Learn*. Portsmouth, NH: Heinemann Educational Books.

White, Burton, B. Kaban, J. Marmor, and B. Shapiro. 1972. *Child-Rearing Practices and the Development of Competence: Final Report (Grant No. CO-9909 A12)*. Washington, DC: Office of Economic Opportunity, Head Start Division.

Winnicott, D. W. 1987. *Babies and Their Mothers*. Reading, MA: Addison-Wesley.

Related Reading

Hauser-Cram, Penny. 1998. "I Think I Can, I Think I Can: Understanding and Encouraging Mastery Motivation in Young Children." *Young Children* 53(4, July): 67–71.

Hohmann, Charles. 1999. *Learning Environment Grades 4–6*. Ypsilanti, MI: High/Scope Educational Research Foundation.

Hohmann, Mary, and David P. Weikart. 1995. *Educating Young Children: Active Learning Practices for Preschool and Child Care Programs*. Ypsilanti, MI: High/Scope Press.

Mahler, Margaret S., Fred Pine, and Anni Bergman. 1975. *The Psychological Birth of the Human Infant: Symbiosis and Individuation*. New York: Basic Books.

As these young active learners decide for themselves how to negotiate the steps to the outdoor play yard, through their senses and actions they learn about climbing. A trusted caregiver serves as their safety net.

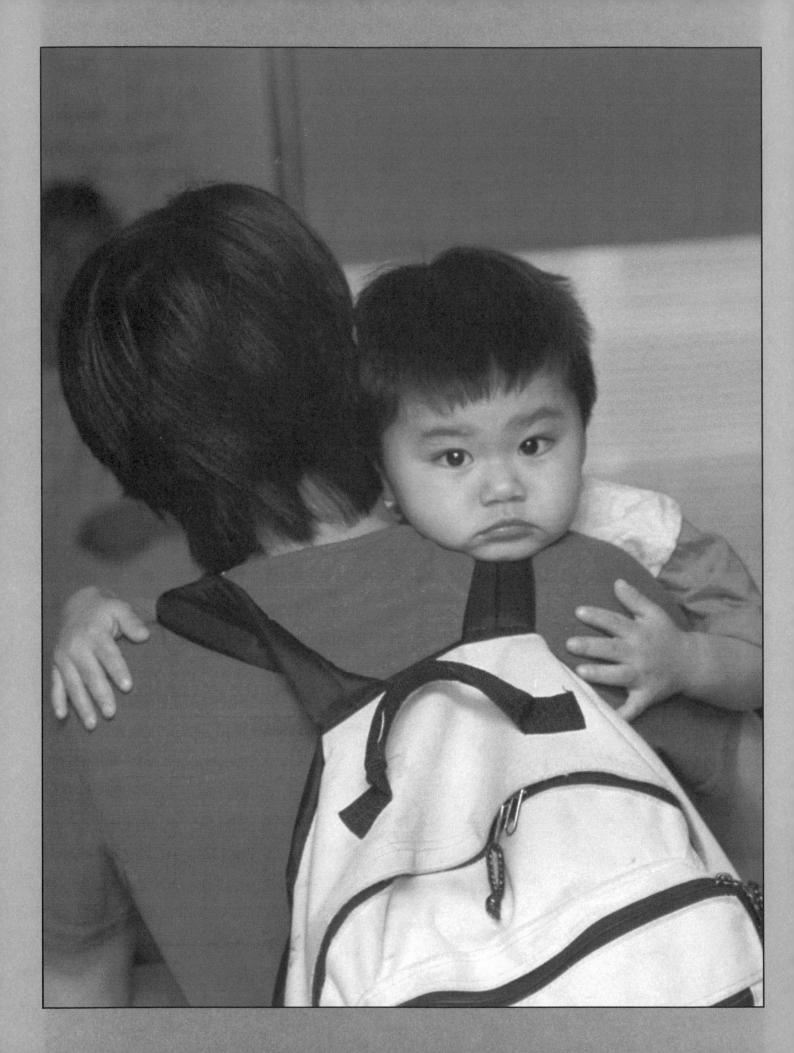

2
Supportive Adult-Child Interactions

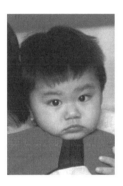

*Consistent, nurturing relationships with the same caregivers,
including the primary one, early in life and throughout childhood
are the cornerstones of both emotional and intellectual competence,
allowing the child to form the deep connectedness that grows into
a sense of shared humanity and, ultimately, empathy and
compassion. Relationships with both parents and day-care
staff must have this stability and consistency.*

—*Stanley Greenspan (1997)*

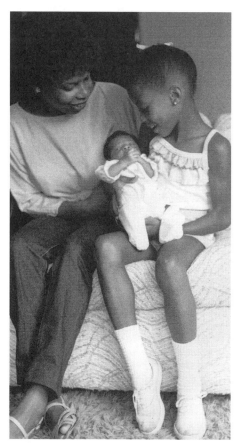

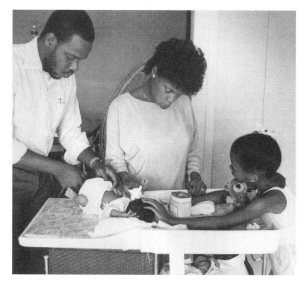

When all goes well, a child has the same supportive family throughout childhood, and the family grows together over the years. Infant-toddler programs strive to provide children with similar continuity of care.

What do infants and toddlers in group care need from their caregivers? In every interaction, these very young children need to be treated with great care and respect. Only then can they form the trusting human relationships that allow them to develop curiosity, courage, initiative, empathy, a sense of self, and a feeling of belonging to a friendly social community. Infants and toddlers who experience adults' daily, ongoing support and respect are free from undue stress. This allows them to devote their energy to the all-important work of sensory-motor exploration, through which they construct an understanding of their social and physical world. They also have the opportunity to form healthy working ideas about themselves and others: *I am a good person. People are generally trustworthy and pleasant to be with. The world is full of interesting possibilities. With help from trusted friends, I can meet life's challenges.*

Treating children well so they can grow and learn is the primary aim of caregivers in an active learning setting. How caregivers go about this task may vary from person to person and from setting to setting. In general, though, caregivers use four broad strategies for building and sustaining supportive, respectful relationships with the ever-changing infants and toddlers in their care. They

- Establish policies that promote continuity of care.

- Create a climate of trust for children.

- Form partnerships with children.

- Support children's intentions.

Establishing Policies That Promote Continuity of Care

When all goes well, a child has the same supportive parents (or parent) throughout childhood.[5] The child-parent threesome (or pair) grow together and come to know one another's interests and interaction styles as the days, months, and years unfold. Infant and toddler development proceeds most smoothly when directors and caregivers make every possible effort to replicate the continuity of care represented by the stable, ongoing parent-child relationship. At home, for example, infants and toddlers typically do not exchange one parent for a new parent every 6 to 8 months; so at the center they should not be expected to exchange one caregiver for a new caregiver every couple of months or even every year. Infants and toddlers cared for away from home by a series of ever-changing caregivers have, for a good part of their lives, little chance to experience trusting relationships, and this

---

[5]In this book, we use "parent" to refer to whatever parent-figure a child may have, whether it be a mother, a father, a grandparent, a foster parent, an adult sibling, or a legal guardian.

can cause them undue stress and confusion. This is particularly true for infants or toddlers whose parents are unavailable or not consistently able to care for them at home.

A child care and early learning setting that is organized in a way that provides continuity of care benefits everyone involved—children, caregivers, and families. Children form trusting relationships with the primary caregivers who are with them day after day, from one year to the next. Being surrounded by known and trusted people enables children to explore the novelties and challenges that promote their growth. At the same time, caregivers come to know "their" children and accumulate a growing store of very useful, specific knowledge about each one of them as they change from creeper-crawlers, to cruisers, to walkers, for example, or from nonverbal communicators, to cooers and babblers, to talkers. Families have the opportunity to form trusting relationships with their children's primary caregivers—caregivers and parents come to know each other, form common expectations, and learn to communicate effectively about the children who draw them together.

The following specific strategies for promoting continuity of care are easiest to implement if you have a new center where no other staffing policies and expectations yet exist. If you have an established center, however, these strategies might be implemented gradually, one at time, over a year or so, with small volunteer groups of existing staff or with newly hired staff. (See "Steps Toward a Policy of Continuity in an Infant-Toddler Program" on the facing page.) In either case, implementing continuity of care is greatly aided when a program has in place the factors that promote low staff-turnover—administrative support and professional working conditions for caregivers, including appropriate salaries and benefits.[6]

Anchor each child's day around a primary caregiver

Infants and toddlers feel at ease when they are surrounded by interesting materials and familiar supportive adults. To ensure that each child develops a close, reliable, affectionate relationship that will sustain him or her while away from home, it is important to assign each child to a *primary caregiver* for the duration of enrollment in the program. Having such a stable relationship reduces the considerable stress on the infant or toddler of having to adjust to an ever-changing stream of caregivers. It also helps to provide the trust and predictability that enable children to live through the frustrations and challenges necessary for growth and development, according to child therapist and pediatrician Judit Falk (1979): "A stable system of relations is a precondition . . . to the child's ability to assimilate the society's pattern of accepted

---

[6]Low staff-turnover was cited as part of the explanation for the long-term positive effects of early child care reported by the Abecedarian Project (Campbell, 1998). Teachers in the project received ongoing training and were compensated at rates higher than is typical in this field.

values, its norms, its rules of behavior, its set of prohibitions, by means of imitation, assimilation, and identification" (p. 117).

In group care, the primary caregiver is the child's anchor, the person on whom the child can rely for reassurance, guidance, and basic care. She is attuned to the child's personal cues, interests, and strengths. She knows, for example, that Maria's diaper-changing routine includes cuddling and playing This Little Piggy . . . ; she knows that Demetrius says "de" when he wants a drink; she knows that Jennifer says "beboo" when she means "peek-a-boo" and that she rubs her eyes when she is tired, naps fitfully when she's teething, can find and retrieve the "blankie" she left in the chair, and needs more lap time when she's coming down with a cold.

The primary caregiver plays a major role in the child's life at the center but is not the child's exclusive caregiver. Because of illness, vacations, parent meetings, conferences, or other unavoidable circumstances, she may need to be absent from the center from time to time. Therefore she shares that

In group care, the primary caregiver is the child's anchor, the person on whom the child can rely for reassurance, guidance, basic care—and enjoyable times outdoors!

Steps Toward a Policy of Continuity in an Infant-Toddler Program

- Develop caregivers' competencies with children from birth to age 3.
- Promote caregivers' professional pride through training.
- Make supportive staff relationships a priority of your program.
- Train and support caregivers in their communications with parents.
- Begin the changeover to continuity with one or two caregivers who are interested in "moving up" with their small group of children.
- Expand the length of time children stay together with a caregiver team. For example, have a group of infants remain together until age 2 instead of moving to another caregiver team upon reaching age 1.
- Hire new staff with the expectation of continuity, for example, with the expectation that they will work with the same small group of children for 3 years.
- Purchase toys and equipment adaptable for children of a wide age-range.

—Sheila Signer (1995, p. 6)

child's caregiving (and thus forms a team) with one or two secondary caregivers. Each child, then, interacts daily with one primary caregiver and one (or two) secondary caregivers, all of whom know the child and provide consistent care and support. As educator J. Ronald Lally (1995) said, "It is crucial that there are other relationships the infant can fall back on when the primary caregiver is missing. This way, a secondary attachment is available, and the child won't feel abandoned" (p. 64). (See "Why a Primary Caregiver?" on the facing page.)

Create small groups of children who share a caregiver team

Each caregiver takes primary responsibility for two, three, or four children. (The actual number is usually related to the ages of children and to county, state, or federal licensing requirements, accreditation standards, and available funding.) To create a team, the primary caregiver and her children join with one (or, at most, two) other primary caregivers and their children, and the adult team members act as secondary caregivers for one another's children. Working with a small group of children allows caregivers and children to establish trusting relationships and, according to Lally (1995), "promotes personal contact between children, quiet exploration, and one-to-one attention from a caregiver. . . . Instead of the confusion of many people, small groups offer comfort and a sense of belonging to everyone in the group." He went on to say that the caregiver "(1) is able to see the infant's cues from afar, (2) makes eye contact and provides emotional support from a distance, and (3) is available if the child needs to return for emotional refueling" (p. 65). (For more about how the caregiver team works together, see Chapter 5.)

Keep children and caregivers together from year to year

When an infant or toddler enrolls in the center, the child joins a small group, or cluster, of one, two, or three other children under the care of one primary caregiver. This adult-child cluster, together with a second (and possibly third) adult-child cluster, remains together from year to year. Depending on how the center is organized, this might mean all moving together from one room to another room each year, or all remaining together in the same room year after year, until the children leave the program. Also, children within each cluster may be close in age, or they may range in age. In either case, children remain with their primary caregiver as long as they are enrolled at the center. (See Chapter 5 for a discussion of specific ways to keep children and caregiver teams together.)

Arrange caregivers' schedules around children's needs

Children in group care are often content to spend time with various caregivers or on their own, exploring materials and interacting with peers, but for regular reassurance and when things go wrong, they want their primary caregiver. Only *she* will provide consolation when they are are tired, hungry, hurt, or ill. Therefore, it is important to schedule caregivers so they are present when their primary care children arrive and/or depart, eat, and go to sleep, and so they are at least "on call" when one of their children becomes sick or injured. For example, in the "Sample Daily Schedules for an Infant-Toddler Program" on pp. 196–197 of Chapter 4, caregivers Yvonne and Leanne are present at the beginning of each day for children's arrivals (Yvonne alone for the earliest children), caregivers Kim and Yvonne are present at the end of each day for children's departures (Kim alone for the latest departures), and Yvonne and Kim are present for breakfast and for the transition from outside to lunch to naps; during naps, all three caregivers are available to meet together for ½ hour of daily team planning. Consistent, harmonious greetings and goodbyes from the same caregivers each day, as shown in this example, help to build a sense of trust and security for children and their families.

Tell children and parents about caregiver absences and returns

Caregivers are of course absent from time to time because of illness, emergencies, vacations, or attendance at conferences and training. On these occasions, it is important to inform even the youngest children. When Yvonne, for example, was out with the flu, Kim told each child and parent as they arrived, "Yvonne's not feeling well, so she won't be here today. Kelly (the center's permanent substitute caregiver) will be here all day in her place. She and I

Why a Primary Caregiver?

"Most of us have, or would like to have, a special relationship with some person on whom we can rely, a relationship which is significant and precious to us. If we are parted from that person we have ways of preserving continuity even through long separations. We use telephones, letters, photographs, recollections, dreams and fantasies to keep alive the comfort we derive from such human relationships. When we lose them, we experience sadness and often deep feelings of despair. If we look back we may recall important people in our early lives who, though they are not there in person, give continuity and significance to how we conduct our present lives. Often we seek to repeat and to enjoy again the warmth of those relationships in a different form.

"The young children with whom we work, and who do not yet have language to express what they are experiencing, need to have these special relationships too, and [they] deeply need to have them in a very immediate and concrete way. It is against this back[drop] of what we know from our own experience, that we have to consider the meaning of a key person [primary caregiver] for a young child. We can never remind ourselves too often that a child, particularly a very young and almost totally dependent one, is the only person in the nursery who cannot understand why he is there. He can only explain it as abandonment, and unless he is helped in a positive and affectionate way, this will mean levels of anxiety greater than he can tolerate."

—Elinor Goldschmied and Sonia Jackson (1994, p. 37)

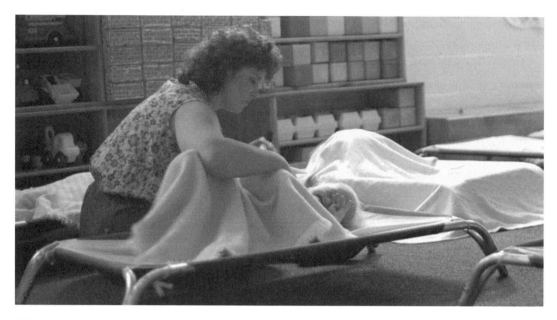

While children in group care are often content to spend time with various caregivers, when it's time for sleep, they want the reassuring touch of their primary caregiver.

will take care of you." (Even infants are comforted by the reassuring tone of such statements.) Children and families need to know very clearly who is caring for children in the absence of their primary caregiver.

Staff at one active learning infant-toddler program use photographs and a pocket-board to let children and parents know who will be at the center each day and who will not. A box containing photographs of individual children and caregivers is located in the entrance area. As each child or caregiver arrives for the day, that person's photograph is taken from the box and placed in a pocket on the "in" side of the board, so all can see who is in that day. (Toddlers enjoy placing their own pictures in the pockets.) The "out" side of the pocket-board is draped with a transparent scarf. When a child or caregiver is absent, his or her photograph is placed in an "out" pocket, under the scarf. The children soon learn that the "out" people (under the scarf) will not be at the center that day. They also learn that, as in the game of peek-a-boo, the absent people *will* come back!

Have primary caregivers record observations of their children

To better focus on her small group of children, each primary caregiver records daily brief anecdotal observations of her individual children. These observations then serve as a basis for the caregiver team's daily planning and for conversations with parents. (See Chapter 5 for more details.) In one active learning center for infants and toddlers, for example, each primary caregiver records brief anecdotal observations related to the infant-toddler key experiences. Parents eagerly read these observations each day to find out what their child has been doing at the center. (See "Interesting Things Your Child Did Today!" on p. 66.) Parents, in turn, also write brief observations about their child in the morning as they sign in. This fills in caregivers about what the child has been doing at home. (See "Sample Parent Sign-In Sheet" on p. 67.)

Creating a Climate of Trust for Children

To carry out the principles of active learning, caregivers treat children in ways that help them to develop a sense of trust in their caregivers and in themselves. They use the following strategies, which spell out what it means to treat children "with great care and respect." Regardless of the organization of your care setting, these strategies in themselves will help to promote continuity of care when they are put to use by everyone, including caregivers and all other adults who interact with children throughout the day.

This caregiver enjoys her children's interests in soap bubbles and water play.

Interesting Things Your Child Did Today!

Child's Name: *Nora G.*   **Date:** *5/28/___*

Reporter's Name: *Yvonne L.*

Sense of Self

At choice time, Nora figured out a way to get the big rubber ball into the climber. She tried to fit it through the ladder rungs, but it was too big, so she rolled it up the slide.

Social Relations

When Nora saw Coty crying at outside time, she brought him his "blankie."

Creative Representation

Nora made scribbles with a marker and a crayon on a big piece of white paper.

Movement and Music

Nora fit corks through the openings of some plastic pop bottles. She also shook the bottles, listening to the sound of the corks.

Communication and Language

Each time Nora put another ball inside the climber, she said, "Aw gone!"

Exploring Objects

At outside time, Nora searched for and found Coty's blanket inside the ball tub.

Early Quantity and Number

Nora put one cork in each of several small yogurt containers.

Space

Nora emptied all the yogurt containers of corks and filled them again with stones and shells.

Time

After lunch, Nora anticipated diaper change by getting a diaper from her cubby and giving it to me.

Sample Parent Sign-In Sheet

Child's Name: *Nora G.*　　　　　**Date:** *5/29/___*

Reporter's Name: *Elizabeth S.*　　**Relationship to Child:** *mother*

Let me tell you about my child!

- *Nora wanted me to hold her in the grocery store, didn't want to sit in the cart as usual. She also fell asleep early last night, so she may be coming down with something. This morning she ate fine, though.*

- *In the car on the way here, Nora spotted 4 "doggies." One was a cat, but I didn't correct her!*

Touch, hold, speak to, and play with children in a warm, unhurried manner

Caregivers interact with infants and toddlers in very physical ways, knowing that holding, touching, cuddling, hugging, rocking, singing, speaking kindly, and being within sight and reach is essential to very young children, who experience everyone and everything in sensory and active ways. While infants and toddlers may not understand *all* of what adults say to them, they comprehend body language immediately and thoroughly. Caregivers strive to carry out every adult-child interaction—a game of peek-a-boo, a trip to the bathroom, a look out the window, a temper tantrum—in a warm, unhurried manner, because no matter what is happening, they want children to feel, hear, and see that they are loved and cared for. Instead of pushing a child to respond, caregivers try to match their pace to the pace of the infant or toddler they are engaged with, responding to the child's actions and cues at the tempo set by the child. This gives caregivers an opportunity to understand and respect what the child is doing and communicating. The child, in turn, experiences being seen, heard, and understood.

Take pleasure in your interactions with children

Caregivers of infants and toddlers tend to genuinely enjoy and appreciate the unique characteristics of very young children—their energy and curiosity, their rapid spurts of growth, their physicality, their unique means of communicating. Interactions with these children can be as varied and diverse as the children themselves, and caregivers find themselves tailoring their interaction styles to fit individual children. Since children of this age are too self-involved to be treated as a "group," caregivers enjoy the challenge of engaging in one-to-one interactions with them even when they have more than one child to feed, read to, or pull in a wagon at one time. In dealing with each child, caregivers exhibit authenticity, an essential human quality psychologist Carl Rogers (1983) defined as "a transparent realness . . . , a willingness to be a person, to be and live the feelings and thoughts of the moment. When this realness includes a prizing, a caring, a trust, a respect for the learner, the climate for learning is enhanced" (p. 133). Further, since infants and toddlers learn through sensory-motor exploration and play, caregivers, in their own manner, are genuinely playful with children rather than stern and demanding, or efficient and businesslike.

Respond supportively to children's needs and attention-getting signals

Caregivers strive to give infants and toddlers their undivided attention during each interaction. This practice allows them to notice and attend to each child's needs and unique attention-getting signals.

Whether they express themselves nonverbally or in words, infants and toddlers in active learning settings know they can count on caregivers to answer their calls of distress. Instead of viewing a child's distress as an annoyance or interruption, caregivers, even when they are engaged with another child, show a genuine concern for the distressed child through eye contact, or verbal reassurance, or some more direct action, such as holding, rocking, hugging, or touching. They acknowledge children's feelings and ask even the youngest children what is troubling them. ("You're crying hard, Lissa. I can

 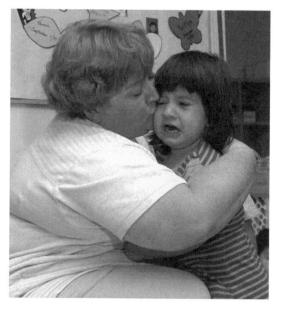

In times of distress, this toddler turns to her primary caregiver for comfort and reassurance.

see you're upset. What's the trouble?") Even when a child cannot yet answer in words, he or she is reassured by the caregiver's presence, calm voice, and focused attention. Eventually, according to Magda Gerber (1979), "the child will learn to give better cues, and you will learn to understand the child better. This is how dialogue between infant and [caregiver] develops" (p. 16). In this scenario, James's cue consists of wanting to be close to his caregiver:

> *After his mom leaves, James clings to his caregiver's leg. "It's sad when mommy leaves for work," she says to James as she bends down and encircles him with her arm. "Would you like to cuddle, James?" she asks gently. When he nods yes, she picks him up. "Rock," James says, pointing to the rocking chair. He spends a good while on his caregiver's lap, looking at books and watching the other children. Instead of trying to push James away or brush off his concerns, his caregiver provides the extra comfort he needs. When she leaves the rocking chair to greet another child, Kara, and later to change Kara's diaper, she invites James along with her. Throughout these interactions, James clings to his caregiver's leg, and she strokes his head when she has a free hand. When she completes Kara's diaper change and Kara has returned to her play, she lifts up James and holds him on one hip while she makes an entry on Kara's diapering log. By midmorning, after a nap, James feels ready to leave his caregiver and venture off on his own to play at the sand table.*

By responding supportively in this manner, James's caregiver gives him a sense of hope and significance. "A fussy infant," observed infant and toddler specialist Peter Mangione (1990), "may turn out to be a hungry infant. A caregiver's prompt response will satisfy much more than hunger. As the caregiver finds out what the child needs, the child learns that someone is there for him or her. In other words, the child is learning basic trust" (p. 11).

Give children time to interact and respond in their own way

Each infant or toddler has a unique way of acting or interacting and does so on his or her own timetable. An older infant, Michelle, for example, initiates a game of scarf peek-a-boo with her caregiver. Natalie, an infant of about the same age, watches the game with apparent interest but does not join in, even when the caregiver offers her a scarf. Her caregiver, however, accepts Natalie's response, realizing, that Natalie *has,* in a sense, joined the game simply by choosing to watch it.

Caregivers also understand that infants and toddlers, craving repetition, often spend a long time repeating an enjoyable action—banging a spoon, turning the pages of a board book, filling and emptying a basket of shells.

Therefore, caregivers might play endless games of peek-a-boo with children or willingly look at their favorite books or read their favorite stories again and again, because they understand that with child-initiated repetition comes understanding and mastery.

Support children's relationships with peers and other adults

Infants and toddlers thrive on supportive relationships, and with each relationship, their world-to-explore expands. Caregivers, therefore, help children form and sustain relationships with peers and with other adults at the center. For example, a caregiver might acknowledge one toddler's preference for another: "Tejas and Emily, I see you like to sit together at lunch!" Or a caregiver might think of ways to provide ongoing opportunities for a particular

Settled comfortably on the floor feeding the baby, this caregiver enjoys the company and "help" of a sociable young toddler!

child to interact with a peer as the two children's interest in each other emerges and develops. Over several days, for example, a caregiver observes that young infant Anil looks in another infant's direction every time that infant, Raina, cries, coos, or makes a noise, so today the caregiver places Anil on a blanket next to Raina. Both babies look at each other, wiggle, and coo with pleasure.

Caregivers resist the temptation to lure "their" children away from playing and interacting with other caregivers. While they may feel a twinge of jealousy, primary caregivers acknowledge this feeling and then set it aside in favor of the child's need to explore and connect with other trusted adults. It is important to remember that your role as a primary caregiver is not an exclusive one. It is meant to guarantee continuity of care rather than to limit children to one trusting relationship at the center.

When a child shows preference for relating to a program director, volunteer, or student teacher whose participation with your cluster of children is intermittent or temporary, it is important that you acknowledge the child's sense of sorrow and loss when that person is not present and provide opportunity for the child and his or her parents to say goodbye on that person's last day at the center. At the same time, whenever possible, you may want to schedule ancillary caregivers so their participation with the children is regular and ongoing. In one setting, for example, the director arranged for a foster grandparent to spend the same 4 hours of the day with the same cluster of children 4 days a week, instead of having her switch from one cluster of children to another on a daily basis. Another child care center that was connected to a college arranged to have two student teachers work with the same cluster of children for two semesters instead of having one student with the cluster for one semester and then another student with them for the next semester. The same center also relegated some other early education students to the observation room (instead of having them "on the floor" with children) to complete the observations they needed to make as part of a course requirement. This plan avoided overwhelming children with a changing stream of unfamiliar adults.

Forming Partnerships With Children

Caregivers and children share many kinds of interactions. Even though caregivers are the experienced senior members in these interactions, they strive to structure their relationships with infants and toddlers as *partnerships*. This means making every effort to create a sense of shared control with children so that children are free to initiate ideas as well as to try out and adapt others' ideas to fit their own needs. Following are some caregiver practices you can use to establish partnerships and share control with infants and toddlers.

Interact at the child's physical level

Very young children spend a lot of time on or close to the floor. Since communication is generally aided when the participants can see each other clearly, caregivers find themselves sometimes holding or lifting up an infant or toddler for a face-to-face exchange and sometimes lowering themselves to kneel, sit, or lie on the floor beside the child. By getting on the child's physical level as often as possible, caregivers share control. And children in turn are less likely to perceive adults as giants who swoop down without warning to impose a change of activity or carry them off to "faraway places."

Respect children's preferences and individual temperaments

Caregivers try to respect rather than to alter children's preferences for certain companions, foods, or activities. One day 6-month-old Hunter, for example, eats all of his strained peaches. The next day he closes his mouth and turns his head away when his caregiver offers a spoonful of strained peaches. "I see you don't want these peaches today, Hunter," she says, sensing that either the taste, or the texture, or being spoonfed isn't to Hunter's liking on this particular day. When she then puts some banana slices in front of him, Hunter picks them up and feeds fruit to himself.

Sometimes children express conflicting needs and preferences: Hanna, a toddler, wants to fall asleep at her usual nap time because she is tired; she also wants to stay awake to watch Tommy play next to her with his stuffed

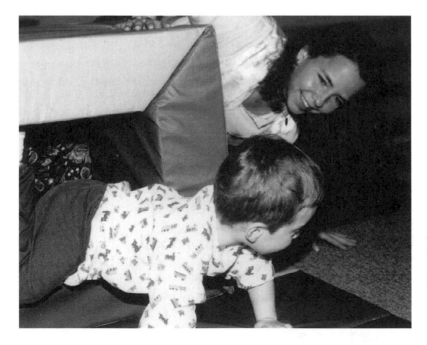

Down on her hands and knees, this caregiver matches a young toddler's enthusiasm for crawling through the tunnel.

bear. In such cases, the caregiver strives to understand the child's internal conflict of *I'm tired but I don't want to miss anything!* She verbally acknowledges the child's dilemma. "Hanna, you want to go to sleep, but you want to watch Tommy." Instead of exasperation and an ultimatum, she offers sympathy and comfort: "It's really hard when you want to be asleep and awake at the same time, Hanna." She strokes Hanna's arm. "I'm going to cover you with your blanket so you can watch Tommy until you go to sleep." While Hanna may still fight to stay awake, she does so with the sense that her real feelings have been acknowledged and accepted, rather than with the sense that now she must fight against sleep *and* her caregiver.

In one center, caregivers found that although their toddlers are sleepy right before lunch, *after* lunch many children are too energized to fall asleep directly. Therefore, while several children leave the lunch table and go right to their cots, the others play vigorously about the room for a short time until, one by one, they too settle down for naps. Even then, Jacob requires less sleep and rarely naps. Instead, he plays with toys or looks at books on the floor while the caregiver team meets nearby. This child was particularly happy throughout a neighboring building's renovation. During nap time, he was glued to the window, watching the workers and their machines.

Caregivers understand that children's temperaments affect how they interact with people and materials. They know that children vary as to activity level, biological rhythms, approach and withdrawal, adaptability, quality of mood, intensity of reaction, sensitivity threshold, distractibility, and persistence, which are the aspects of temperament defined by child psychiatrists Alexander Thomas and Stella Chess (1970). (See "Aspects of Temperament" on p. 74.) Because children's temperaments are a normal part of who they are, caregivers strive to adjust their interaction style to accommodate and support each child's pace and style. An energetic caregiver, for example, does not try to prod a deliberate, cautious child into action. And a quiet, deliberate caregiver does not try to slow down an energetic child. If a child finds a certain pair of socks intolerably tight, his caregiver, who may not be bothered by wearing tight socks, does not try to persuade him otherwise. Instead, she helps him to remove the irritating socks and to select a comfortable alternative.

Whether children are naturally "easygoing," "quiet," or "always on the go" (Brazelton, 1969), caregivers in an active learning setting try to accept rather than alter the child's overall orientation toward life. For example, caregivers accept and support the child who is fairly active, tries out new foods with interest, naps at predictable times, is not easily distracted when exploring self-selected materials, and is generally happy except before and after naps. At the same time, they slow themselves down and patiently support the child who moves very deliberately and only when necessary, who tends to withdraw initially from new people and materials, likes to eat a few familiar foods, naps regularly twice a day, plays alone or watches others play, and

Aspects of Temperament

- **Activity level:** How much a child moves. Many infants or toddlers, right from the start, are all over the place. For example, they turn themselves completely around in their sleep and rarely keep a blanket on for any length of time. Others are less active. They wake up in the same position they went to sleep in, with all the covers still tucked in.

- **Biological rhythms:** The regularity or irregularity of a child's eating, sleeping, and eliminating cycles.

- **Approach and withdrawal:** How a child reacts to new people or materials. For example, a child may eagerly approach a new toy, cautiously approach it, avoid it altogether, or gradually warm up to it.

- **Adaptability:** The ease and speed with which a child adjusts to new situations. Some children fall asleep wherever they happen to be when they become tired. Others require their own crib or cot and a specific comfort item, such as a favorite "blankie," stuffed animal, or book.

- **Mood:** The child's general state of mind or feeling. For example, some children are usually pleasant and in a cheerful frame of mind. Some are usually quiet and thoughtful. Some generally fuss and worry. Some children shift from one mood to another in response to people and circumstances, while other children are less apt to swing from one mood to another.

- **Intensity of reaction:** The energy level with which a child expresses his or her mood. For example, some fussy children become very upset when their food is not at the temperature they prefer. Other fussy children are only mildly upset when this occurs.

- **Sensitivity threshold:** The child's tendency to react to potentially irritating stimuli. Some children are very frightened by sudden loud noises like thunder and lightning; others are not perturbed by a storm. Some children cannot tolerate a wet diaper and need to be changed right away; others hardly seem to notice diaper wetness, even when it causes a rash.

- **Distractibility:** How easily a child's attention is interrupted. Some children continue to drink from a bottle or to finger-paint, for example, without regard for ringing phones or people coming through the door. Other children must stop whatever they are doing to check out each new noise or event.

- **Persistence and attention:** How long a child will stick with a difficult activity without giving up and how long a child will concentrate on something before shifting interest to something else. For example, some children become so absorbed in what they are doing that they resist stopping for a wash or a diaper change. Other children flit from one thing to another and are less resistant to caregiving interruptions.

—Adapted from Stella Chess (1990, pp. 7–9)
and Judith Evans and Ellen Ilfeld (1982, pp. 39–43)

is generally quiet and self-contained. And they also energetically support the child who is active all day long except for one 20-minute nap, enjoys some new people and not others, loudly disputes any attempt to interrupt his or her play, and is generally either very involved or very frustrated.

Follow children's lead

Another way to build partnerships with children is by following children's cues throughout the day. That is, during play and caregiving routines,

- **Imitate what the child is doing.** As 9-month-old Elizabeth gets her diaper changed, she blows a kiss to her caregiver, who blows one back to her.

- **In interactions, pause and wait for the child to take a turn.** Toddler Sean's caregiver Marina rolls a ball toward Sean, who is sitting opposite her on the floor. As he reaches for the ball, she waits to see what he will do with it, instead of urging him to roll it back to her or quickly rolling another ball to him.

- **Follow the child's pace and interests.** Sam, a caregiver, sets a small basket of blocks next to infant Jessica, and Jessica immediately dumps out the blocks. She then looks at Sam, crawls to the bookshelf, takes down a book, and hands it to Sam. "You want to read this book now, Jessica?" he asks. She nods affirmatively and crawls into his lap.

- **Play with the same materials the child is using.** Marnie, a caregiver, sits down next to Josh, an older toddler, who is using sponges to daub paint on a piece of newsprint. Marnie watches Josh for a few moments, then picks up a sponge, dips it in paint, and applies it to another piece of newsprint. Josh stops to watch Marnie briefly, then continues painting.

Watch and listen to children

Communication is a complex process, especially when one of the partners is just learning the ropes. Infants and toddlers rely heavily on patient listeners to understand and respond appropriately to the intent of their messages.

Caregivers in High/Scope active learning settings try to be especially alert to children's nonverbal communications, because they are so easy to miss. Through careful attention, they learn that infants communicate interest, pleasure, and excitement by looking, smiling, making noises, or wiggling—and that turning away is an infant's way of saying *That's enough.* In one setting, for example, caregivers observing their children at mealtime documented the following ways that a child nonverbally communicates *I'm finished eating:* accepting the nipple without sucking, turning away from the bottle, playing with the bottle, gazing at other children, pulling the bottle out of

During feeding, this caregiver pays close attention to nonverbal communication. She returns the baby's gaze and accepts the baby's light touch of her hand.

his/her mouth, turning away from the spoon, not opening his/her mouth for the spoon, holding food in the cheeks but not swallowing it, letting food drip out of his/her mouth, dropping bits of food on the floor, leaving the table, putting the bowl on his/her head, pulling at or removing the bib. As their children learned to talk, the caregivers documented them using such words as these to bring an end to eating: "all done," "no," "no more," or "bib off."

Through watching and listening, caregivers also learn to fill in the context for toddlers' often elliptical utterances. For example, they learn that Tommy's "Tata!" means *I see a tractor!* and that Eleanor's "Me! Bag!" means *I want to carry the bag!* As early educators Elinor Goldschmied and Sonia Jackson (1994) have reminded us, "Giving full attention to a child as he tries haltingly to express himself can be difficult for a [caregiver] amidst the distractions and demands of a group, but it is essential if we aim to help a child gain command of language" (p. 110).

Communicate and converse in a give-and-take manner

In the spirit of partnership, caregivers try to converse with children in a style that does not overwhelm an infant or toddler with adult talk. They communicate and converse in a balanced, turn-taking manner, allowing enough time for the child's responses. Here is an example of how Dina, a young infant, and her caregiver communicate:

Dina: (Smiles at her caregiver.)

Caregiver: (Smiles back.) *I see a smile!* (Pauses.)

Dina: (Smiles and wiggles.)

Caregiver: (Smiles, nods her head.) *I see a smile and a wiggle!* (Pauses.)

Dina: (Smacks her lips.)

Caregiver: (Smacks *her* lips.)

Dina: (Smiles, then turns her head away.)

Caregiver: (Smiles.) *That was fun!*

Notice that the caregiver leaves room in her exchange with Dina to allow the infant to shape the direction of the dialogue. She also adopts the same pace as Dina, leaving pauses before and after responding, to match the infant's pauses. Each young child communicates at his or her own pace. A child needs time, for example, to decide whether to respond, how to respond, and (if verbal) what words to use. Here is an exchange, for example, between young toddler Nomi and her caregiver Ann at the "waving window" as they wave goodbye to Nomi's mom.

Nomi: *Byyye!* (She waves.)

Caregiver: *Bye, bye.* (She waves. Nomi's mom gets into her car.)

Nomi: *Uppy! Uppy!* (Holds her arms up to her caregiver.)

Caregiver: (Picks up Nomi.) *Now you can see better.*

Nomi: *Ma. Bye. Ma.*

Caregiver: *Bye, bye, Mom.* (Mom's car disappears around the corner.)

Nomi: *Aw gone.* (Looks at Ann.) *Back?*

Caregiver: *Mommy's all gone. She'll come back to get you.*

Nomi: *Get me, get me, get me.*

Caregiver: (Begins singing.) *Your mom will come back to get you. Your mom will come back to get you. Your mom will come back to get you, at the end of the day.*

Nomi: (Rests against Ann, then squirms to get down.)

Caregiver: (Puts Nomi gently on the floor.)

Nomi: (Touching Ann's leg, looks around. Sees Laramee, another child.) *La-me, La-me!*

Caregiver: *There's Laramee!*

Nomi: (Heads toward Laramee.)

Make comments and acknowledgments

Caregivers who want to encourage dialogue, instead of asking lots of questions of children, offer them comments, observations, and acknowledgments. They do so because factual comments or observations ("You're watching the rain splash against the window") and acknowledgments ("I see!" and "You did it!") leave opportunity for children to respond without actually pressuring them to respond in a certain way or at a particular pace. A question, by contrast, requires children to produce an answer that satisfies the questioner. Therefore, it is important to ask questions sparingly and to make comments, observations, and acknowledgments generously.

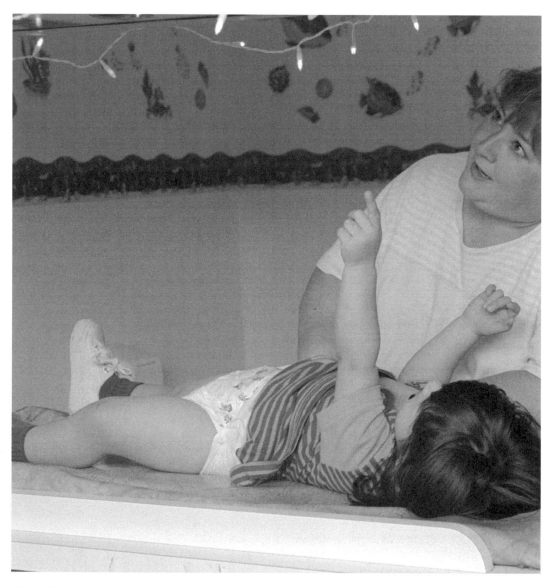

"Yights!" exclaims this toddler. "There are the little lights!" replies her caregiver. "Yots!" says the child. "Lots of lights!" affirms her caregiver. In an active learning environment, there are many opportunities for comment and conversation.

Caregivers who are tuned in to children's active learning find there is no shortage of "material" for adult comments and observations. They describe what children are seeing and doing: "You see your Daddy, Peter!" "You're kicking your legs!" Or they describe what they themselves are observing or doing: "I see you, Jacob, lying on your bunny blanket!" "Now, I'm pulling your shirt off over your head, Katie." They also talk with children about what will happen next: "I'm going to put your sweater on you so we can go play outside, Max." "I'm going to lift you up and take you to the changing table for a dry diaper, Deedee." With this kind of support, infants and toddlers develop the ability to communicate and talk by playing with interesting objects and with interacting adults who leave space and time in conversations for them to respond at their own pace, in their own way.

You may have noticed the factual nature of the sample comments and observations in the previous paragraph. In these and other examples, caregivers strive to speak to children about what the children are doing ("You're washing your hands with soap") rather than to praise their efforts ("You're doing a good job washing your hands"). Although praising children is tempting because it seems to motivate desired behavior (like hand washing), it also serves to break down the trusting relationships that are so important to build. For one thing, giving praise puts children in competition with one another to gain your praise. It also undermines the self-trust children are building as they do things for themselves. With praise, for example, the child's self-perception *I can wash my hands whenever I need to* is apt to turn into *I can wash my hands to gain the love of important adults*. Children need to feel loved and respected regardless of their specific actions.

Caregivers are able to best support an infant's or toddler's rapidly growing repertoire of actions and ideas by focusing on what the child is doing at the moment. This child is making green dots!

Look at children's actions from their viewpoint

Two people often see the same situation from differing viewpoints, depending on their individual experience, culture, problem-solving approach, and temperament. Imagine the disparity of viewpoints between two individuals who are as far apart in age and experience as an infant or toddler and an adult caregiver! Caregivers in active learning settings are keenly aware of this disparity and know that an infant or toddler cannot assume another person's viewpoint very easily, if at all. For very young children, the world revolves around themselves and the present moment. They react to how people, places, and things affect them personally. Fifteen-month-old Jamie, for example, wants her mom to stay and play a while longer after bringing her to the center. Her caregiver understands Jamie's point of view, remains physically close to Jamie while her mother is departing, and verbally acknowledges Jamie's feelings of rage and sadness at her mother's departure. Throughout this difficult time, the caregiver does not assume Jamie's feelings herself or become angry at Jamie as she cries furiously after her mom leaves. Jamie accepts her caregiver's embrace, then sits in her lap. Eventually, Jamie's crying subsides as she begins to watch Ryan finger-paint; she is signaling that she is at last ready to move into the life of the child care setting.

Give children choices when they have to do something

Sometimes, an infant or toddler resists doing something that needs to be done, such as getting a diaper changed, taking a bath, or coming in from outdoors. When this happens, a caregiver can encourage the child's partnership and control over the process by giving, in simple words, a reason for the necessary action and then giving the child some choice about how he or she will participate in that action. Here is what happened one day at the end of outside time when Jack, an older toddler, was having such a good time pulling a wagon that he didn't want to go indoors for lunch:

Caregiver: *Jack, it's time to come inside for lunch!*

Jack: *No! Play!*

Caregiver: (Squats next to Jack.) *I need you to come in now because your lunch is on the table.*

Jack: (Looks at her but makes no move toward the door.)

Caregiver: *You can pull the wagon up to the door, or you can get in the wagon and I can pull you up to the door.*

Jack: (Considers a moment, looks around the play yard, and sees no other children.) *Me pull!* (He pulls the wagon, and together he and his caregiver head for the door.)

Supporting Children's Intentions

In active learning settings, caregivers are observing, interacting with, and learning about their children throughout the day—during mealtime, choice time, outside time, group time, dressing, and diapering. Here are the strategies you can use to continually give as much support as possible to children's interests and ideas.

Focus on children's strengths and interests

A child progressing from infancy through toddlerhood demonstrates an amazing capacity to learn new skills within a relatively brief time. Throughout this period of rapid development, caregivers are able to best support the child's growing repertoire of actions and ideas by focusing on what the child is doing at the moment instead of looking for and commenting on what he or she is not yet able to do.

Children's strengths and interests rather than their deficits provide adults with positive guideposts to follow in adult-child interactions. Through their actions, children let caregivers know that *Hey, this is me. This is what I like to do right now.* Tia's caregivers, for example, note that Tia is pulling herself up to stand. They provide her with low chairs and tables, sturdy boxes and blocks, and their own bodies to steady herself with as she cruises around the room. They watch for her first steps and are happy when they occur, but they do not pressure her or expect her to walk alone until she herself demonstrates that she is ready by taking her first unaided step. Similarly, a caregiver's observation that "Frankie is figuring out how to use both hands to hold the pitcher when pouring juice" is more supportive and informative than the observation that "Frankie cannot pour his juice without spilling it."

Caregivers also support children's continued interaction with the materials and activities they show interest in, instead of focusing on and urging children toward things they show no interest in. For example, Connie observes that 1½-year-old Jake often chooses to play at the water table and push the little plastic boats from one end of it to the other. Based on this observation, she and her teammate discuss ways to support Jake's specific interest in water, boats, and perhaps other objects that can float in water. Focusing on boats and water, they decide to add to the water table two *wooden* boats and some little wooden "passengers" who fit into the boats. The next day, when Jake again goes to the water table, he exclaims, "Boh! Boh!" He picks up first one wooden boat and then the other, and eventually pushes these new boats through the water. He shows no interest, however, in putting passengers into the boats, until another day, when he sees another child doing so. When caregivers introduce new materials or experiences into the setting, they anticipate that children will warm up to and explore the new challenges on their individual terms and time schedule. Through their actions, children let caregivers know when they are ready to try something new. Caregivers therefore provide the materials and experiences that allow children to pursue their own interests instead of trying to stimulate or over-load them with the things adults want children to be interested in. (See "Experience Versus Stimulation" on the facing page.)

Anticipate children's explorations

Caregivers providing an active learning setting understand that sensory-motor exploration drives infant-toddler growth and development. Throughout the day, therefore, they try to anticipate what their children will want to explore, so they can make appropriate preparations. For example, one caregiving team knows from experience that the first time they offer their toddlers pieces of mixed fresh fruit for lunch, most of the children will check out the new con-coction, exploring it with their hands as well as their mouths. Some children will pick out only certain pieces of fruit to eat, liking the feel and taste of some fruits but not others. Some children will mash and smoosh bits of fruit, getting their hands, arms, faces, and even hair sticky. The satisfaction of this will distract some of the children from actually *eating* the fruit. The caregiving team allows for the fact that washing up children and equipment before naps will probably take a little longer than usual! Because they value this fruit ex-ploration as a learning experience for children, they remain calm and good-

For toddlers, an outdoor water faucet and a section of wet pavement are well worth exploring!

spirited about how little or how much fruit children eat or smoosh—and about the extra cleanup it creates. They also know that at another time, after the novelty wears off, children will most likely eat rather than "wear" their fruit.

Encourage and acknowledge children's choices in exploration and play

In the course of their active learning, within the setting provided by adults, infants and toddlers make choices about what and how to explore. For example, one summer day, at outside time at a child care center, this scenario takes place:

> *Karina and Melody offer their eight toddlers dish tubs of blue and red (nontoxic) tempera paints and new fly swatters, thinking the children might use these to paint on large pieces of white butcher paper that hang at the children's level on the board fence surrounding the play yard. Initially, as three of the children gather around one of the paint tubs, Karina says, "Here are some big brushes for painting." The children look at her, but make no move, so she takes a fly swatter, dips it in the paint, and uses it to spread paint on the paper. Two of the children then get fly swatters for themselves and begin to use them to smear paint on the paper and on the wooden fence. The third child watches awhile, then dips a fly swatter into the paint, looks at the paint-dipped fly swatter, and feels it with her free hand, thus covering her hand with paint. Eventually she tastes the paint on her hand. "How does that paint taste?" Karina asks her. "Sour," the child replies, wrinkling her nose.*
>
> *In the meantime, the other five children (who also could have joined the painting if they had chosen to) have decided to engage in other pursuits: one fills a bowl with grass, sits at the toddler-sized picnic table, empties the bowl, leaves the table, fills the bowl with grass again, and so forth; another drives a big*

Experience Versus Stimulation

"Stimulation is something you do *to somebody else. It's experience the child needs."*

"I don't think it's healthy to be *at* the child too much, to have him taste this, and smell that, and feel this, trying to enrich all aspects of his life. It's too much, it's intrusive. The normal kind of interaction that takes place in the course of routines, where there is some conversation and smiling back and forth and perhaps a little play, or in periods that are consciously devoted to play—I think that is what the infant needs in the way of stimulation. That doesn't mean the child's interest in other things shouldn't be encouraged, but he'll have that interest if he just has a chance to explore. Stimulation is something you *do* to somebody else. It's experience the child needs."

—Mary Ainsworth interviewed by Robert Karen (1990, p. 69)

These toddlers and their caregiver splash in a puddle of water.

wooden truck across the play yard and back; another is busy opening and closing the doors and shutters of the little play-house; a fourth is digging in the sand; one child "waters the grass," turning on the outdoor faucet, filling a small bucket with water, and dumping it out on the grass.

Eventually, two of the painters join caregiver Melody at the water faucet, where they become involved in rinsing the paint off themselves. "Paint!" says one child, showing her hands to Melody. "You painted your hands red and blue!" Melody says, admiring the child's hands. After the painters rinse off under the faucet, Melody offers them Handi Wipes to complete their cleanup. Later, the child who has been filling and emptying the bowl with grass carries the box of Handi Wipes to the little pic-nic table. She pulls the remaining few wipes out one by one and uses them to clean the table top. When the box of Handi Wipes is empty, she looks at it awhile, then takes one of the used table-cleaning wipes, stuffs it back into its box through the hole in the top, pulls it out again, and again cleans the table. Watching this process, Melody says to this child, "You really like the wipes, Angela. You figured out a way to get more!"

Help children achieve what they set out to do

When infants and toddlers attempt to do things they are not able to complete or accomplish, caregiver support can be invaluable. Through careful observation, caregivers consider when they might help children follow through on their intentions. Children may need additional materials or a caregiver suggestion to complete their task, or as in the story that follows, they may simply need a caregiver's attentive presence.

Jenny, an older infant, sits on her blanket, touching and patting a colorful cloth ball. At one point she pats it so hard that it rolls away out of sight, whereupon she looks up at Ann, her caregiver, who is sitting on the floor close by. "The ball rolled away," says Ann. Unperturbed, Jenny turns back to where she was playing with the ball, sees a small plastic bowl, and picks it up and contentedly puts it in her mouth. As Jenny explores the bowl, Ann quietly places the ball so it is again within Jenny's sight. She does this because she knows that Jenny focuses all her attention on things she can see—"out of sight, out of mind" is quite literally true for her. Ann interprets Jenny's intention as not just wanting to play with the ball, but wanting to play with anything she can see and reach. Therefore, because Jenny is now content playing with the bowl, Ann simply puts the ball within Jenny's reach (instead of distracting her by handing it to her). Jenny continues playing with the bowl for a while, then picks up a spatula. For a moment, she holds the bowl in one hand and the spatula in the other. Then she drops the bowl and uses both hands to guide the spatula to her mouth. After chewing on and playing with the spatula for quite some time, Jenny drops the spatula and again reaches for the ball that Ann retrieved.

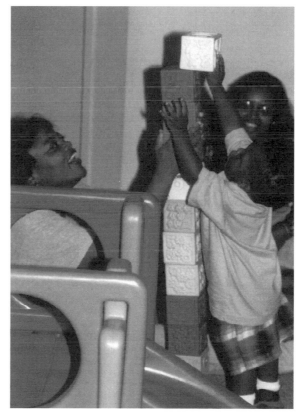

With caregiver support, this toddler adds another block to his stack!

Give children time to solve problems they encounter with materials in exploration and play

A toddler may be struggling to fit a block into a shape-sorter, or an infant may be straining to touch an out-of-reach toy. For adults, deciding whether or when to intervene in these situations can be difficult. Caregivers want to protect children from unreasonable frustration, but they also want to provide children with enough time to solve these child-sized problems on their own. If a caregiver always quickly steps in and "rescues" the infant or toddler, the child does not get a sense of being an active agent in his or her own life. Part of the equation is knowing each child's temperament (activity level, adaptability, intensity of reaction, persistence, and so on) and current level of development. In the following scenario, Ann, a caregiver, responds differently to two different problem solvers.

> *Ann watches Theo, a toddler, as he tries to fit a wooden rectangular block into its slot in a shape-sorter box. He tries turning the block this way and that; he bangs the block and pushes it, but to no avail. He persists with this problem without apparent frustration. Finally, he puts the block down, picks up a spoon, and easily pushes it through the slot. He also drops some keys through the slot, along with several wooden beads. When he looks up briefly at Ann, she says, "You fit lots of things into that hole." He continues contentedly putting things into the slot.*
>
> *Later that same day, Neal, an older toddler, plays with the same shape-sorter box and bursts into tears after numerous unsuccessful attempts to fit the rectangular block through its slot. "It's really upsetting when the block won't go through the hole," Ann says, stroking his back. His crying abates somewhat. "Won't go!" he says. "I wonder what would happen if you stand the block on its end, she says," knowing Neal has often placed building blocks in this position. Ann stands a block on end on top of the shape-sorter, next to the slot. Neal looks at the block in his hand and slowly, using both hands, turns it to an upright position on the shape-sorter, next to Ann's block. Then, as Ann holds her block still, with both hands he slides his block into the slot. Then he pushes Ann's hand away and slides her block in as well. His whole body seems to relax with relief. He opens the lid, takes both blocks out, and puts them in again and again.*

Sometimes, the problems children solve involve other people:

> *At snack time, when caregiver Sonja picks up the napkins to pass them out, Alex tugs at her arm and says, "Me do!" So Sonja gives Alex the napkins, saying "Alex wants to give each*

person a napkin today." Alex gives one napkin to Rob, two napkins to Megan, and a small pile of napkins to Kris. When he sits down, he sees that he himself does not have a napkin and so takes several from Kris's pile. While this is not standard napkin-distribution procedure, Sonja notes that Alex and the rest of the children are satisfied with the results. Having encouraged Alex to try something on his own, his caregiver supports his particular solution.

Support toddlers in resolving social conflicts

As toddlers gain a sense of self and begin to claim things as "Mine!" they also become entangled in social conflicts. When toddler disputes lead to crying, hitting, or biting, caregivers calmly approach the toddlers in conflict, stop their hurtful actions, acknowledge the children's feelings, gather information, engage the children in describing the problem and finding a solution, and offer follow-up support. Here is an example of these problem-solving strategies in action:

> *Two toddlers, Kyle and Tony, both want the same blue toy racing car. As Kyle takes it out of the car box, Tony says "Mine" and tries to grab it away. "No!" says Kyle, pulling the car away from Tony and hiding it under his shirt. Tony cries and repeats*

"Mine, mine!" Sandy, their caregiver, hearing Tony's distress but unaware of its cause, approaches the two boys calmly and sits down on the floor with one child on either side of her, an arm gently around each one. "You seem pretty upset, Kyle," Sandy says to Kyle as she gently strokes his arm. "And Tony, you're sad and crying," she says to Tony while stroking his hand. Both boys nod their head up and down, and Tony's crying subsides. "It looks like Kyle has something that Tony wants," Sandy says, noting the bulge under Kyle's shirt. "Is that

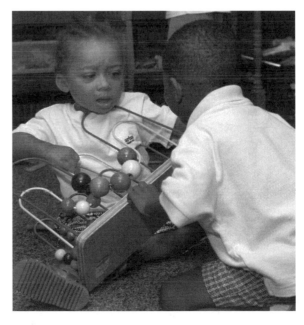

Toddlers have a strong sense of self and "their" possessions. "Mine!" this toddler says with his whole body when an older child attempts to take the bead maze.

right?" Both boys look at her and nod yes. "Kyle, what do you have under your shirt?" she asks with genuine curiosity. Kyle immediately pulls out the car. "My car" he says, clutching it tightly in his hand. "Mine!" says Tony, his eyes filling again with tears. "Oh, a car," says Sandy. "Let me hold it for you." She takes it carefully from Kyle, and holding it in one hand, she addresses both children: "So the problem is, you both want the car." Kyle and Tony look at Sandy and nod in agreement. "What can we do to solve this problem?" she asks them. The boys are quiet and still, taking in the situation. "You seem to be thinking very hard," Sandy comments quietly. Eventually, Kyle turns to the car box, carefully selects a red racing car, and hands it to Tony. Tony accepts the red car with a broad smile. "Would you like to play with this red car, Tony?" Sandy asks. Tony nods yes. "So, Kyle will have the blue racing car, and Tony will have the red racing car," Sandy says. The boys nod their head in agreement. Sandy looks at both boys clutching their cars and says, "You solved the problem!" Kyle and Tony squat down, push their cars along the rug, and make car noises. Sandy watches them for several minutes, then joins two other children at the nearby art table.

In this scenario, Sandy uses a six-step problem-solving approach to conflict (see "Steps in Resolving Conflicts Between Toddlers," p. 90). First, she *approaches calmly,* positions herself at Kyle and Tony's physical level, and establishes gentle contact with each child. She knows that her relaxed, unhurried manner and gentle touch will help reassure the children and create a positive climate for working out the problem. She remains neutral instead of blaming one child or the other for causing the problem. Her neutrality allows her to mediate the dispute, which she could not do if she were to take sides. Her gentle touch, calm body-language, and kind concern speak directly to the children of her genuine regard for their powerful feelings and the dilemma they are facing.

Sandy's first words, gentle and concerned, *acknowledge the children's feelings.* ("You seem pretty upset, Kyle. And Tony, you're sad and crying.") Hearing their feelings described gives these toddlers names for their emotions. Once they get the message—through gentle touch and a voice that registers genuine concern—that an adult understands how strongly they feel, children are generally able to let go of these negative feelings. They are then free to devote their energies to thinking clearly about what to do about the problem.

When their feelings subside, Sandy *gathers information* from the children about what is happening. Since toddlers' verbal communication is still in its formative stages, Sandy does not ask Kyle and Tony a question that requires more than a single word, nod, or gesture to answer. (For example, she does not ask, "What's the problem?") Instead, she describes the information she gathers from carefully observing their actions. ("It looks like Kyle has something that Tony wants.") She asks the children for confirmation. ("Is that right?") And she asks Kyle a fact-finding question that he can answer with a single word or an action. ("Kyle, what do you have under your shirt?") Once Kyle reveals the car, she requests to hold it herself. This puts the disputed object in neutral hands and allows the children to focus more freely on the problem the car presents to them.

Sandy *restates the problem* for clarity. ("So the problem is, you both want the car.") Then she *asks for ideas for solutions.* ("What can we do to solve this problem?") Toddlers are new to the problem-solving process. They take time to comprehend what might work next, and they are apt to offer some action as a solution to the problem rather than to state their solution in words. After a long moment, without saying anything, Kyle finds and gives Tony another car, which Tony accepts. Sandy sees that Tony appears to be

When the dump truck driver and the sweeper attempt to drive and sweep in the same spot, their caregiver crouches calmly between them and stops the truck to clear the way for problem solving.

Steps in Resolving Conflicts Between Toddlers

1. Approach calmly, stopping any hurtful actions.

- Place yourself between the children, on their level.
- Use a calm voice and gentle touch.
- Remain neutral rather than take sides.

2. Acknowledge children's feelings.

- "You seem pretty upset."
- Let the children know you need to hold the object in question.

3. Gather information.

- "It looks like the problem is . . . Is that right?"

4. Restate the problem.

- "So the problem is . . ."

5. Ask for ideas for solutions, and choose one together.

- "What can we do to solve this problem?"
- Encourage *children* to think of a solution.
- Check to make sure the solution is acceptable to both children.

6. Be prepared to give follow-up support.

- "You solved the problem!"
- Stay near the children.

happy, but she checks with him to make sure Kyle's solution suits him. ("Would you like to play with this red car, Tony?") Assured by Tony's nod, Sandy confirms their solution with them in words. ("So, Kyle will have the blue racing car, and Tony will have the red racing car.")

Notice that Sandy *prepares to give follow-up support*. She verbally brings closure to the problem-solving process by recognizing the significance of the work the two boys did together. ("You solved the problem!") Note also that the *children* resolve the conflict, not Sandy. She interprets what has happened without making judgments or imposing her own ideas for a solution. As Kyle and Tony play with their cars, Sandy remains directly within their reach for several minutes and then goes to the art table where Kyle and Tony can still see her and gain her attention if they need it.[7]

Most caregivers are new to this problem-solving approach to conflict. They are finding, however, that with thought and practice, they and the children get used to it, and they are finding that toddlers can be capable problem solvers. With the support of their caregivers, toddlers can develop and practice the ability to solve many of their own social conflicts. Throughout their efforts, they exercise thinking and reasoning skills, gain a sense of control over the solution or outcome of the problem, experience cooperation, and develop trust in themselves, their peers, and caregivers.

---

[7]For more on the six conflict-resolution steps, see Betsy Evans's article "Helping Children Resolve Disputes and Conflicts" and the video *Supporting Children in Resolving Conflicts* listed on pp. 93–94.

Seven Irreducible Needs of Childhood

"*First*, every child needs a safe, secure environment that includes at least one stable, predictable, comforting, and protective relationship with an adult, not necessarily a biological parent, who has made a long-term, personal commitment to the child's daily welfare and who has the means, time, and personal qualities to carry it out. . . .

"*Second*, consistent, nurturing relationships with the same caregivers, including the primary one, early in life and throughout childhood are the cornerstones of both emotional and intellectual competence, allowing a child to form the deep connectedness that grows into a sense of shared humanity and, ultimately, empathy and compassion. Relationships with both parents and day-care staff must have this stability and consistency. . . .

"*Third* is the need for rich, ongoing interaction. . . . [Children] cannot develop a sense of their own intentionality or of the boundaries between their inner and outer worlds except through extended exchanges with people they know well and trust deeply. . . .

"*Fourth*, each child and family needs an environment that allows them to progress through the developmental stages in their own style and their own good time. . . .

"*Fifth*, children must have opportunities to experiment, to find solutions, to take risks, and even to fail at attempted tasks. From trying different approaches, seeking out allies, and assessing all options emerge the perseverance and self-confidence needed to succeed at any serious endeavor. . . .

"*Sixth*, children need structure and clear boundaries. They learn to build bridges among their thoughts and feelings when their world is predictable and responsive. . . .

"*Seventh*, to achieve these goals, families need stable neighborhoods and communities. The appropriate, consistent, and deeply committed care that a child needs to master the developmental levels requires adults who are themselves mature, empathic, and emotionally accessible. . . .

—Stanley Greenspan (1997, pp. 264–267)

Supportive Adult-Child Interactions: A Summary

Establishing policies that promote continuity of care
❏ Anchor each child's day around a primary caregiver.

❏ Create small groups of children who share a caregiver team.

❏ Keep children and caregivers together from year to year.

❏ Arrange caregivers' schedules around children's needs.

❏ Tell children and parents about caregiver absences and returns.

❏ Have primary caregivers record observations of their children.

Creating a climate of trust for children
❏ Touch, hold, speak to, and play with children in a warm, unhurried manner.

❏ Take pleasure in your interactions with children.

❏ Respond supportively to children's needs and attention-getting signals.

❏ Give children time to interact and respond in their own way.

❏ Support children's relationships with peers and other adults.

Forming partnerships with children
❏ Interact at the child's physical level.

❏ Respect children's preferences and individual temperaments.

❏ Follow children's lead.

❏ Watch and listen to children.

❏ Communicate and converse in a give-and-take manner.

❏ Make comments and acknowledgments.

❏ Look at children's actions from their viewpoint.

❏ Give children choices when they have to do something.

Supporting children's intentions
❏ Focus on children's strengths and interests.

❏ Anticipate children's explorations.

❏ Encourage and acknowledge children's choices in exploration and play.

❏ Help children achieve what they set out to do.

❏ Give children time to solve problems they encounter with materials in exploration and play.

❏ Support toddlers in resolving social conflicts.

References

Brazelton, T. Barry. 1969. *Infants and Mothers: Differences in Development.* New York: Dell.

Campbell, F. A., R. Helms, J. J. Sparling, and C. T. Ramey. 1998. "Early-Childhood Programs and Success in School: The Abecedarian Study." In *Early Care and Education for Children in Poverty: Promises, Programs, and Long-Term Effects,* eds. W. Steven Barnett and S. S. Babcock, 145–66. Albany, NY: SUNY Press.

Chess, Stella. 1990. "Temperaments of Infants and Toddlers." In *Infant and Toddler Caregiving: A Guide to Social-Emotional Growth and Socialization,* ed. J. Ronald Lally, 27–56. Sacramento, CA: California Department of Education.

Evans, Betsy. 1996. "Helping Children Resolve Disputes and Conflicts." In *Supporting Young Learners 2,* ed. Nancy A. Brickman, 27–36. Ypsilanti, MI: High/Scope Press.

Evans, Judith, and Ellen Ilfeld. 1982. *Good Beginnings: Parenting in the Early Years.* Ypsilanti, MI: High/Scope Press.

Falk, Judit. 1979. "The Importance of Person-Oriented Adult-Child Relationships." In *The RIE Manual for Parents and Professionals,* ed. Magda Gerber, 115–24. Los Angeles: Resources for Infant Educarers.

Gerber, Magda, ed. 1979. *The RIE Manual for Parents and Professionals.* Los Angeles: Resources for Infant Educarers.

Goldschmied, Elinor, and Sonia Jackson. 1994. *People Under Three: Young Children in Day Care.* London: Routledge.

Greenspan, Stanley I., with Beryl Lieff Benderly. 1997. *The Growth of the Mind and the Endangered Origins of Intelligence.* Reading, MA: Perseus Books.

Jackson, Beverly Roberson. 1997. "Creating a Climate for Healing in a Violent Society." *Young Children* 52(7, November): 68–70.

Karen, Robert. 1990. "Becoming Attached." *The Atlantic Monthly* (February): 35–70.

Lally, J. Ronald. 1995. "The Impact of Child Care Policies and Practices on Infant/Toddler Identity Formation." *Young Children* 51(1, November): 58–67.

Mangione, Peter. 1990. *Child Care Video Magazine, It's Not Just Routine: Feeding, Diapering, and Napping Infants and Toddlers.* Sacramento, CA: California Department of Education.

Rogers, Carl R. 1983. *The Freedom to Learn for the 80's.* Columbus, OH: Merrill.

Signer, Sheila. 1995. *Strategies for Implementing Continuity of Care in Infant/Toddler Programs.* A paper developed by participants at the Program for Infant/Toddler Caregivers Graduate Conference Seminar on Continuity, November. Sausalito, CA: WestEd.

Thomas, Alexander, and Stella Chess. 1970. *Temperament and Development.* New York: Bruner/Mazel.

Related Reading

Da Ros, Denise, and Beverly Kovach. 1998. "Assisting Toddlers and Caregivers During Conflict Resolutions." *Childhood Education* 75(1, Fall): 25–30.

Goleman, Daniel. 1995. *Emotional Intelligence.* New York: Bantam Books.

Hohmann, Mary, and David P. Weikart. 1995. "Establishing a Supportive Climate: The Basics of Positive Adult-Child Interactions." In *Educating Young Children: Active Learning Practices for Preschool and Child Care Programs,* Mary Hohmann and David P. Weikart, 43–67. Ypsilanti, MI: High/Scope Press.

Honig, Alice Sterling. 1993. "Mental Health for Babies: What Do Theory and Research Teach Us?" *Young Children* 48(3, March): 69–76.

Honig, Alice Sterling. 1996. *Behavior and Guidance for Infants and Toddlers.* Little Rock, AR: Southern Early Childhood Association.

Howes, Carollee. 1998. "Continuity of Care: The Importance of Infant, Toddler, Caregiver Relationships." *Zero to Three* (June/July): 7–11.

Miller, Karen. 1999. "Caring for the Little Ones: Continuity of Care." *Child Care Information Exchange,* Issue 129 (September/October): 94–97.

Raikes, Helen. 1996. "A Secure Base for Babies: Applying Attachment Concepts to the Infant Care Setting." *Young Children* 51(5, July): 59–67.

Sanchez, Sylvia Y., and Eva K. Thorp. 1998. "Discovering the Meanings of Continuity: Implications for the Infant/Family Field." *Zero to Three* (June/July): 1–6.

Related Videos

First Moves: Welcoming a Child to a New Caregiving Setting. 1988. Color videotape, 27 min. Sacramento, CA: California Department of Education.

Getting in Tune: Creating Nurturing Relationships With Infants and Toddlers. 1990. Color videotape, 24 min. Sacramento, CA: California Department of Education.

The High/Scope Approach for Under Threes, U.S. Edition. 1999. Color videotape, 68 min. London, England: High/Scope Institute U.K. (Available from High/Scope Press, Ypsilanti, MI.)

On Their Own/With Our Help. 1976. Black-and-white videotape, 14 min. Los Angeles: Resources for Infant Educarers.

Supporting Children in Resolving Conflicts. 1998. Color videotape, 24 min. Ypsilanti, MI: High/Scope Press.

Learning to stand puts this toddler face to face with his caregiver. She doesn't have to tell him "Lean on me!" He already knows he can count on her support no matter what he is doing.

3
Arranging and Equipping an Environment for Infants and Toddlers

We believe that childcare centers should provide infants and toddlers with beautiful environments that support child-directed, child-initiated, and teacher-facilitated play. We also believe that childcare providers deserve highly functional, easy-to-use, and aesthetically attractive work environments.

—*Louis Torelli and Charles Durrett (1998)*

Jn a High/Scope program for infants and toddlers, caregivers arrange and equip the environment to provide children with a sense of comfort and well-being and at the same time offer ample opportunity for active learning. Such an environment neither unnecessarily restricts children from their natural inclinations to wiggle, roll, crawl, cruise, balance, toddle, walk, climb, and run nor pushes children to do things before they are ready; children can pursue their interests and act at their individual levels of development. The environment is consistent enough to give children a sense of security and mastery and yet flexible enough to accommodate children's changing needs and interests. The environment's furnishings and materials are in many cases child-oriented and child-sized, and they provide comfort and convenience both for children and for adult caregivers. Within the physical boundaries of the setting, both indoors and out, the infants and toddlers are able to move, explore, create, communicate, and solve problems with as much freedom as possible. The adults, trained in child development, are free to interact with and give full attention to children.

Active Learning Environments for Infants and Toddlers

In creating an active learning environment for infants and toddlers, caregivers need to consider several practical issues: Given our space and resources and the children in our program, how can we arrange areas, equipment, and materials to best support children's growth and development? How can we ensure that we meet all requirements for the health and safety of children and staff? How can we involve families in the program? How can we make the setting a welcoming and responsive one, where children are encouraged to interact with materials, with adults, and with other children, and where adults are encouraged to interact with children and with one another? If caregivers have carefully worked through these issues, the physical space they design will be one that proclaims its own purposes. According to educator Jim Greenman (1988),

> One should be able to enter the room in the evening with no staff present and marvel at the learning environment, *the world at the child's fingertips*—the built-in opportunities for motor and sensory experiences, the range of places to be with different visual and auditory stimulation, the number of protected spaces for young babies, and the problem-solving opportunities for small detectives of varying interests and skills. Lying on the floor you should see pathways and small divided spaces—opportunities to go in and out, up and over, and so on; to be alone, to be enclosed on three sides, and to peer over thirty-inch walls. (p. 55)

A well-set-up environment promotes children's progress in physical development, communication, cognitive skills, and social interactions. It allows children to do what they are currently able to do yet grows with them as they grow. Remove the children and the caregivers, and the physical environment alone shows how it supports the basic development of infants and toddlers—through softness; child-sized furnishings; a variety of levels, vistas, and materials for children; and distinct areas for their eating, sleeping, bodily care, and play. Add the children and the knowledgeable, trained adults back in, and you have a complete picture of an active learning setting in operation—a pleasant setting where adults observe, value, and support children's actions, choices, and ideas.

A well-set-up child-centered environment promotes children's physical development, communication, cognitive skills, and social interactions.

Broad Guidelines for Organizing Space and Materials

This chapter looks at arranging and equipping specific spaces for children's eating, sleeping, bodily care, and play. It expands on these three basic guidelines for setting up and maintaining infant-toddler settings:

- Build *order and flexibility* into the physical environment.

- Provide *comfort and safety* for children and adults.

- Support children's *sensory-motor approach* to learning.

Build order and flexibility into the physical environment

While the need to explore and play remains constant throughout infancy and toddlerhood, *what* very young children want to explore and play with changes continually as they grow and develop. Therefore, the environment needs to provide both order and flexibility if it is to respond to children's changing interests, promote child choice, and help children gain a sense of control over their immediate world. As you assess, modify, or arrange your infant-toddler setting, consider the following ways to build order and flexibility into the physical environment.

✦ *Distinct care and play areas*

It is essential that a group-care environment for infants and toddlers include *clearly designated areas* for food preparation and eating; for sleeping and napping; and for bodily care—diapering, dressing, and using the toilet. For health reasons, it is necessary that any area having to do with food (preparation or eating) be clearly separate from any area used for children's bodily care. Organize each of these types of areas (food and bodily care) around a sink with hot running water. It is also important to locate sleeping areas away from play areas so children can sleep undisturbed. Once these areas are clearly defined, devote the rest of the space to exploration and play, and if possible, set off a reception area near the door, to help ease children's and families' arrivals and departures.

Make sure that play areas include ample space for children to move about, to use materials, and to have social interaction, but also provide some private places, where a child can be alone. According to Louis Torelli (1992), a designer of children's environments,

> " . . . we often expect infants and toddlers to function well in group care situations for upwards of ten hours a day, five days a week. Private spaces in the group care environment support

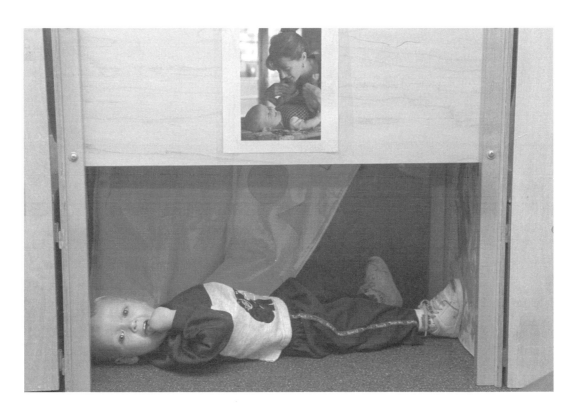

Very young children need private space—like this nook for time alone under the climber—and social space—like this small table to share with others.

the development of the young child's self-concept and personal
identity. . . . Instead of experiencing the stress of being in a
large group all day, the infant can withdraw to a private space
to rest, observe, and recharge emotionally. With access to a
private space, two toddlers who are just beginning to develop
a relationship can go off together. (p. 40)

One way to provide a private place is to use low shelving units and
pillows, for example, to create a small space enclosed on three sides—just
the right size for one child. You can also provide a mattress in a corner
or a cozy loft for infants to lie on;[8] provide a box, crate, barrel, or tunnel
for mobile infants and toddlers to "hide" in, crawl through, and sit in; cover
a table or a climber with sheets or blankets to create a "tent"; set up small
climbers indoors and out for children to crawl under and inside of; hang
sheets to enclose the space underneath a loft to make a "little house" with
a door just big enough for a small child; or leave some "crawl space" between the wall and an easy chair or couch. Greenman (1988) emphasized
the importance of such provisions: "Nooks and crannies and their makeshift
equivalents are not frills, but psychological necessities" (p. 149).

Very young children also want to spend time with others. To support
this desire, provide cooperative play equipment—small tables, rocking
boats, side-by-side easels, and connecting riding toys. Arrange couches,
chairs and tables, pillow groups, and small mattresses to create spaces
for pairs and threesomes. Design sink areas to accommodate more
than one child at a time so washing and cleaning up can be social
occasions, too.

✦ *An open floor plan*

Keep the floor plan as open and uncluttered as possible instead of using
every bit of space for shelves, furniture, equipment, and toys. One way to
do this is to locate eating, sleeping, bodily care, and fixed specialized play
areas (the block, book, toy areas, for example) along the edges of the
room, leaving the middle of the room, or space, open for crawling, balancing, and walking. This allows the areas around the periphery of the
room to remain fairly stable and thus familiar while the middle of the room
is open to change as, for example, walkers become runners and climbers,
or block carriers become block arrangers and stackers. J. Ronald Lally, cre-
ator of the Program for Infant and Toddler Caregivers, and writer Jay Stewart (1990) explained further advantages of this arrangement:

---

[8]For specifications for safe lofts for infants 3 months and older, see pp. 39–40 of *Landscapes for
Learning* by Louis Torelli and Charles Durrett, which is listed on p. 186.

An open center lets the children see what activities are available throughout the room. The children can also get where they want to go easily. They can see the caregiver across the room, and the caregiver can see and respond to any child who needs attention. An open center creates maximum flexibility and lets children navigate easily between areas. (p. 25)

✦ *Moveable furnishings, equipment, and storage containers*

Keeping built-in and heavy furnishings to a minimum and equipping shelves and platforms with casters allows caregivers to rearrange low shelves, platforms, large pillows, and mats as needed. Remember, however, to remove any wheels or casters or, if possible, to lock them in place once you have used them to move a piece of equipment, so it becomes stable. Shelves, in particular, need to be immovable and untippable for infants and toddlers who hang onto them to pull themselves up to stand.

Older toddlers pursue some fairly delicate tasks, such as stacking blocks, assembling a puzzle, or spreading out on the floor to paint with brushes on a large sheet of butcher paper. One caregiver team supported their toddlers' need to be undisturbed in this kind of play by creating a "delicate work

Baskets provide handy storage for small toy collections—they taste good, too!

zone" in one section of the room. The area was surrounded by low, moveable partitions, one of which incorporated a "latched" gate that older toddlers could open and close but younger toddlers could not. This provided the older toddlers with a safe, semisecluded space to work in and to access art supplies without being entirely separated from the other children. Another team used similar low, hinged, moveable partitions to set off a large safe area for nonmobile infants. The active toddlers played outside the infant area, but since a number of the partition panels were Plexiglas, children on opposite sides could still see each other.

Store small collections of toys and materials suitable for nonmobile infants in individual baskets, bins, or bags. This allows you to handily provide a range of appealing items to the child who is not yet crawling, wherever he or she might be. With this kind of flexibility, it is not unusual to see a crawling child settle next to a shelf containing interesting objects to explore while a nonmobile child sits nearby playing with items selected from a basket his caregiver has placed within his reach.

✦ *Easy outdoor access*

Infants and toddlers need daily play outdoors, where the opportunities for sensory-motor exploration are endless. Therefore, if possible, every indoor infant-toddler space should have access to an outdoor play area. "A trip outdoors provides a complete change of scene for infants," observed psychologist Thelma Harms (1994), "with different things to watch, and changes in temperature and air movement to experience" (p. 157). The outdoors provides a variety of surfaces (grass and wooden decks for lying, sitting, crawling, and walking; paths for wheel toys; sand for digging and making soft landings); a changing "ceiling" (the sky, clouds, branches, and leaves); softness (grass, fine ground cover, sand, blankets, and plants); and natural lighting. Though weather is always a factor, it is important for children to experience whatever variety the local climate affords. Snow and warm light rain, for example, can be very exciting for this age group, so include "a translucent overhang that provides shelter from sun and rain" (Torelli and Durrett, 1998, p. 131). Such an overhang can serve as a transition from indoor to outdoor play.

Provide comfort and safety for children and adults

To promote active learning, caregivers strive to combine the requisite physical and psychological comfort and safety for children with practicality and convenience for adults. Soft furnishings, fresh air, soothing colors, pleasant sounds and odors, for example, tend to evoke a sense of well-being for infants and toddlers, who learn about the world directly, through their senses and actions. When the environment provides an array of interesting sights, textures, sounds, smells, and tastes and also warmly invites and safely supports children's active exploration of these things, this enables children to feel psychological comfort. Protected from cramped spaces, sharp corners, toppling or falling objects, and slippery surfaces, they venture to examine their immediate sensory world. In a physically friendly setting that doesn't "bite back," children can feel pleased with their adventures and confident in themselves as adventurers. At the same time that caregivers are providing new interests and safe adventures for children, they can also include some features that children are used to, to make them feel at home in group care (see "Pleasant reminders of home," p. 110).

Torelli (1992) has reminded us that "a developmentally appropriate space is designed to be emotionally supportive for both children and adults" (p. 39). Thus, a psychologically comfortable environment also includes practicality and convenience—things that make the setting work for adults. As you assess, set up, or modify your setting for comfort and safety, consider the following elements.

✦ *Inviting floors, walls, and ceilings*

Since infants and toddlers spend a lot of time on the floor, it is important that the floor be clean, warm, and comfortable. One safe and straightforward way to provide an infant/toddler-friendly floor surface is to cover your indoor space for children with long-wearing, relatively low-pile, stain-resistant, wall-to-wall carpeting laid over carpet padding. Such carpeting provides warmth, muffles ambient sound, is easy to vacuum and shampoo, cushions falls, and provides a suitable surface for children's exploration and play and for barefoot babies' first attempts at walking.

A carpet, quilt, floor mat, and pillow; some balloons hung in mesh bags; and a graceful gauze drape add softness to this space.

When selecting carpet, look for solid colors or heather tones. Carpet that is multicolored or has bold patterns or figures (animals, numbers, letters) not only is expensive but also can cause visual overload and make it difficult for children to distinguish playthings from the carpet. While the parts of the floor that are around toilets, sinks, and eating areas are usually covered with vinyl tile or wood for easy cleaning, it is important that the tile or wood be in good condition, clean, and finished with wax or polish that is *nonskid*. (Also see "A floor-level focus" on p. 112.)

Walls and ceilings painted in a soft, light color (with lead-free paint that is not chipping or peeling) generally provide a more soothing atmosphere for children and adults than do walls and ceilings painted in one or more bright colors or covered with bright, busy wallpaper. Plain walls and wall coverings, such as bulletin boards and cork strips painted in soft colors, also complement rather than compete with the materials displayed on them (mirrors, wall hangings, photographs, children's creations, samples of various textures). Electrical outlets need to be covered with child-proof covers or installed high on the wall, well above children's reach, so children cannot poke things into them. Acoustical ceiling tiles also help to muffle ambient sound.

◆ *Soft places*

Both children and adults appreciate soft places. These may include a corner of the room furnished with pillows and comforters; a mattress on the floor covered with a mattress pad and fitted sheet; couches, easy chairs, and low, deep, cloth hammocks (hung over a carpeted surface). Air mattresses and large vinyl-covered mats and cushions in a variety of shapes and sizes can be used singly or in various combinations to build soft structures for children to explore and climb on. Outfitting the diapering and infant-dressing area with a thick, cleanable pad provides a soft surface for children to lie on during diaper and clothing changes. At higher levels, easy-to-grow house plants, sheer curtains and valances, and fabric wall hangings can be used to soften the look of corners and edges and add a pleasant texture and movement to windows, walls, and corners. (Any curtains or wall hangings should comply with local fire regulations.)

Remember, too, that caregivers' laps, arms, and bodies serve as soft vantage points and places of repose for infants and toddlers. Natalie, for example, crawls over to her caregiver, climbs into her lap, and settles in to watch Mona and Chad negotiate the climber. Natalie herself is not interested in climbing, but from the safety of her caregiver's lap, she is interested in watching Mona and Chad in action.

◆ *Soft and natural lighting*

Infants are especially sensitive to light. While they need light to see, they are less fussy and more comfortable in spaces lit by soft and natural light. In an infant-toddler setting, it makes sense to light the space as you would a home—with windows, window walls, skylights, and shaded lamps. Install dimmer switches on overhead lights or, better yet, avoid them altogether in favor of sturdy wall and hanging lamps strategically placed about the space. "In planning the lighting," said Greenman (1988), "it is important to consider the plan from all angles, literally. Will there be glare in the sight lines of the children, including infants staring straight up into the ceiling?" (p. 112). Torelli and architect Charles Durrett (1998) made these suggestions:

We recommend incandescent lighting rather than fluorescent because the quality of light contributes to a child's visual development. Nearly every classroom we remodel is overlit initially by a flood of fluorescent light at the ceiling, which makes the space look and feel more like a hospital or an office than a place where children play. Incandescent lighting will make your classroom look and feel more like a home, which is especially important for children who spend up to ten hours a day in your care. (pp. 13–14)

✦ *Infant- and toddler-sized equipment and furnishings*

Children are likely to feel they belong and have some control when the setting has furnishings and equipment that are sturdily constructed and downsized especially for them. For infants and toddlers, this includes very low sinks, drinking fountains, and toilets. There should also be very low tables, chairs, stools, benches, toy shelves, and bookracks. All these furnishings need to be well-balanced and sturdy enough to accommodate mobile infants who hang on to furniture to pull themselves up to stand. To an adult caregiver, infant and toddler furnishings may appear to be extremely close to the ground, and they are—infants and toddlers, after all, are very short human beings!

Torelli/Durrett, Inc. & Spaces for Children

Child-sized furnishings provide children with a sense of belonging and control.

Furnishings sized to infants and toddlers help create an environment children can oftentimes manage on their own, but adult help will still be needed. Sturdy, low, accessible toy shelves, bookracks, baskets, and bins encourage mobile children to find and use (and sometimes even return) play materials they have chosen. Child-sized furnishings and child-accessible storage also enable older toddlers to join caregivers in cleanup routines. After meals and snacks, for example, toddlers will often help to wipe off tables and chairs that are within their reach.

✦ *Adult-sized furniture*

The setting, of course, also needs to have some adult-sized furniture for adults' physical comfort! Adult-sized chairs and couches also serve a purpose for children by providing them with physical challenges *(How can I get myself up onto that comfortable-looking couch?)* as well as a cozy place to cuddle with a caregiver, a blanket, and a book. Having some adult-sized furniture also makes the setting look home-like. As Greenman (1988) observed, "A mixture of adult and child scale is valuable for both caring and learning and minimizes the teacher as an outsized Gulliver in a Lilliputian world" (p. 62).

Adult-sized furniture provides a comfortable spot for adults and children! (This sofa is "one of last year's floor models" donated by a local furniture dealer.)

✦ *Storage for caregivers' belongings, children's belongings, extra toys and supplies*

Adequate and accessible storage space plays a big part in making the group-care setting workable for everyone. For their own sense of order and control, caregivers need a place to store their personal belongings. Adult-height shelving and cupboards and safety-latched closets can meet these needs as can adult-height hooks in the entrance area.

Caregivers and parents also need a set of conveniently located cubbies, tubs, or storage bins—one per child—clearly labeled with each child's name and photograph. These provide a storage place for extra clothing for the child, along with whatever personal items parents and the child may bring in from home—an extra pair of mittens, a special bear for nap time, spare pacifiers, clothes for the weekend away from home, and so on. (Children's medications and topical creams are stored on shelves above their reach or in the refrigerator, as needed.) Generally, the younger the child, the more space the child needs for storing personal belongings!

Most infant-toddler centers have toys and supplies that are not in use with the children at the moment. By keeping these materials in a storeroom, in a closet, or on high shelves well above the children's reach, caregivers can cut down on clutter, and dedicate floor space and low shelves to children's play and the materials intended to be child-accessible.

✦ *Safe, convenient adult access to appliances and everyday supplies*

To keep the day running smoothly, caregivers need easy access to basic appliances (sinks, refrigerators, microwaves) and everyday supplies (bottles, diapers, wipes). In a well-designed infant and toddler setting, said Greenman (1988), "the environment needs to be furnished, equipped, and organized to maximize the caregivers' time and ease of providing care: no sinks down the hall; no looking for bottles, training pants, or materials" (p. 54). Locate clipboards, notebooks, and other information-recording materials where caregivers can easily reach them as they care for and play and interact with the children. Careful placement of appliances and supplies not only reduces caregivers' steps but also enables them to focus their attention on children's actions and communications.

✦ *A welcoming entrance or reception area*

When space allows, having a defined place for parents and other family members to meet and mingle as they come and go with their children can help families feel connected to one another and to center staff, who have thought to provide this pleasant space. If you establish such a place, whether it be a foyer, hallway, or room, consider ways to make its decor and furnishings welcoming. Incorporate comfortable seating; plants; soft and natural lighting;

photos of families, children at play, and staff (labeled with individuals' names); a bulletin board for posting parent-friendly notices and reminders to parents in the languages they speak and read; one or more tables to gather around; and space for strollers, diaper bags, and all the things parents and very young children routinely travel with.

✦ *Pleasant reminders of home*

Not everything in your care setting should present novelty to children. Consider ways to incorporate the following familiar materials throughout your infant-toddler setting:

Children's comfort items. Many infants and toddlers feel more at home when they can have at hand or carry around some personal comfort item, whatever it might be—a particular striped blanket, a stuffed gray dog with floppy ears, a pacifier on a green ribbon, or a blue ring-shaped teether. When children cling to these items, it is as if they are holding on to a piece of themselves, something intimately connected to home and Mommy. They are happier with these comfort items in hand or nearby, even though *what* they choose to cling to may look insignificant and even grubby to anyone but themselves! Understanding this, caregivers permit children to hold on to or let go of these items at will.

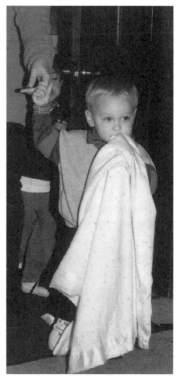

Comfort items help children soothe themselves throughout the ups and downs of daily life away from home.

Everyone, young and old, likes family photos! Poring over a photo album at their family child care home, two toddlers point out people they know.

Family photographs. Young children take pleasure in photographs of themselves and their families. They touch, look at, and if they can talk, name the people they see as they connect the images in these pictures with the loved ones they represent. To protect photographs from bending or smearing by eager fingers and hands, cover them with clear plastic sleeves or Con-Tact paper, or laminate them. Using Velcro, reusable plastic adhesive, or foam mounting tape, mount the pictures where children can easily see and touch them: low on walls or corkboard alongside children's play areas; on the wall alongside the diaper-changing table; on walls in the sleeping area, where children can study them as they fall asleep and wake up; on the floor, for creeping and crawling infants. Also, collect photographs of children and their families in small easy-to-handle albums so infants and toddlers can look at them on their own and with others. Some caregivers suggest to families that children bring to the center or child care home a small photo album of their family, pets, and residence to ease the transition from home. If families do not have such photographs, consider taking some, with the family's permission, on a home visit or at the care setting. For this, an instant camera (like a Polaroid) or an automatic-focus, "point-and-shoot" camera is an invaluable tool.

Here's another way to add a homey touch—put laminated family photos where a baby goes to sleep and wakes up!

◆ *Space for children's creations*

Seeing their own creations on display can help to give very young children a sense of belonging. When they crawl or toddle over to a wall or bulletin board containing samples of their art exploration (their papers covered with marks and scribbles or streaks and blobs, for example), they see familiar things that have emerged through their own actions. When a toddler exclaims "Mine!" while examining a personal creation mounted low on the wall of the play space, he or she refers not only to the paper filled with color, for example, but also to the space itself. In a setting that includes examples of their creative explorations, children can see reflections of themselves just by looking around.

◆ *A floor-level focus*

Since infants and toddlers spend lots of time on or near the floor, it is important to establish and maintain a warm, interesting floor-level setting. To achieve such a setting, look at your environment from the child's perspective. For example, crawl around on the floor yourself, lie down on your back, roll over. Examine what you see, feel, hear, and smell from a variety of floor-level positions around the play and care space. Make whatever adjustments are necessary so that from the very young child's vantage point, the surroundings present inviting sights, sounds, smells, textures, objects, and spaces.

Support children's sensory-motor approach to learning

To create an environment that holds and engages infants and toddlers, it is essential for caregivers to understand that infants and toddlers are eager to explore and learn directly using their whole body and all their senses. Because these very young children grow and change rapidly and individually, they need a dynamic environment with people and materials and equipment that provide the challenges they seek when they are ready for them. At the same time they need enough consistency in their environment to allow them to return again and again to familiar things and experiences. As you assess, set up, and modify your setting based on these characteristics of infants and toddlers, consider the following environmental elements that support their sensory-motor development.

◆ *Appealing to children's senses*

To support very young children's natural desire for sensory exploration, include the following kinds of experiences and materials for exploration and play: aromatic materials and experiences; sound-producing materials and experiences; materials to touch, mouth, taste, and look at, including a wide variety of found and natural materials so children experience more than plastic playthings, which have limited sensory appeal. Think also about providing an environment with open-ended materials, textural variety, and a variety of vistas.

Open-ended materials. Open-ended materials are objects or playthings whose use is not predetermined or narrowly limited in action or purpose; rather, children can use them in many different ways. A set of blocks, for example, is open-ended because growing children can see and use them in different ways: Infants reach for, grasp, mouth, drop, and bang blocks; toddlers carry, stack, and make simple structures with blocks; preschoolers pretend and build with blocks, making increasingly complex structures, and use blocks for pretend-play props; elementary-school children build elaborate designs, structures, and cityscapes and use blocks for tools.

A basket of large wooden beads is another example of an open-ended plaything. Infants and toddlers can do many things with the beads—handle them, hold them, mouth them, drop them, roll them, dump them out of the basket and put them back in, hide them under the basket, offer them to another child, bang them against the floor, carry them in their hands or in a bucket or purse. A bead maze, by contrast, is less open-ended. A young child can sit next to this toy and slide some attached wooden beads along a series of winding wire tracks. This device calls for a limited set of actions (sliding one or more beads along a track or spinning beads) and therefore engages a child's creativity less than the basket of beads does.

Providing infants and toddlers with a variety of open-ended materials like the set of blocks or basket of beads enables them to explore and manipulate the materials in ways that are personally meaningful and suited to their individual levels of development.

A many-textured environment. Another way to support infants' and toddlers' direct sensory-motor method of

The beauty of open-ended materials is their flexibility. Here's just one way to use sand, a cake tin, a spatula, a bucket!

learning is to include in their environment a lot of different textures for tactile exploration. Consider the following opportunities to incorporate or make use of textural variety in and around your setting:

- **Varied floor surfaces,** such as carpet, vinyl tile, and wood; outdoor walkways with small mirrors, ceramic tiles, or smooth stones embedded in them

- **Various types of moveable surfaces to sit on, lie on, crawl on, play on,** such as tatami (straw) mats, blankets, pillows, comforters, fleeces, mattresses, futons; a plastic wading pool containing sand or filled with crumpled newsprint

- **A variety of outdoor surfaces,** such as grass, fine ground covers, wooden decks and pathways, flat stone pathways, areas of sand, areas of soil, leaf-covered areas

- **A variety of low-level wall surfaces/coverings,** such as metal mirrors, cork, wood, butcher paper, foil, cardboard egg cartons, pegboard, glass brick, fabric, Con-Tact paper with the sticky side out

- **Various types of outdoor barriers or fences** made of such materials as board, stone, brick, chain link, rubber tile, straw bales, tree stumps (with bark or without)

- **A variety of fabrics used for drapery, upholstery, and pillow/mattress coverings,** such as corduroy, chenille, polished cotton, seersucker, ribbon, felt, silk, velveteen, leather, vinyl, suede, knitted or crocheted pieces

Interesting vistas. Include lots of windows that are accessible to children for peeks into the outside world, which they usually find captivating. Infants and toddlers like to crawl or toddle over to a window or climb up to a window to see who is going by; to watch the rain come down and the trees tossing in the wind; to observe the activities of birds, butterflies, squirrels, and other local animals; and to check out passing people, trucks, cars, and buses.

To provide very young children with interesting things to see, the following types of windows can be included in the design of an infant-toddler setting: skylights, floor-to-ceiling windows or sliding glass doors, low-level windows in walls and doors, a sunroom or sun porch (good for plants *and* people). Also think about including child-level windows that look into other children's indoor and outdoor play spaces, allowing children to watch their peers at play. These kinds of windows "can function as an additional learning center," in the opinion of Torelli (1992, p. 40).

Even an adult-level window can be accessible to mobile infants and toddlers if a broad, sturdy platform, loft, window seat, or climber is placed in front of the window to allow children to safely climb up to stand or sit at window level. Also, consider locating the diapering and dressing area next

Although this window is high, the strategic placement of the climber allows children to climb up and enjoy the view, or sit on the stairs and watch others in action!

to or near an adult-level window so, during washing and diapering, children can choose to look outside and perhaps talk about what's going on outside.

Be sure to also think about what you might place or plant outside the windows for children's viewing and observing over time. You can, for example, add a window box planted with flowers or establish a flower bed, some flowering trees and shrubs, a meadow with grasses and flowers, or a rock garden with ferns and a small waterfall. To build some action into the scene, add a windsock, a windmill, a wind chime, a birdbath, a bird or squirrel feeder, a fishpond, or a rabbit hutch.

For an interesting and soothing indoor vista, set up an aquarium with a secure top. Include low-maintenance fish, aquatic frogs, aquatic plants, stones, and pebbles. Children are fascinated and soothed by the colors and motions of the fish and the plants.

✦ *Providing space and materials for movement*

Children of all ages have a built-in need for movement. For sensory-motor infants and toddlers, however, learning how to move, control their body, and get from one place to another are major developmental tasks that take up a

These sturdy cartons, stuffed with newspaper and painted by the toddlers, create opportunities for climbing, balancing, and surveying the scene from a safe height!

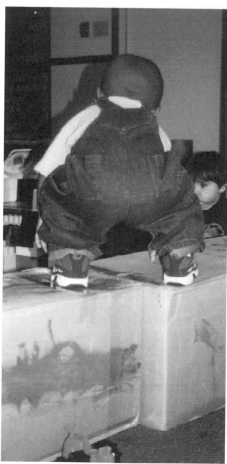

good deal of their time and energy. Therefore, it is absolutely essential to include space and materials that support the movement tasks very young children are striving to master. Infants need to have freedom and room to wave their arms and kick their legs, turn themselves over, and roll. Eventually, they want to sit, scoot, and crawl, pull up to stand, cruise, and walk. Once toddling, children are soon climbing, jumping, running, riding, and rocking. Add to this all the tasks they perform in gaining control of arm, hand, and finger movements. To give infants and toddlers opportunities for all these kinds of movement, think about ways that your environment can provide variety in scale, multiple levels, and places for active and quiet play.

Variety in scale. On pp. 107–108, we discussed reasons for having both child-sized and adult-sized furnishings. This variety in scale provides infants and toddlers with important movement experiences and allows them to relate positively to both their own close-to-the-ground world and the out-of-reach world of the taller people around them.

Caregivers can also provide variety in scale by supplying infants and toddlers with equipment, toys, and materials that vary in size. There should be cardboard boxes small enough for children's hands to carry or put things in and cartons large enough for children to get inside of; blankets sized for dolls and stuffed animals, blankets sized for infants and toddlers, and blankets large enough to drape over a small table to make a tent. Include large rubber balls that are big enough to push or sit on as well as small, easy-to-handle tennis and rubber balls. Small buckets, pots, and pans are easy and fun for toddlers to carry, but also provide some large buckets, pots, and pans (like the ones adults use) to give toddlers a chance to test their strength and balance. Small, light, high-impact plastic wagons are ones that new walkers can pull, but larger, heavier, wooden wagons that require more strength, balance, and walking experience to pull present a challenge to older toddlers. When an infant-toddler setting includes this kind of variety in scale, children have both chances to succeed and opportunities to be challenged.

Multiple levels. An environment that has multiple physical levels for young children provides them with opportunities to see and reach things above floor level, to balance and coordinate their bodies, to use their muscles to climb, and to experience safe heights. Infants enjoy the change of view afforded by multiple levels and eventually enjoy the challenge of crawling from level to level. Toddlers like to climb up to view their environment from different vantage points and to sometimes feel as tall as adults or relate to adults face to face. To create a variety of levels (both indoors and out) for children, use mattresses, raised platforms, decks, climbers of all sorts, ladders, lofts, hammocks, slides, ramps, hills, benches, balance beams, large blocks, and carpeted steps leading to sunken play areas.

Places to suit different activity levels. Very young infants who are not yet creeping or crawling need safe floor and outdoor space where they can lie or sit to play on blankets, mats, or mattresses without being crawled over, stepped on, leaned on, or sat on by the more mobile infants or by toddlers.

One way to create a safe play place for nonmobile infants is to provide them with their own room and outdoor area; if young infants, older infants, and toddlers share one room or outdoor area, try surrounding some part of the floor or outdoor space with low soft barriers, such as large pillows or bolsters. Low, hinged partitions made of framed Plexiglas serve the same purpose and may be more effective in the case of particularly curious toddlers. Being within this "buffered" space allows very young infants to see the activity going on around them, to see and be seen by their caregivers, and yet to play safely without being as isolated or confined as they would be if left to play in a crib or playpen. To promote active learning, cribs should be used as comfortable places for sleeping, *not* as playpens or holding areas for infants who are awake and interested in interacting and exploring. Regarding the use of playpens as play areas for nonmobile infants, this is what Goldschmied and Jackson (1994) have written:

> One great drawback of the [wooden] playpen is that it is a too convenient way of ignoring a baby or of restricting a crawling child. . . .
>
> The other type of playpen, . . . is usually called a "lobster pot." A baby confined there sees the world through a rather dense white netting, which is something none of us would want to do for more than a few moments. Remember how when we want to see outside we always lift back a net curtain from a window? A playpen has its use as a secure place. . . . But secure places can so easily become prisons, and even if a seated baby is supplied with a well-stocked Treasure Basket, [the baby] is still cut off from adult contact. (p. 79)

Mobile infants need large, open space for their active, noisy play but also smaller, separate space for their quiet, more stationary play. By providing soft quilts, mattresses, and pillows and lowered lighting in one or more corners of the room, caregivers can provide opportunities for quiet, less active pursuits, such as looking at books, exploring a basket of rocks and shells, filling a tin cup with walnuts, or simply observing and listening to what is going on in the rest of the room. This leaves the middle of the room open for more active, noisy pursuits.

Toddlers also need their places for active versus quiet play. For them, the corners of the room and areas along the sides of the room can serve as specific interest areas for looking at books, playing with small toys, exploring art materials, sand and water play, block play, and pretend play, while the middle of the room can serve, as it does for mobile infants, as a place for active play.

Guidelines for Organizing Space and Materials: A Summary

Build order and flexibility into the physical environment with

- ❏ Care and play areas that are distinct
  - ❏ Food preparation and eating, napping and sleeping, bodily care
  - ❏ Places for social interaction, private places
- ❏ An open floor plan
  - ❏ Fixed, specialized areas along perimeter
  - ❏ Middle space left open for active play
- ❏ Moveable furnishings, equipment, and storage containers
- ❏ Easy access to an outdoor play yard

Provide comfort and safety for children and adults with

- ❏ Clean, inviting floors, walls, and ceilings
- ❏ Soft places (pillows, couches, easy chairs, mats)
- ❏ Soft and natural lighting
- ❏ Infant- and toddler-sized equipment and furnishings
- ❏ Adult-sized furniture
- ❏ Storage for caregivers' belongings, children's belongings, extra toys and supplies
  - ❏ Children's cubbies
  - ❏ Child-accessible shelves, containers
  - ❏ Adult-height shelves, cupboards, hooks

- ❏ Safe, convenient adult access to appliances and everyday supplies
- ❏ A welcoming entrance or reception area
- ❏ Pleasant reminders of home
  - ❏ Children's comfort items
  - ❏ Family photographs
- ❏ Space for children's creations
- ❏ A floor-level focus

Support children's sensory-motor approach to learning with

- ❏ Materials that appeal to children's senses
  - ❏ Things to smell, hear, touch, taste, see
  - ❏ Open-ended materials (found/natural as well as commercial)
  - ❏ A many-textured environment (indoor, outdoor surfaces; furnishings)
  - ❏ Interesting vistas (windows, skylights, aquarium)
- ❏ Space and materials for children's movement
  - ❏ Variety in scale (equipment, furnishings, playthings)
  - ❏ Multiple physical levels
  - ❏ Places to suit different activity levels
    - ❏ Active play
    - ❏ Quiet, stationary play

Applying the Guidelines to Specific Areas

The specific areas in your infant-toddler setting might be these: eating places and food preparation areas, sleeping and napping areas, bodily care areas, infant indoor-play spaces, toddler indoor-play spaces (including their movement area, sand and water area, book area, art area, block area, house area, and toy area), infant outdoor-play areas, and toddler outdoor-play areas. The rest of this chapter describes how the broad guidelines summarized on p. 119 apply to each of those areas.

Eating places and food preparation areas

Infants spend a significant amount of time each day eating, and what and where they eat affects their growth and development. Overall, infants' personal nutritional needs are best met in a safe, relaxed, peaceful environment in which a thoroughly familiar nurturing caregiver plays a major role.

Nutritious food gives toddlers energy for exploration and growth, and a pleasant dining space supports children in eating, exploring their food, feeding themselves, and socializing. Small groups of toddlers generally enjoy sitting with their caregivers while eating and sharing observations: "Charlie, cup!" "What this?" "Annie, me, chicken!" "Big!"

✦ *Location*

In a group-care setting, infants do not necessarily eat in or even near the food preparation area. Caregivers generally prepare bottles in a fixed location, but they bottle-feed infants in a variety of locations. For young infants,

the bottle-feeding takes place in the arms of the primary caregiver, anywhere that the pair can find a peaceful place to settle—in a comfortable chair; on a couch; or on the floor or grass, nestled against a few pillows. Some infants are highly sensitive to their surroundings and prefer to settle with their caregiver in the same place for each feeding. Other infants are content to be held and to drink from their bottle in any comfortable location. As long as the infant is in the caregiver's arms, bottle-feeding takes place wherever it works best for each particular infant-caregiver pair.

Bottle-feeding takes place in the arms of the primary caregiver.

Beginning spoon-feeding is still an intimate one-to-one interaction between child and caregiver.

For infants who are sitting and trying out solid foods, eating generally takes place in a consistent location that is close to the food preparation area and that has an easily cleaned floor. Early on, the sitting infant might be propped up in the caregiver's lap, against a pillow, or in an infant seat while the caregiver offers food on a spoon. When infants are able to sit by themselves and are interested in picking up finger foods, guiding the spoon to their mouth, and exploring food with their hands, caregivers can provide them with very low tables. This allows children to sit on the floor or on low chairs or stools while eating and to move away when they have had enough. (See "Tables and Chairs for Mobile Infants and Toddlers," p. 122.) Magda Gerber (1996) has suggested setting adult breakfast-in-bed tray-tables directly on the floor, with the infants then sitting comfortably on the floor to eat from them.

It is a good idea to locate the toddlers' eating tables close to the food preparation area, to minimize the distance food travels from the refrigerator or microwave and to make running water accessible for cleanup. The toddlers' eating area needs to have an easily cleaned floor, since food and drink inevitably end up there as toddlers explore their food and try to master a variety of ways to convey it from the table to their mouth.

The bottle and food preparation area itself is conveniently located in an area with a sink, at a distance from the changing area and within sight of the children on the floor at play. Such a location separates food preparation from activities involving bodily waste. It also allows caregivers to warm bottles and prepare food in full view of the very young children in their care (these are the children who cannot yet hold a mental image of their caregivers in mind and are therefore likely to become distressed if their caregivers "disappear" around the corner or into another room). If infants and toddlers share the same space, locate and set up one food preparation area to serve both infants and toddlers.

Tables and Chairs for Mobile Infants and Toddlers

"At RIE [Resources for Infant Educarers] classes we use small plastic molded chairs and a low, rounded table. If a child can creep or walk, she can climb into one of the chairs.

"I feel that a child-size table and chair promote respect because children see the world from their own perspective. Why should a child sit at a dining room table in a high chair or a booster chair? A high chair is a convenience for the [caregiver], but it's a little prison [for the child]. Why not have a little chair and table [the] child's size, where she can sit down and get up on her own?

"By using a child-size table and chair, you adjust to [the] child's level, which makes her feel more comfortable. Picking her up and fastening her into a restraining device may underscore her helplessness. The table and chair encourage competence by letting her [crawl or] walk to the table herself. She chooses whether to sit and eat and decides when she wants to get up and leave. She also knows that [the little table] is her special eating place.

"Giving a child appropriate choices is important. Having choices gives children power and promotes self-confidence. The little table and chair aid in doing this."

—*Magda Gerber and Allison Johnson*
(1998, pp. 153–154)

✦ *Materials and equipment*

A well-stocked infant food-preparation area includes, for each child, a set of bottles, a set of bibs, and a set of towels (to protect caregiver's clothing and wipe away drool), and these are all labeled with the child's name. Private bottles (bibs and towels) restrict the spread of germs and accommodate infants' individual formula or breast milk requirements. The area also includes the tableware for children who are beyond bottle-feeding—unbreakable (usually plastic) plates with upward-curved edges, short-handled spoons, shallow bowls, and cups with weighted bottoms and spouted tops. For toddlers who have graduated from spouted-top cups, include chunky, plastic drinking glasses that are wide enough in circumference so that children can hold them with both hands. Additional equipment or utensils may be needed based on the individual eating habits of the children in the program. Provide napkins, smocks, aprons, or hand towels for children who no longer wear bibs. Also continue to provide personally labeled bottles for toddlers who still prefer bottles to cups or who are in the process of switching from a bottle to a cup.

A refrigerator provides necessary storage for prepared bottles and food. Caregivers also need an appliance such as a bottle warmer (a Crock-Pot can substitute), a microwave oven, a sink with hot running water, a dishwasher, and cleaning supplies.

To minimize time spent on cleanup and maximize time with children, stock the area with enough bottles, spoons, bowls, utensils, to last the day, or run the dishwasher periodically throughout the day. For older toddlers who regard cleaning up the eating area as water play and fun with tools, provide cloths and buckets of warm soapy water along with child-sized brushes, brooms, and dustpans.

The type of furniture needed for infants' and toddlers' mealtimes has already been described (see pp. 120–121). We might add here, however, that the tables for toddlers should be big enough to seat three or four toddlers and a caregiver.

A table and chairs that are toddler-sized give these children a sense of control as they share a meal together. The table's proximity to counter space and a sink also makes serving and cleaning up easier for adults.

✦ *Storage*

Since infants follow individualized eating schedules, caregivers need to prepare their bottles and food throughout the day. Organizing all the spoons together, all the bowls together, all the clean cloths together, for example, and making them easily accessible in one place minimizes the time that must be spent away from children in food preparation tasks. Sorting food preparation items in baskets or on racks helps organize cupboards, drawers, shelves, and counter tops so caregivers can easily locate what they need. Store bibs and towels in baskets or on hooks labeled with individual children's names. Label with specific infants' names any unopened bottles or cans of formula, and store these on a shelf or in a cupboard.

Store toddlers' tableware and a clean supply of their slip-on bibs (dishtowels with neck-holes) in an organized fashion in cupboards or on shelves in the food preparation area, as close to the eating tables as possible. If parents provide toddler bibs, smocks, or aprons, label them with children's names and store them in children's individual cubbies, in a bib "mailbox," or on individual hooks close to the eating tables. If parents provide food for meals or snacks, have them label their child's food with the child's name, and store it in the refrigerator until needed.

Store cleaning supplies together, away from food supplies and above toddlers' reach or in a cupboard or closet fitted with a child-proof latch. (See p. 170 for a summary checklist of equipment and materials for the eating and food preparation area.)

Sleeping and napping areas

For all children, sleeping is natural and vital, but sleep needs vary considerably from child to child and from month to month. Infants generally spend more time sleeping than toddlers and older children do. As children grow, their need for daytime sleep gradually decreases, although it continues to fluctuate for a variety of reasons, including illness, nighttime sleep-patterns, special events, and changes in routine. The group-care environment needs to include a time and place for toddlers to sleep or rest for an hour or so at least once a day. Whatever is happening in their world, infants and toddlers depend on their caregivers to support their individual sleep schedules and to provide them with peaceful, comfortable places to sleep whenever the need arises.

✦ *Location*

The location of the sleeping area varies from program to program, depending on the layout of the physical space. Caregivers set aside a separate and accessible room for sleeping, if such a room is available. In temperate climates and dry weather, the sleeping area may be outdoors on a shaded deck or screened porch. In either case, caregivers remain accessible. They also check on children frequently so as to be available when children awake. If a separate room is not available, the sleeping area may be located in an alcove or corner in the program's main room, where lights can be dimmed and noise and distractions minimized.

Caregivers place infants on their backs for sleeping because this position has been found to decrease the incidence of sudden infant death syndrome (SIDS). Infants, may, however, roll over and change their sleeping position without jeopardizing their health.

Some parents may wish their children to sleep, or at least fall asleep, in their caregiver's arms or cuddled up next to another infant or older child, on the couch, on the floor, or wherever they are when

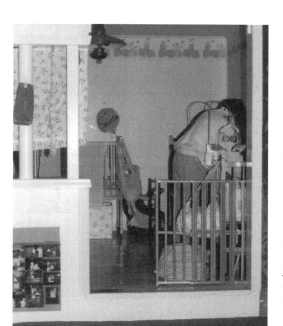

This center's infant napping alcove is set off by a half wall, curtains, and a childproof gate across the entrance. A sign above each crib designates who sleeps in it, and that child's personal sleeping supplies are in a bag hanging on the crib's corner post. Today, Samantha's car seat rests next to her crib, because Mommy brings her in one car, and Grandpa takes her home in another.

Torelli/Durrett, Inc. & Spaces for Children

Outside this nap room, a hammock takes the place of a rocking chair.

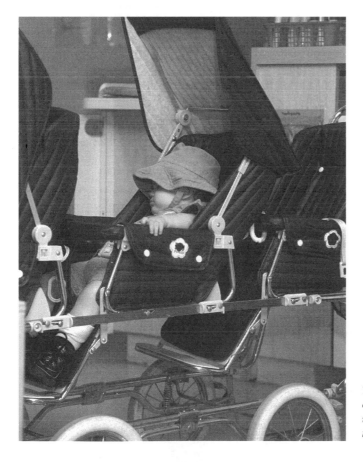

This older infant naps in a carriage—where he fell asleep while riding in from an active time in the play yard.

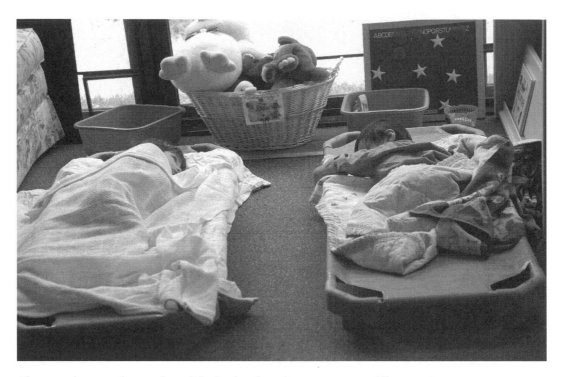

The space between the couch and the bookrack makes a cozy two-toddler napping spot.

sleep overtakes them. When this is the case, listen carefully to parents, and together find a sleeping place in the group-care setting that works for parents, children, and caregivers. (See "Responding to Families' Values About Sleep Routines," p. 127.)

In settings where toddlers are in a separate room from infants, at nap time the toddlers' central play area may be set up with cots to become the napping area. This arrangement works when all the toddlers within a given small group of toddlers rest at approximately the same time each day. While this approach to napping is an efficient use of space, it can be somewhat disconcerting to toddlers unless they can each nap in the same, familiar spot every day. Even then, some children may find it difficult to fall asleep when they have a full view of inviting toys and play materials; for such children, some shelves and equipment might need to be temporarily turned to the wall or covered with a sheet or drape. Locate cots out of the pathways children and adults use going to and from the bathroom.

✦ *Equipment and materials*

The sleeping equipment and materials needed for each infant generally include a cradle, basket, or crib (depending on the age and comfort needs of the infant), a snugly fitting mattress, bedding (mattress pad, fitted sheet, blanket), and the infant's particular comfort items ("blankie," teddy, soft toy) from home. Cribs (cradles, baskets), bedding, and comfort items are labeled to help prevent the spread of germs and to create a familiar, personalized place where each child can fall asleep and wake up comfortably. At the same time, there may be occasions when the parent-caregiver team, following the cues of the particular child or children involved, takes exception to the one-child-per-crib practice, and for example, puts siblings or twins to sleep in the same crib or sleeping space.

Young toddlers may continue for some time to nap in the cribs they slept in as infants. However, somewhere between their first and third year, most toddlers in group-care settings generally move from a crib to a cot. Bedding includes a sheet to cover the cot and a blanket for the child to snuggle under. These are labeled for individual children. Like infants, most toddlers prefer to nap with some personal item that gives them comfort.

If center staff, rather than parents, launder soiled bedding, a washer and a dryer for this purpose need to be located somewhere in the center. Alternatively, some centers may keep a large supply of clean bedding on hand and use a laundromat or a laundry service on a regular basis.

◆ *Storage*

In an adult-accessible cupboard in the sleeping area, store extra clean bedding and extra comfort items for each child. These can be on a shelf or in a basket labeled with the child's name. Soiled bedding can be placed in a closed hamper that is located in the changing area or next to the washer and dryer. Some centers keep soiled items in sealed bags until they can be put in the hamper or until they can be taken home by parents to launder and return.

If the sleeping area is not permanently set up, stack the cots, stripped of bedding, in a clean, out-of-the-way but accessible place. The bedding currently in use on cots can be folded and put on a shelf above the stored cots, or it can be folded and placed on top of each cot; in this way, when cots are stacked, one child's bedding does not come in contact with another child's. Crib bedding currently in use need not be stripped if the cribs are

---

Responding to Families' Values About Sleep Routines

"Values about sleeping and napping routines often cause a conflict when the caregiving practices at home do not match those at the child care setting. In many programs in the United States, the policy of the child care program, the licensing requirements, or the interpretation of child care licensing regulations dictate separate sleeping arrangements for infants and toddlers. Consequently, when children come from home settings with different caregiving practices for sleeping, they experience a major inconsistency in care. The situation becomes difficult for all concerned—baby, caregiver, and parents—when babies are accustomed to being held and rocked to sleep at home but in the child care setting are placed alone in a crib in a quiet, separate sleeping room. No wonder the children have difficulty falling asleep when they first come into group care.

"Again, it is important to be sensitive and responsive to the needs of individual parents and babies and to be realistic about what is possible and best for the child in the child care setting. Together you and the parents will need to explore how you can come to a mutually satisfying solution. With this particular issue you may have to include your licensing person in your discussions to be sure the requirements are truly appropriate to the infant's needs and consistent with the family's child-rearing practices and are not simply a culturally biased interpretation of the regulation."

—Janet Gonzalez-Mena
(1995, pp. 17–18)

permanently set up. Similarly, children's comfort items can be kept in their individualized cribs or in their cubbies. (See p. 171 for a summary checklist of equipment and materials for the sleeping and napping area.)

Bodily care areas

The infant diapering and dressing area should be convenient to use and easy to keep clean. It is also important that the diapering and dressing area be inviting and interesting enough that infants willingly spend time there even though they might rather be on the floor playing and moving about.

Each toddler moves from diapers to underpants at his or her own pace. As walkers and active learners, toddlers are generally eager to take on the self-help tasks involved in their own bodily care. They rely on caregivers to set up changing areas and toddler bathrooms in ways that allow them to exercise their developing motor abilities and growing desire to do things for themselves.

✦ *Location*

For the sake of sanitation, the diapering and dressing area needs to be located next to a sink and at a distance from eating and food preparation areas. So that the caregiver who is diapering or dressing an infant can provide reassurance to other children in her care, locate this bodily care area where other children can look up from their play and see her while she is at the changing table. Additionally, locating the diapering and dressing area next to a window or mirror provides a view for children and caregivers to enjoy while engaged in these tasks.

Locating the toddler bathroom directly off the main toddler play area gives children the easiest access to toilets. Otherwise, they would have to wait for caregivers to take them out of the room and down the hallway to the bathroom. If the toddlers' bathroom is not directly accessible to their play space, allocate space in or next to the diapering area for small portable toilets or potty chairs for toddlers to use as needed throughout the day.

If you are building or creating a new infant-toddler facility, consider combining the diapering area and the toddler bathroom into one room within or off the main indoor play space. Make the bathroom large, and divide it from the rest of the room with low walls (around 48 inches high) so children in the main play space can easily see and be seen by caregivers as they assist children in bodily care routines.

✦ *Equipment and materials*

The focal points of the diapering and dressing area are the sink and a sturdy changing table or counter about 36 inches high, with low, raised sides (to prevent the child from rolling off). Equip the changing table with an easily

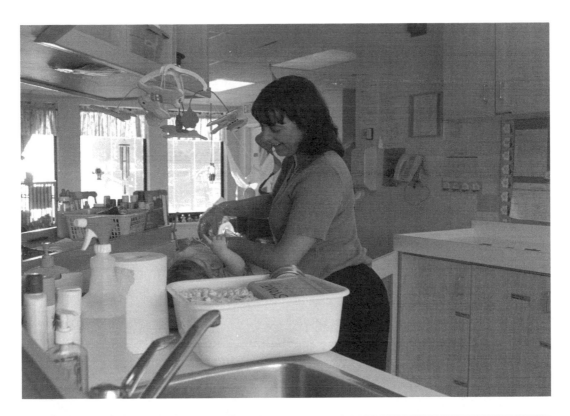

Torelli/Durrett, Inc. & Spaces for Children

Both of these infant diapering and changing areas (top, and bottom right) are well organized for adults and pleasant for children.

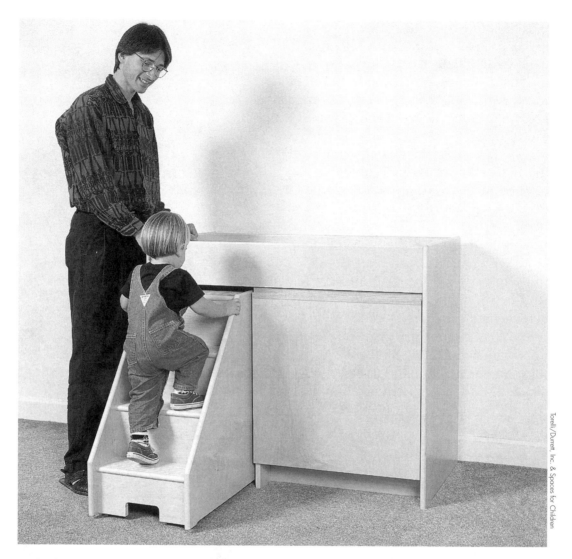

A climb-up changing table supports toddlers' "me-do-it" spirit and *saves caregivers' backs!*

cleaned soft pad. If the changing table is used for toddlers as well as infants, include a moveable set of steps that the toddlers can climb to get themselves up to the changing table. Or have a separate, climb-up changing table for toddlers. Having steps or a climb-up changing table for toddlers both supports toddlers' physical development and sense of control and helps prevent caregiver back-strain.

Materials for this area include a supply of clean diapers and extra clean clothes and a hairbrush (as needed) for each child; creams, diaper fasteners, and diaper covers, as needed; disposable wipes, or soap and a supply of individual washcloths for each child; disinfectants and cleaning supplies, such as a spray bottle of water and bleach or a roll of clean paper for covering the diaper-changing surface; disposable, protective gloves for the caregiver; closed, foot-operated containers for the soiled disposable diapers, soiled

In this child-friendly bathroom, toddlers can reach everything they need—toilet paper, faucets, soap, and towels—all by themselves!

wipes, and the used changing-table covers; hampers and sealable bags for soiled wash-cloths, clothes, and cloth diapers that are on their way home or to the washing machine.

Caregivers may also stock the area with one or more containers of small toys and objects for children to hold and play with while they are being changed. These items should be washable and frequently cleaned to prevent spreading any contamination from bodily waste. While cleanliness is a particular concern for the small toys kept in this area, it is important to provide a choice of objects for infants to play with to help children retain some control over diaper changing, an event about which they have little choice.

In the toddlers' bathroom, include very low, toddler-sized toilets and toilet paper in dispensers children can easily reach. If your facility's toilets are too high for toddlers, add step stools, or provide low, portable toilets or potty chairs. (Empty potties into the full-sized toilets and disinfect them after each use.) In the toddlers' bathroom, include a low sink or a stable set of steps leading up to the sink to enable toddlers to easily reach the tap (it should be an automatic tap or a lift tap that is easy for children to use and, for safety, the hot water should be no more than 110°F). At the hand-washing sink, include pump soap and a paper-towel dispenser mounted within toddler reach, or hang a set of cloth hand towels on low pegs labeled with individual children's photographs, so each child can recognize and use his or her own towel. Having a mirror over the sink allows toddlers to watch themselves as they wash.

✦ *Storage*

Store each infant's diapers, extra clothing, and other diapering supplies in a clearly labeled container, large Ziploc bag, or pillowcase. Store these in cupboards or on shelves that are easily accessible to the caregiver as she stands at the changing table. These cupboards and shelves can be restocked daily, or as necessary, from some larger, less convenient storage areas. Store older toddlers' supplies of extra diapers, underpants, and clothing changes in their cubbies, so the children can get these items themselves and bring them to the bathroom or diapering area as needed. Store the extra hand-washing soap, paper towels, toilet paper, and cleaning supplies for this area safely out of toddlers' reach. (See p. 172 for a summary checklist of equipment and materials for the diapering, dressing, and bathroom area.)

Infant play spaces

Any indoor play space intended for infants needs to be on or near the floor, where infants can safely move and explore their immediate environment, still keep their caregiver in sight, and engage her attention. When their play space provides comfortable surroundings and interesting materials, this piques infants' curiosity and encourages them to interact with people and materials. It may help to think of this indoor play space as the essential laboratory where, through their senses and actions and movement, infants learn about their physical and social world.

✦ *Location*

An indoor play space for infants (including those nonmobile and those mobile) may be located any place within the group-care room or setting that meets the following criteria:

- It is physically separate from the food preparation/eating, sleeping, diapering/dressing areas.

- It is out of the path of major traffic.

- It is large enough for three or four infants to lie, move, roll, sit, creep, crawl, or play without crowding.

With these criteria in mind, it often makes sense to locate the areas for food preparation/eating, sleeping, and diapering/dressing, and also any specialized or fixed play areas, along the edges of the room, as discussed on pp. 102–103, leaving the middle of the room open for mobile children to creep, crawl, balance, and play on moveable mats, ramps, steps.

Safe space for nonmobile infants. A play space for infants who are not yet creeping or crawling may be established in a fixed location, for example, on a raised carpeted platform or a covered mattress bounded by walls, low

An infant-sized "little house" with openings on all four sides creates a safe place for this creeper-crawler to explore.

windows, and/or cushions. Another play space may be defined by a large blanket or quilt on which an infant or a small group of infants are lying. Caregivers may change the location of this blanket play space from day to day to accommodate whatever else is going on in the room and to provide the infants on the blankets with a variety of interesting vistas. If there are also mobile infants and toddlers playing in the immediate vicinity, encircle the nonmobile infant's play space by buffering, as described on pp. 117–118.

Safe space for mobile infants. Creepers and crawlers require more space than nonmobile infants do. Mobile infants may start out on their own low platform, mattress, or blanket and gradually work their way across the floor to the couch, the window, the fish tank, or any object that attracts their attention. It is important to locate their play space where it is clear of such hazards as swinging or opening doors and where it can accommodate a variety of levels and things to crawl into and behind. Again, an open central area may best serve this purpose.

✦ *Equipment and materials*

As active learners, infants need a variety of open-ended materials that support their exploratory, sensory-motor approach to learning. The following types of playthings meet these criteria:

- *Pleasant reminders of home.* See pp. 110–111 for a discussion of comfort items and family photographs.

- *Materials that appeal to children's senses.* This includes the general kinds of items discussed earlier, on pp. 112–113. For a checklist of specific materials that appeal to children's senses, see pp. 174–175. Note that many of the materials on this list appeal to more than one sense. Also, most of the materials suggested are ones that can be found at home and in nature rather than purchased from toy stores or catalogs. Commercial toys are usually (but not always) durable,

Babies take great interest in everyday materials. Tins, empty food containers, a strainer, and a paper towel tube are easy to grasp and appealing to look at, touch, smell, taste, or listen to.

colorful, safe, and washable, but they should not be the only types of things infants explore and play with. Inexpensive materials found both indoors and out often hold a special fascination for children. However, in providing either found or commercial playthings to infants (and toddlers), adults need to be alert to safety issues and potential health hazards, such as allergies. (See "Choosing Safe Materials for Infants and Toddlers" on p. 136.)

- *Materials and equipment that encourage movement.* Infants spend a lot of time rolling, maneuvering themselves into a sitting position, scooting, crawling, and pulling themselves upright. As discussed on

pp. 115–118, they need equipment and materials that, instead of restricting them, allow them to move in these ways on a variety of physical levels and surfaces. (See "Why Not Infant Swings and Walkers?" on p. 138.) Also, because infants enjoy initiating and repeating satisfying actions, they

An infant-level ledge and a low, sturdy water table encourage these infants to pull themselves up to stand—now they can explore shaker bottles and play in the water with nesting cups, rubber ducks and fish, and a whisk.

Choosing Safe Materials for Infants and Toddlers

Here are some guidelines for choosing materials, objects, or toys that infants and toddlers might safely handle and explore:

1. They should be sturdy.
2. They should be too large for a child to swallow, too short for child to strangle in.
3. They should not have sharp edges or points or be easily torn or broken into small pieces or easily splintered. Look for durability and smooth, rounded corners.
4. An infant should be able to handle an object with one hand, since working with two hands is not a well-developed skill at this stage. The infant should be able to grasp the object in more than one place. It should be light enough to be shaken and small enough not to knock the child over if he or she pulls on it.
5. Examine objects or toys closely to make sure there are no detachable parts. Look out for button eyes not securely sewn on, a tassel or bell clapper that can be pulled off, a part of an object that could break off and leave an exposed staple or nail. Do not assume that a commercial toy is safe even if it is made by a well-known toy manufacturer who presumably knows about safety issues.
6. Infants and toddlers enjoy brightly colored objects, but be sure that the paint or dye will not come off and is not toxic.
7. Assess flowers, leaves, bark, for toxicity. Check with a local botanical garden, poison control center, landscape architect, or see Appendix C in the High/Scope Press publication *Let's Go Outside!* by Tracy Theemes (1999).
8. Consult with parents to learn whether any children are sensitive or allergic to nontoxic plants or other natural items, including things they might mouth or inhale.

—Adapted from Judith Evans and Ellen Ilfeld
(1982, p. 71)

need objects and materials that readily respond to their movements rather than playthings that are self-propelled or controlled by adults. (See p. 173 for a checklist of movement-supporting materials and equipment for children at various stages.)

Balloons enclosed in mesh bags and hung from the ceiling invite exploration!

• *Balls.* Balls deserve special mention as toys that encourage children's movement. Wiffle balls, as well as cloth, wool, leather, rubber, and tennis balls, are wonderfully responsive infant toys. As perfect spheres, they are always poised for action and easy to set in motion. Young infants enjoy both tracking their movement and making them move. Once infants are mobile, they enjoy setting balls in motion and crawling after them as they roll across the floor. In a sense, balls serve as infant guides through space.

• *Wheeled vehicles and animals.* Like balls, simple, sturdy, easy-to-grasp toy vehicles and animals with large wheels or rollers are easy and satisfying for sitting children to set in motion. Practiced crawlers also enjoy pushing them or rolling them along under one hand as they crawl.

• *Mirrors.* An infant's reflection in a mirror responds immediately to the infant. When the infant looking into the mirror moves, the reflected baby magically moves! Infants regard their own reflections with great interest long before they begin to understand that the reflected eyes and faces and motions that hold their attention are their own. Older infants reach out to play with their reflections; they may even "converse" with them. Positioning firmly fastened, metal mirrors on the floor, walls, and closet doors and next to or over the changing table and securely mounting large mirrors low on walls in infant play spaces allows children to re-

On their blanket in front of a mirror, these infants are in a good position to enjoy cloth balls, one another, and their reflections.

gard themselves and their reflective play partners from a variety of vantage points. If a low railing is near a low, wall-mounted mirror, infants can watch as they pull themselves up to a standing position.

- *Soft dolls and stuffed animals.* Small, simple, soft washable dolls and stuffed animals appeal to infants for a number of reasons. The softness feels good. The toys' facial features reflect the features infants

This slightly deflated beach ball is big, light, and easy to grasp!

Why Not Infant Swings and Walkers?

When making decisions about equipment and materials for infants, remember that it is through whole-body movement that babies learn about what their bodies can do. Given their need to wave their arms, kick their legs, turn their heads, arch their backs, roll over, push themselves up with their arms, sit, creep, crawl, and pull themselves upright, it makes sense to put infants in a safely watched, comfortably cushioned place that allows free whole-body movement—on the floor, a bolster-surrounded platform, or a grassy space—for exploration and play whenever they are not eating, sleeping, or being changed, bathed, dressed, or held. In contrast, infant swings (and seats), *when used as places for play,* confine infants to one position, severely restricting many of the kinds of movement they are ready and eager for. While walkers allow infants to scoot themselves from place to place with their feet, they actually prevent children from practicing many of the motions vital to learning to walk—pulling themselves into a standing position, balancing, and bearing their own weight. Further, they physically restrict exploration, because they prevent infants from touching and grasping things on the floor. (They also permit scooting to precarious places, such as edges of steps and ramps.)

study in the faces of their parents, siblings, and caregivers. Further, as infants learn to grasp and wave these soft toys around, the blows they inadvertently deliver to themselves are gentle and sometimes even soothing. Older infants tend to converse with their dolls and stuffed animals, probably because infants associate faces with "talk."

- *Cloth and board books.* Small, sturdy, easy-to-handle cloth and board picture books provide infants with their first literacy experiences. At first, lying in a caregiver's arms, on the floor, or on the changing table, nonmobile infants may simply look at a picture on the cover or open page of a book as a caregiver holds or props the book up. Infants tend to prefer simple, bright, high-contrast pictures of people, animals, and familiar objects. (Very young infants see black-and-white pictures best.) Initially, they treat these first books as they do any other object of interest— looking at them, batting at and reaching for them, touching them, grasping the edges of pages, and mouthing the books' corners. Once infants can sit up and have both hands free, they often like to turn the pages, especially with a caregiver holding the book. During page turning, they gradually begin to pause, examine the pictures, and imitate the caregiver as she points to and talks about the objects pictured. As reading specialist Cathleen Soundy (1997) has noted, "During these early reading sessions, infants often smile, reach, point and babble. With repeated exposure, babies will pat the book, show pleasure in familiar favorites, turn the pages and jabber at the pictures. . . . Older infants and toddlers who have been introduced early to books take great pleasure in being read to, often requesting that one book be read repeatedly during the same session" (p. 151). (See "Books for Babies" on the facing page.)

- *Hinged doors and boxes.* Infants, when old enough to sit with both hands free, develop a fascination with doors and hinged lids they can readily open and close over and over again. Given the satisfaction this action brings, it makes sense to provide wooden boxes or tins with hinged lids, toy cupboard doors, dollhouse doors, and small climber doors, for example, that infants can safely operate as much as they like. (See photos on p. 269.)

- *Lightweight blocks.* Sitting infants enjoy the challenge of stacking or attempting to stack two or three lightweight blocks or cubes they can easily grasp. The sound and sight of toppling them over is equally rewarding.

- *Open containers.* Infants' initial interest in open containers centers around grasping and mouthing them. This is relatively easy to do, since empty juice cans, cottage cheese containers, butter tubs, and small wicker baskets, for example, have thin sides that are easy for infants to grasp with one hand. When an infant puts a shell or rattle into a container, it is usually accidental, and a young infant may not even be aware of the item in the container once it can no longer be seen. Gradually, however, with maturation and experience, babies remember out-of-sight objects, and they begin to fill and empty containers deliberately.

Here's a cozy spot for examining a selection of sturdy picture books.

✦ *Storage*

In an active learning setting, play materials for infants are stored in ways that allow children to choose what they want to explore and play with. For non-mobile infants, this means creating a portable storage system of small baskets, boxes, buckets, cloth bags, and tins, so wherever the infant is lying or sitting, the caregiver can readily supply a container of appealing sensory materials. For mobile infants, along with using the portable storage system, store toys and play materials directly on low, sturdy shelves or in baskets or clear plastic containers on shelves. Infants can then crawl over to get particular items they wish to explore and play with.

Store infant books where they are easy for creepers, crawlers, or cruisers to see and reach. Place them in plastic tubs or boxes for easy access, or stand them up on very low shelves, on

---

Books for Babies

"Books for infants and toddlers usually have minimal text; the words often function more like labels or captions for the pictures. [The books'] plots, when they exist, are often a single event from the child's daily experience, such as getting dressed or taking a bath. Although short texts and bold illustrations provide the mainstay, older babies and toddlers will benefit from books that include some narrative. Toddlers who have been read to since birth are ready for more advanced story lines with increased amounts of text."

—*Cathleen S. Soundy (1997, p. 153)*

This infant knows exactly where to find the little books—in the small box on the floor-level shelf!

forward-facing bookracks, or in clear, hanging pockets (available from supply catalogs). Using any of the latter three book-storage options may require more adult involvement, but these options do allow children to see all the covers and make a choice based on what they see. (See p. 176 for a summary checklist of indoor play equipment and materials for infants.)

Where and how do toddlers play?

As babies gain their feet and turn into toddlers, their world expands. With their increasing ability to move, communicate, and engage in complex play, toddlers continue to look for the comfort and security of known people and materials but also are ready for the challenge of bigger spaces and new materials. If they share the group-care setting with infants, toddlers need both shared play space and space of their own, where they can pursue "toddler only" activities.

Toddlers therefore play in appealing interest areas set up around the room but also on the floor, on the couch, at small tables, in a loft, on the grass, on a climber, in a sandbox, and along riding-toy paths. Caregivers set up specific toddler play spaces to reflect and encourage toddlers' increased mobility and interest in the physical and social world, their growing sense of themselves as doers, and their emerging cognitive capacities. Toddlers are beginning to explore and understand categories—how things are the same or different—and to develop a spatial sense of where things are, so having consistently located play areas stocked with accessible materials that are organized around specific types of play begins to make sense.

Toddlers often repeat satisfying actions both to gain a sense of mastery and to challenge themselves by introducing slight variations in their play, so they rely on a consistent stock of open-ended materials and playthings they can locate on their own and play with or explore as often as they choose.

"Toddlers need more space for their size than children of any other age; they should not have to spend the day in one small room."

Toddlers also need more play space than infants do. In fact, in the opinion of developmental psychologist Doris Bergen and her colleagues (1988), "Toddlers need more space for their size than children of any other age; they should not have to spend the entire day in one small room" (p. 202). The following sections describe some specific play areas that support toddlers' expanding interests.

The toddler movement area

The movement area should be a safe, accessible, open place where toddlers can do their first, tentative walking without bumping into people or things and, as they become increasingly sure on their feet, where they can run, climb, push, pull, rock, and ride. Large-muscle movement—walking, running, climbing, carrying—defines, in large part, how toddlers explore and construct knowledge about themselves and their world.

✦ *Location*

The toddlers' indoor movement area is best located in the middle of the center's floor plan so toddlers can easily move into it from other activities. After all, for toddlers, movement time is all the time. Their movement area may also

Torelli/Durrett, Inc. & Spaces for Children

Toddlers need things to climb, ride, and crawl through.

extend toward the side of the room to include a sunken play area and particular pieces of equipment, such as a dowel climber attached to a wall, or a toddler loft placed against a wall. Depending on the layout of the center, caregivers might dedicate an alcove or an entire room to the toddler movement area, as long as it opens directly onto the rest of the toddler play space.

✦ *Equipment and materials*

Aside from open space in which to walk and run, a toddler movement area needs things for toddlers to climb on. In the absence of appropriate climbing structures, toddlers will climb anyway—on tables, chairs, and shelves—so it is up to caregivers to provide sturdy, appropriate climbers! Toddlers also need objects to jump off of, things to get into, balls for rolling and throwing, wheeled toys to push and pull, rocking toys, and riding toys. The riding toys should have at least four wheels widely spaced for stability, and at least some of them should not require use of a steering mechanism (although older toddlers enjoy and can generally manage steering). When sitting on the rocking or riding toys, toddlers should be able to rest their feet flat on the floor.

In addition to having recorded music that they can move to (for an example, see p. 363), toddlers also need a set of sturdy, high-quality musical instruments they can play while sitting down or as they move about. Though many of these materials are initially expensive, their impact on children and their durability over the years make them wise investments.

✦ *Storage*

Store climbers and large pieces of movement equipment in the movement area, where they are used. Store riding toys and pull- and push-toys in a designated "parking" area next to a loft or along a wall. Store musical instruments on a low shelf or in open containers or baskets. (See p. 177 for a summary checklist of equipment and materials for the movement area.)

The toddler sand and water area

Toddlers like to muck about in sand and water, enjoying the look and soothing feel of sand and water and the continuous changes that occur as they pat, splash, dump, and pour. In fact, the sand and water area is one toddler play space where play with squishy, messy materials is encouraged!

✦ *Location*

If possible, locate the sand and water area on a tile floor and close to a sink to simplify cleanup and the process of adding and draining water. If a space with tile floor is not available, prepare the area by securely fastening down a piece of nonskid waterproof floor-covering of some kind.

◆ *Equipment and materials*

This area centers around a toddler-height sand and water table partially filled with sand and/or water. (If space permits, provide two tables, one for sand and the other for water.) If you do not have a suitable table, substitute a baby bath tub or a child's plastic wading pool placed on the floor or on a low table. If the table, tub, or pool is some distance from the sink, provide small buckets with handles so children can participate in adding to and draining the supply of water. For children's play with sand and water, include containers to fill and empty, things to hide and find, things to float, things to soak and squeeze. For older toddlers who are beginning to pretend, include rubber or plastic animal and people figures.

In nice weather, caregivers wheel the water table outside, where it is easy to fill with the hose.

◆ *Storage*

At the end of the day, remove all the containers and objects from the sand and water table and store them where children can easily see and reach them, for example, in baskets or dish tubs next to the table or on a low nearby shelf. This allows children to see and feel the sand or water itself and to make choices about what materials they wish to add to their sand and water play on any given day. (See "Sand and Water Area Tips" on the facing page. Also see p. 178 for a summary checklist of materials and equipment for the sand and water area.)

The toddler book area

The book area should be a cozy place where toddlers can easily find and enjoy picture books. For toddlers, handling books, carrying them around, looking at the pictures, sitting on a caregiver's lap pointing to and "talking" about things in pictures, hearing stories, and "reading" stories are immediately pleasurable experiences that have a lasting impact. When toddlers have had these early experiences on a regular basis, it facilitates their learning to read in the elementary school years. A study by linguists Dorothy Allison and J. Allen Watson (1994) found that the earlier parents began reading aloud to their infants and toddlers, the higher the children's emergent reading levels were at the end of kindergarten. Further, in a study of reading in 15 countries, psychologist Robert Thorndike (1973) found that children who had been read aloud to from an early age became the best readers. And in a longitudinal study of literacy achievement, linguist Gordon Wells (1986) found that the best readers had heard approximately 6,000 stories between birth and age 5. So, a pleasant, well-stocked toddler book area can make a real difference in children's lives.

✦ *Location*

Locate the toddler book area in a corner or along the perimeter of the toddler play space so that major traffic patterns and active play will not interfere with book exploration and reading. Use bookshelves and other furnishings as boundaries for the area. One boundary might be formed by a large open carton tipped on its side and furnished with pillows to create a comfortable nook where children can retreat with books.

Remember that toddlers will spend some time using books in the book area, but they will also carry books about with them as they play in other areas. For example, they may "read" to baby dolls in the house area, drive books around in dump trucks, or look at books outside on the deck while sitting on a caregiver's lap.

Sand and Water Area Tips

"Sand needs to be washed regularly. . . . This is a task with which even small children (not more than two together) much enjoy helping. Shovel some of the sand into a bucket, take the bucket to the sink, fill the bucket with water and leave the tap running until it overflows the rim. Turn off the water while stirring up the sand lying in the bottom of the bucket to release the dirty bits and accumulated dust. Running the tap again, the dirt coming to the surface will gradually clear away. Some drops of disinfectant can be added.

"The equipment for use in the sand tray should be appropriate to its size, that is, not buckets and spades scaled to the outdoor sandpit. . . . The small plastic plant pots from garden centers come in a useful variety of sizes and serve very well for filling and emptying of sand and making 'castles' and 'cakes.' Because the plastic splits easily, it is a good idea to glue one container inside another. Plastic scoops are less satisfactory than the metal ones used in hotel and restaurant kitchens for flour and sugar. Stores specializing in catering equipment are often a better source of items for the sand table than toyshops. . . .

"If the . . . [sand table] is on legs, it is sometimes too high for the youngest children to reach comfortably. Low wooden boxes turned upside down make a helpful platform for them. . . .

"[Water play] can take place throughout the . . . day: helping to wash and wipe toys and tables, washing dolls' clothes, watering plants, and above all in the bathroom. The key person [primary caregiver] with her small group can allow the children unhurried time for experimentation with running water. Only taps provide the experience of trying to catch with finger and thumb the descending column of water and watching the swirl as it disappears down the drain."

—*Elinor Goldschmied and Sonia Jackson*
(1994, pp. 31–32)

A quilt-covered platform makes a cozy reading spot.

A sturdy forward-facing bookrack works for toddlers—all you need is one hand!

No matter where books are stored, toddlers read them all over the room!

Books in clear hanging pockets are easy for children to see and reach.

Torelli/Durrett Inc. & Spaces for Children

✦ *Equipment and materials*

However large or small the book area, it should be furnished comfortably. This might mean providing the carton nook (described earlier), or simply a mattress or quilt and some pillows, or some low easy chairs, or a couch. Children will want to sprawl or sit comfortably with a book alone, with peers, or snuggled up with a caregiver. Equipping the area with several stuffed toys and toddler-sized puppets representing familiar story characters offers the opportunity for pretending.

Provide a variety of books for toddlers to handle and look at. You will want to have a permanent collection of books in your book area, but don't neglect to use the local children's library for adding to your collection. (See "Library Visits" on p. 148.) When selecting books, look for board books with clear, well-drawn pictures or photographs. If text is included, it should be a simple description of what is pictured, or a simple story or rhyme. If you select an alphabet or counting book, choose it for the quality of the pictures, which will be of more interest to toddlers than the letters or numbers. For older toddlers, you may also wish to provide a selection of regular (non-board) picture books (both with and without text) and some catalogs and magazines with lots of illustrations.

Along with books, include small albums of photos you have taken of the children at the center. Also provide a box or album of postcards depicting animals, flowers, places of interest to children, and art reproductions (which often hold interest for young children—see "Museum Visits" on p. 148). Children, staff, and families can be invited to add to this picture collection.

Because it is a relatively peaceful setting, the book area is also a natural place to locate the aquarium suggested on p. 115. Also, caregivers who provide a computer for toddlers' use sometimes locate it in the book area, although a computer is *not necessary* in group-care settings for toddlers. "While we have been supportive of computer use for children of preschool

Library Visits

"Trips to the local children's library can start very early in a child's life, whenever possible involving a parent too. . . . The nursery [child care center or child care home] will probably already have a good relationship with the Children's Librarian and may have an arrangement for a stock of books changed periodically. Some parents may need convincing that a child is never too young to have a book borrowed on his behalf and read or shown to him at home."

—Elinor Goldschmied and Sonia Jackson (1994, p. 169)

Museum Visits

"Museums and art galleries are not often thought of as places to take very young children, but are full of objects and pictures which can hold great interest for them. . . . The [caregiver] leading the outing should discuss with the person responsible for the educational work of the museum or gallery what is likely to appeal to small children and ask if possible for a guided tour [for herself]. She can then make her own selection from her knowledge of the children and compile a list of exhibits to last over several visits, taking the children to look at no more than two or three different things on each occasion. This of course is entirely different from most people's past experience of visiting museums, either in school parties or as tourists, when we tend to rush around the whole place ending up exhausted and with no clear impression of what we have seen."

—Elinor Goldschmied and Sonia Jackson (1994, pp. 169–170)

age [3 years and above]," said educational psychologist Charles Hohmann (1998), "computer use by toddlers may not make developmental sense. . . . Even an inexpensive computer priced at under $1000 is an expensive (and delicate) toy for a toddler" (p. 5). However, if you already have a computer for toddlers (or if they share one with older children in your center), choose toddler software that includes music activities, peekaboo games, and creative art activities rather than preacademic content like letter, number, and shape recognition.

✦ *Storage*

Store books in ways that allow toddlers to see their covers—propped in forward-facing bookracks, hanging in clear pockets, or standing up on low shelves. Store overflow books in baskets or tubs, and rotate the toddler books between forward-facing display and tub (or basket) storage. Because toddlers enjoy hearing the same stories over and over, whatever you do, make sure to save display room for children's favorite books. If infants and toddlers share the same space, it may be necessary to store any non-board books above the reach of mobile infants. (See p. 179 for a summary checklist of equipment and materials for the book area.)

The toddler art area

The art area is where toddlers in group care have the chance to experience and explore basic art materials, get their hands messy and sticky, and enjoy the sensation of making motions that leave a mark—smearing finger paint across a large sheet of paper, making dots and scribbles with markers, kneading and squeezing dough and clay, crumpling and tearing paper. Through these sensory-motor experiences, children discover the essential nature of paint, paper, dough, clay, and markers. This sensory-motor understanding of the properties of basic art materials provides them with a body of experience to turn to when they reach the point of wanting to use these materials to represent their ideas, make things for play, and solve problems.

It is particularly important for caregivers to appreciate that toddlers are involved in *exploring* art materials rather than using them to make something. This means they are interested in feeling the finger paint, hearing paper rip and crunch, squeezing dough or clay and watching it smoosh through their fingers, and moving the brush across the paper. For toddlers, the actions of art seem to matter more than the outcomes.

✦ *Location*

Locate the toddler art area on a tile floor or on some other permanent or taped-down, easily cleaned, nonslip floor surface. Having the area close to a sink gives children and adults easy access to water for mixing paints, washing hands, and cleaning up; if possible, it should also be close to a window or skylight so children can easily see colors and materials. Since the requirements for toddlers' art and eating areas are similar, it may make sense to locate these two areas close to or overlapping each other. Alternatively, it might make sense to locate the art area around the corner from the toddler bathroom. In warm weather and temperate climates, locate the art area outside on a deck or in a shady area and close to a water source (a tap or a bucket of water).

This toddler art area is located on a tile floor, next to a window, and around the corner from a bathroom. Art materials are easily accessible on low shelves, and there is room for children to work on the floor and at the table or easels.

Outdoors there is a lot of light and space for painting.

✦ *Equipment and materials*

To protect children's clothing during any messy art activities, have them push up their sleeves, and provide them with one-piece, plastic or vinyl smocks that are easy to put on. If the smocks fasten, make sure buttons or Velcro pieces are fairly large so toddlers can manipulate them. If it is warm enough, children might simply remove their shirts before launching into messy art activities.

A table in the art area can provide children with a stable, smooth work surface. Depending on the space available, the art table may be dedicated to art activities or serve as a mealtime table as well. In either case, make sure to leave space for children who prefer to spread out and work with art materials on the floor.

Basic art materials for toddlers to explore fall into these broad categories: painting and drawing materials, paper, and dough and clay.

Painting and drawing materials. Finger painting lets toddlers experience the paint directly on their palms and fingers, feel the way it moves across the painting surface, and clearly see their actions making a mark. Provide children with finger paints in the primary colors (red, yellow, and blue) and large sheets of white paper spread on the table, floor, or ground. They need large sheets of paper (for example, butcher paper cut from a roll) because it is easier and more natural for toddlers to make large, sweeping arm motions rather than the small, contained motions required by small sheets of paper. White paper allows them to see the color they are using and also to see what happens when primary colors overlap and combine to make orange, green, and violet. If finger paints are given to toddlers on paper or plastic plates or in rectangular plastic food containers, they can put their palms and fingers directly into the paint.

For brush painting provide toddlers with tempera in the primary colors and short-handled brushes or small house-painting brushes in several widths. They also need large sheets of white paper, such as butcher paper, and a flat painting surface, such as a table, the floor, or ground. Some older toddlers may enjoy painting at free-standing or wall-mounted easels or on a wall- or fence-mounted piece of paper. If you use powdered tempera, mix it (away from children) with just enough water to make a fairly thick, nonrunny paint. Pour paints into low, flat containers that do not tip (muffin tins, cut-down yogurt containers, or tuna cans snugly arranged in a small square cake tin; baby food jars set in cut-out holes in sponges). Some toddlers prefer to use their fingers and hands instead of brushes. Others enjoy spreading paint with scrub brushes, dish-washing mops, feathers, sticks, cotton balls, or pieces of sponge. Provide a bucket for transporting painting tools to the sink to be washed—cleaning brushes and other tools is a task toddlers enjoy as much as painting!

For drawing, provide toddlers with a variety of colors in crayons, non-toxic water-based markers, and pieces of chalk. After children have had many opportunities to mark and scribble with these on large sheets of white drawing or butcher paper, add colored kraft or construction paper to their drawing materials.

For squeeze-bottle drawing and painting, provide children with pieces of cardboard and toddler-sized plastic squeeze bottles (such as small condiment bottles) filled with what educator Karen Miller (1984) described as "salt dribbles": equal parts of flour, salt, and water (with drops of paint for color).

Paper. Children use paper not only as a painting or drawing surface. They use it also as something to explore—by crumpling, tearing, folding, and twisting it to find out how it sounds, feels, changes, or bounces back. Therefore, it is important to provide toddlers with newsprint; white paper; colored construction, kraft, and tissue paper; and stiff cellophane.

Dough and clay. Provide children with play dough and clay to knead, pull, smoosh, squeeze, poke, roll, pat, and pound. Besides poking their fingers into these materials, older toddlers also like to poke objects into them, so it makes sense to provide them with a variety of objects to use in this way.

✦ *Storage*

Though bulk art supplies are usually stored in cupboards or on shelves accessible to staff, the art materials toddlers use each day should be where they can see and reach them. For example, hang toddlers' smocks in the art area on low wooden hooks (made from dowels with knobs on the ends). Store a daily supply of art materials on a set of low shelves in the art area, so children can choose what they want to use. If the set of shelves has wheels or casters, this makes it easy to move the art materials outside on

Easy access to art materials encourages these toddlers to explore and learn about the qualities of dough, paint, and paper.

nice days. A low supply-cart can also serve as portable shelves. At the beginning of each day, prepare the toddlers' art shelves: Set out that day's supply of paints in the nonspill containers described earlier. Store brushes together in small buckets, clear boxes, or racks. To keep markers from drying out, store them upside down with their caps inserted into holes drilled in a block of wood (you can make such a holder or order one from a supply catalog). Store play dough and clay in clear airtight containers (check them at the end of each day to make sure the lids are back on, and replace any dried-out dough or clay). For older toddlers who can hold images in mind, you might label each storage container on the art shelves with a sample item, a picture, or a photo to enable children and staff to easily return items to their designated containers.

Store sheets of paper on racks in the art area. You might stand a roll of butcher paper on an upright paper-holder and cut off strips and pieces each day, or keep the roll on a horizontal paper-holder and have a long piece rolled out on the floor or taped to the wall at the beginning of each day. (See p. 180 for a summary checklist of equipment and materials for the art area.)

The toddler block area

Providing a block area gives toddlers the space and opportunity to explore and work with easy-to-handle blocks, manipulate basic shapes, and begin to construct an understanding of spatial relationships. They like to handle, carry, and balance blocks, sometimes stacking them higher and higher to see when the stack will tip over. They use blocks to make simple enclosures they can get inside of. Older toddlers line up blocks end to end and then walk along the "path" they have made. Toddler block play is a satisfying whole-body experience.

✦ *Location*

Locate the toddler block area away from the book area, in a place where there is space enough for spread-out block structures, and where block play can extend if necessary into the open center of the room. Toddlers are awkward and need plenty of room to maneuver both themselves and their blocks. Make sure the floor surface is smooth and flat to allow stacking and balancing of blocks.

✦ *Equipment and materials*

Stock the block area with large, relatively lightweight blocks that toddlers can lift or handle with two hands. These might be large foam, plastic, or cardboard "brick" blocks that are uniform in size and easy for toddlers to stack. Include also a set of wooden unit blocks to give toddlers satisfying experiences handling denser, heavier blocks in a variety of shapes. (The pine unit blocks are lighter; the maple ones are more durable.) Include sturdy plastic or wooden vehicles for carrying and pushing blocks, and sets of pretend people and animals for filling, emptying, and pretending. (See p. 363.)

✦ *Storage*

Store blocks and large vehicles on low shelves, where children can easily see and reach them. If shelves are not available, stack the large blocks and the vehicles on the floor against a wall and the unit blocks in a basket or sturdy clear container. Store other small items in open baskets. (See p. 181 for a summary checklist of equipment and materials for the block area.)

Toppling blocks is just as much fun as stacking them!

This low shelf holds a variety of blocks and vehicles for toddler play.

The toddler house area

Here toddlers can find and explore dolls, kitchen-related items, and dress-up clothes. They can engage in a lot of filling and emptying—putting dolls in beds and buggies, emptying cupboards, filling the toy sink with dishes and spoons. They can imitate things they see family members doing at home—talking on the phone, putting dishes on the table, turning toy sink faucets off and on, putting on shoes like Mommy's, feeding the baby. Older toddlers may also begin to pretend, for example, using a pillow for a doll bed, or a cooking pot for a hat.

✦ *Location*

Locate the toddlers' house area in a corner or along the perimeter of the central, open play space. Since the play in this area often reflects what adults do at home in the kitchen, consider establishing the toddler house area close to or across from the food preparation and eating area. It may also work to locate the house area in a cozy space under a loft.

✦ *Equipment and materials*

To support children's exploration and imitative play, provide familiar household materials. This includes toy kitchen furnishings, such as a sturdy, stable sink, stove, and refrigerator equipped with hinged doors children can open and close as often as they want; toy and/or real telephones; and a toddler-sized table and several home-like wooden or wicker chairs. Surrounded by these appliances, toddlers can enjoy exploring, combining, and filling and

In the house area, children explore and play with everyday household materials.

emptying a variety of nonbreak-
able real (rather than toy) dishes,
small cooking pots, and empty
food containers. Also provide a
variety of real kitchen utensils and
collections of small items (corks,
shells) to use for "food."

For doll play, include soft-
bodied baby dolls reflecting the
racial and ethnic identities of the
children in the program; simple
doll clothes with Velcro closings;
baby bottles and baby blankets;
and a doll bed and doll carriage
large and strong enough to hold
a toddler, because children will
get into doll beds and carriages
themselves. (See photo on p. 42.)

*Pressing the keys on this old computer keyboard
makes a satisfying clicking noise!*

Keep dress-up materials relatively simple. Toddlers are often content to
wear one thing at a time and also like to use dress-up items such as purses
and bags (with handles or short straps) for filling, emptying, and transporting
materials. Provide a full-length mirror so children can see themselves in their
dress-up attire.

If the house area is near a window, this is also a natural place to include
nontoxic plants children can enjoy and help care for.

✦ *Storage*

Store materials where toddlers can easily see and reach them. For example,
store dishes on low shelves and utensils on low shelves in large open containers; store baby dolls in the doll bed or carriage; store doll accessories and
dress-up clothes in baskets or tubs. Labeling storage containers with a sample
object, picture, or photograph may help older toddlers to put toys away. If
you decide to hang pots and pans, for example, on large wooden pegs, attach
large shower-curtain rings to the holes in the pan handles. (See photo on
p. 188.) Toddlers can then easily slip these large rings onto the hooks. (See
p. 182 for a summary checklist of equipment and materials for the house area.)

The toddler toy area

In their toy area, toddlers explore, manipulate, and play with small toys and
collections. Here they engage in fitting things together and taking them apart,
filling and emptying, and pretending. Children spend time in this area as a
quiet place of play. They also take things from this area to use in other parts
of the play space.

In the toy area, toddlers spread out on the table and floor to play   with poker chips and a can with a slotted top; with a doll house, doll house furniture, and figures.

✦ *Location*

Locate the toddler toy area in a corner or along the perimeter of the central, open play space. Since play in this area tends to be on the quiet side, consider locating it near the toddler book area, and where there is sufficient comfortable floor space to spread out with toys and collections.

✦ *Equipment and materials*

Provide toys, puzzles, and other materials toddlers can fit together and take apart; graduated-size nesting toys and containers (including bowls, cups, and measuring spoons); magnetic blocks and various kinds of large interlocking blocks; a wooden pounding bench; simple off/on, open/close items; boxes with hinged lids and easy-to-work latches or locks; things toddlers can fill and empty; sets of large cubes, beads, and pegs; and figures and vehicles for pretending. Keep in mind that while it is very easy to stock this area with things made from plastic, this is also the place to include collections of a wide variety of household and natural objects of different textures and weights.

✦ *Storage*

To help toddlers find and choose what they need, store toys and other playthings on low shelves in open, easy-to-access baskets and containers. Labeling these baskets and containers with a sample object, picture, or photograph may help older toddlers put toys away on days when they have emptied all the containers. (See p. 183 for a summary checklist of equipment and materials for the toy area.)

Outdoor Play Yards for Infants and Toddlers

The outdoor play area is an important extension of the indoor exploration and play environment. Outside, infants can hear, smell, feel, or see trees, clouds, wind, warm and cool temperatures, and changes in light. Toddlers can run, throw, kick, climb, swing, or dig; they find plants, animals, and insects to examine. (See "Learning About Living Things" on p. 161.) Rich in sights, textures, sounds, smells, and opportunities for movement, an outdoor play yard greatly expands children's store of sensory-motor experiences.

✦ *Location*

To make movement from indoor to outdoor play easy and hassle-free, locate the play yard as close to the indoor play space as possible. Infants and toddlers generally spend more time outdoors when the indoor play space opens directly onto the play yard. If the yard is not directly accessible, you will need to think about how children can safely move (or be moved) there from indoors. Infants can be transported in strollers or wagons, and toddlers will

Indoor exploration and play continues in the outdoor play yard. Infants and toddlers generally spend more time outdoors when the indoor play space opens directly onto the play yard.

be able to walk to the yard with caregivers if it is only a short distance away. If the distance is really too far for toddlers to walk, transport small groups of them in wagons or strollers. If one outdoor play yard serves both infants and toddlers, separate the infants' space from that of the older children by a low barrier of canvas- or vinyl-covered cushions, a low wall or fence, or low shrubs.

Remember that the immediate neighborhood can also be a part of the children's outdoor experience. Pushing infants in a stroller, pulling infants and toddlers in a wagon, or walking with toddlers gives them the opportunity to go places they cannot yet go on their own and to see, hear, or smell a variety of sights, sounds, and aromas. Because of the children's need to move and act on and touch things, however, it is important that stroller and wagon rides supplement rather than take the place of children's on-the-ground exploration and play in a safe outdoor play yard. During this on-the-ground exploration, it is important to ensure that any sticks, leaves, and stones that children pick up to mouth are nontoxic and too large to swallow.

This caregiver shares her respect for a "minibeast" with several fascinated toddlers.

✦ *Equipment and materials for infants*

The playthings that support infants' indoor activity will also work outdoors. They will play outdoors with balls, rattles, and containers, for example, as long as someone brings a basket or tub of these materials outside for them to play with. There are some other things, however, that work particularly well in holding infants' interest outdoors, and they are these:

- *Movement opportunities.* Something as simple as a change in terrain, a gentle grassy hill built into the play area, will provide mobile infants with a good deal of crawling pleasure. For other up-and-down crawling opportunities, consider adding low, flat tree-stump rounds; a smooth log or landscape timber children can straddle; low, flat rocks; a few wooden steps; an inflated inner tube; a low wooden platform; and a canvas- or vinyl-covered mattress. A large carton, a tunnel, or a tent can provide a cozy crawl-through space. Mobile infants who are pulling themselves up to stand can do so beside a sturdy bench or wagon, the seat or bed of which also makes a good place for banging and pushing small wheeled toys while standing and balancing. Infants *who sit well by themselves* may enjoy being pushed gently back and forth in a sturdy, safely suspended outdoor infant swing-seat. (If the caregiver pushes from the front of the swing, the caregiver and child can see and converse with each other.) Infants also enjoy the swings that are designed to accommodate two infants face to face.

- *Things that move in the wind.* Young infants lying and sitting on blankets or mats enjoy watching and listening to the fluttering and flapping of banners, streamers, hanging foil pie tins, or wind chimes. These can be tied to branches, poles, or fences.

- *Crawling surfaces.* The outdoor play area can afford a variety of crawling surfaces, such as grass, aromatic-herb ground covers (such as mint), sand, leaves, wooden decking, and pathways made of smooth flagstone, packed clay, concrete, or wood. Direct contact with each of these surfaces will tell babies that each surface has a distinct look, smell, and feel (some will feel more comfortable than others).

- *Water-play materials.* Supplying a sitting infant with a small container of water and some objects that float provides opportunities for splashing and dabbling where nobody minds if the "floor" gets wet.

- *Garden plants.* Gardens of any type provide infants with a wealth of sights, textures, and smells. Raised garden beds provide young infants with colors and textures to view, and they give older infants who want to reach the flowers an added incentive for pulling themselves up to stand. Plantings can include flowers (nontoxic), vegetables, herbs, grains, and grasses.

Learning About Living Things

"Long before they reach their third year many children will already have learned to dislike and fear crawling and flying insects. Their immediate response to an insect seen in the garden may be to stamp on it. By expressing our own interest in and respect for 'minibeasts' we can play a significant role in re-education, and children will soon pick up our very different attitude. Bees, wasps, ants, beetles, spiders, earwigs, ladybirds, woodlice, centipedes, snails, caterpillars, worms and butterflies all offer scope for conversation, and some for close examination. . . . Under close supervision, . . . children quickly learn to distinguish between insects which must on no account be touched, such as wasps, and those that can safely be picked up (gently) and inspected at close quarters.

"Children old enough to appreciate the need for quiet and stillness will enjoy observing birds if the garden is provided with a feeding tray and bird-bath out of reach of local cats. The children can help to put out different types of food to attract a range of birds. . . .

"Pets such as rabbits and guinea-pigs can be an asset in a nursery, provided the children are involved in their care and feeding and one or more staff members is prepared to take clear responsibility for their wellbeing and especially for care [on] weekends and holidays. This needs to be someone who really loves animals and does not have to be persuaded to do the job as a tiresome obligation. If there is no such person on the nursery [center] staff, it is better to do without pets altogether. An adequate hutch and run are needed, so space is another consideration."

—Elinor Goldschmied and Sonia Jackson
(1994, pp. 166–167)

There are lots of things for a nonmobile baby to watch and listen to outdoors—including another baby sitting in the grass clutching a ball!

Close to her caregiver, this mobile infant explores the texture of sand and the heft of the pan while toddlers play around her.

✦ *Equipment and materials for toddlers*

As walkers and climbers, toddlers are eager to explore a wide range of outdoor equipment and materials, including natural features and things to climb, balance on, swing on, throw and kick, dig, push and pull, or ride.

- *Natural features.* The toddler outdoor play area is more than a fenced-off patch of grass, although this is what you may start with. Shade trees, grasses, low shrubs, and plants (all nontoxic), vegetable gardens, a hill, a very shallow water course, stepping stones, and sand invite toddlers to spend time exploring nature, picking flowers, and enjoying the rigors of outdoor play. The more the area is like a back yard and the more varied its natural features, the more toddlers and caregivers will want to be outdoors.

- *Things to climb.* Include a climbing structure that allows toddlers to safely climb sturdy steps, ladders, or ramps. This climber may include a low-sided, toddler-height slide, or the slide may be free-standing or set into a hillside. To cushion falls, position the climber and slide on a surface such as sand or rubber matting.

- *Things to get inside of.* Toddlers enjoy playing in cozy places (corrugated packing boxes, tunnels, tents) and underneath the low-hanging branches of trees or shrubs. Some climbers also include little "rooms" to crawl into.

- *Things to balance on.* Along with liking the challenge of steps and ramps, toddlers like to try balancing on low tree-stump rounds, flat rocks or stepping stones, planks, flat boards (for example, 1 x 12's), and low balance beams. They also like to straddle logs.

- *Swings.* Provide toddlers with low soft-seat swings to use sitting or lying on their tummies. Underneath these should be a soft surface, such as sand or rubber matting. A very low, deep, cloth hammock provides children with a type of swing they can either sit or lie on—don't forget the soft surface underneath, however, as hammocks may tip their users.

This play yard includes a variety of surfaces, levels, and materials for toddlers to explore.

A child-sized picnic table provides a handy surface for making sand cakes.

- *Sand and water.* Provide toddlers with a sandbox large enough for several children (and perhaps an adult) to sit in comfortably, and include a collection of sand toys. If possible, locate the sandbox close to an outdoor water faucet so children can add water to their sandbox play.

- *Balls.* Provide toddlers with large beach balls, 10" and 12" playground balls, small rubber balls they can hold in one hand, and tennis balls for kicking, throwing, rolling, and carrying. Some toddlers will enjoy rolling balls down the hill, slide, or ramp and through tunnels, and dropping them off the climber.

A play yard like this one surrounds children with the sights, sounds, textures, and smells of nature.

- *Riding and rocking toys.* Provide sturdy rocking toys and riding toys (without steering mechanisms for younger toddlers, with steering mechanisms for older toddlers). Some older toddlers may also enjoy small (10"-wheel) tricycles. Though toddlers will use riding toys on grass, they can generally ride better on decks, paths, walkways, or sidewalks. They also enjoy ringing and tooting vehicle bells and horns.

- *Push- and pull-toys.* Toddlers take pleasure in pulling wagons; filling them with sticks, sand, or leaves; and even turning them over and spinning their wheels. They also enjoy maneuvering small, lightweight wheelbarrows, garden carts, shopping carts, or baby carriages. If it snows, be sure to have small plastic toboggans for pulling, pushing, and sliding.

- *Loose materials.* Some indoor materials are particularly fun and easy to use outdoors, for example, paints and paper, colored chalk, bubble-blowing materials, beanbags, and blankets for tents.

✦ *Storage*

Whenever possible, store all loose outdoor playthings at the play yard, in a shed or watertight storage box. Otherwise, store these materials, along with riding toys, wagons, carts, strollers, sleds, and buggies, as close to the yard as possible. Your storage system should allow caregivers to save steps and time and to focus more on children than on moving materials. Store any indoor materials that you usually want to use outdoors in baskets, bags, or buckets with handles; this makes it easy to quickly sling them over your shoulder or arm, and toddlers are able to help in carrying them outdoors. (See pp. 184–185 for a summary checklist of equipment and materials for the outdoor play yard.)

Creating an Infant-Toddler Active Learning Setting: Where Do You Start?

This chapter has described setting up an environment that offers order and flexibility, provides comfort for children and adults, and supports infants' and toddlers' sensory-motor approach to learning. If you are feeling overwhelmed as you think about setting up or redesigning your environment for infants and toddlers, remember it is a gradual, thoughtful team process. Here are some ideas to keep in mind as you work together with all the caregivers who share your space:

Enjoy your active learning environment. If you look forward to entering it each day, so will the children in your care.

Start simply

Look at the space and resources you have available and the areas you have already established. Decide what is working, and identify just one or two things you might want to, and can afford to, change or modify first-off. Try out your new ideas. Watch to see how they affect the children before you attempt further changes.

Gradually add new items or new arrangements to your setting

Without taking away any of children's old favorites, start by adding a few new materials or perhaps just reorganizing some of the ones you already have. Once you have put out materials for toddlers to use, add to or subtract from them gradually instead of suddenly removing one set of materials and introducing a whole new set. This same approach applies to replacing old equipment with new. Toddlers are choice-makers and rely on a predictable environment. They trust that the materials, toys, and equipment they have played with today will be there for them to play with tomorrow and the next day and the next.

Remember, most toys travel

This chapter has offered many suggestions for storage. But infant-toddler care-givers know that regardless of where things are stored and what area they are associated with, many objects and materials will move about the play space according to the needs and desires of the children. The dolls may be stored in the house area, for example, but toddlers will play with them all over the room. Some art materials, however, you may want children to use only in the art area, where the floor is easy to clean. When materials are consistently accessible to children on a daily basis, children in a group setting quickly learn, for example, that messy materials like paint stay in designated areas where cleanup is easy, whereas materials like blocks, books, and baby dolls can travel with them wherever they choose to play. At cleanup times (described in Chapter 4) things that have "traveled" can return to their storage places.

Provide an appropriate area and materials for *all* the children who use the play space

If nonmobile and mobile infants as well as younger and older toddlers share the same general play space, think of ways to provide, for example, a consistent art area for the interested toddlers, as well as the different kinds of play spaces that both nonmobile and mobile infants need. This may mean storing art materials in see-through drawers that toddlers can operate but infants cannot, or dedicating one ample area to nonmobile infants, another to mobile infants, and another to young toddlers and then surrounding each of these areas with low barriers so children of all ages can still see one another but learn to play and explore within their own area.

Take room-arrangement cues from the children

If toddlers are frequently building block structures that topple over into the book area, think about relocating the books or the blocks, or come up with a way to create a low barrier between the two areas. If infants are tearing picture books, place these more delicate books in pockets on a shelf that is above infant reach but within reach of toddlers. Or, as one caregiver team did, solve this problem by placing non-board books in a toddler loft that is accessible by a short ladder. In another center, when several toddlers developed the habit of emptying their cubbies to play "house" in them, caregivers brought in corrugated cartons for the children to play in. The children liked these cartons and quickly appropriated them as "new houses," leaving their cubbies to serve, once again, as personal storage space.

Enjoy your active learning environment

Enjoy the setting you have created—its indoor and outdoor areas, the comfort and opportunities they provide, the kinds of exploration and discovery children can engage in there. If you look forward to entering your active learning environment each day, so will the children in your care!

Here's another way to add softness to the environment—a big teddy bear with lots of companions!

What You Need for the
Eating and Food Preparation Area

Eating utensils

- ❏ Baby bottles (labeled sets for each infant)
- ❏ Plastic plates with upward-curved edges
- ❏ Plastic shallow bowls
- ❏ Plastic cups with weighted bottoms and spouted tops
- ❏ Plastic drinking glasses wide enough for toddlers to hold with both hands
- ❏ Spoons with short handles

Protective clothing

- ❏ Bibs (labeled sets for each infant)
- ❏ Towels (labeled sets for each infant)
- ❏ Slip-on bibs for toddlers
- ❏ Napkins or hand towels for toddlers not using bibs
- ❏ Smocks or aprons, as needed for toddlers

Cleaning supplies

- ❏ Cleaning cloths
- ❏ Disinfectants
- ❏ Detergents
- ❏ Cleaning solutions
- ❏ Broom, dustpan, mop, vacuum (depending on floor surface)
- ❏ Buckets for warm, soapy water
- ❏ Child-sized brooms, brushes, dustpans
- ❏ Wastebasket

Appliances/furnishings

- ❏ Sink with hot running water
- ❏ Refrigerator
- ❏ Dishwasher

- ❏ Microwave oven
- ❏ Bottle warmer or Crock-Pot
- ❏ Cupboards or shelves above children's reach
- ❏ At least one cupboard/closet with a childproof latch
- ❏ Baskets or hooks for individualized bibs, smocks, aprons

Furniture

For bottle-feeding infants

- ❏ Comfortable chair, couch, or pillows for adult holding child

For infants sitting and trying out solid food

- ❏ Pillows or an infant seat to prop the sitting child

For infants able to sit alone

- ❏ Breakfast-in-bed tray-tables to seat one child, or very low tables (12" high)
- ❏ Infant-sized chairs or stools (seats 5½"–6" high)

For toddlers

- ❏ Toddler-sized tables (14"–16" in height)
- ❏ Toddler-sized chairs or stools (seats 6½"–8" high)

What You Need for the Sleeping and Napping Area

Furnishings
- ❑ Crib, cradle, or basket (one for each infant, labeled with child's name)
- ❑ Crib or cot (for each toddler)
- ❑ Mattress, snugly fitting (one for each crib)
- ❑ Closed hamper, sealable bags for soiled bedding

Bedding
- ❑ Protective mattress pad (one for each bed)
- ❑ Fitted sheet (one for each bed)
- ❑ Blanket or quilt (one for each bed)
- ❑ Extra bedding for each child

Comfort items
- ❑ Items chosen by, reserved for each child (stuffed toy, "blankie," pacifier)

Appliances (optional if parents or a commercial laundry clean soiled bedding)
- ❑ Washer
- ❑ Dryer (or accessible clothesline in sunny, dry climate)

What You Need for the
Diapering, Dressing, and Bathroom Area

Furnishings

❑ Sink

❑ Step stool for sink (if not toddler height)

❑ Mirror over sink

❑ Changing table or counter (about 36" high, low raised sides, cleanable soft surface)

❑ Set of steps for climbing to changing table (or climb-up changing table)

❑ Closed, foot-operated containers for soiled disposable diapers, wipes, changing-table papers

❑ Hampers, sealable bags (for soiled cloth diapers, clothing)

❑ Container of small, washable toys

❑ Child-accessible toilet paper dispensers

❑ Toddler-sized toilets or potty chairs

❑ Step stools for full-sized toilets, if needed

❑ Cupboards or shelves for adults' easy access to changing supplies

Clothing

❑ Diapers and diaper covers, fasteners for each child, as needed

❑ Underpants for each child, as needed

❑ Change of clothes for each child

Personal care items

❑ Soap suitable for children's skin

❑ Disposable wipes or a supply of washcloths for each child

❑ Hairbrush for each child, as needed

❑ Diaper creams (as needed, with written parental instructions)

❑ Hand-washing soap in pump dispenser

❑ Child hand towels, paper or cloth

❑ Toilet paper

Cleaning supplies

❑ Disinfectants

❑ Spray soaps and cleaners

❑ Cleaning cloths

❑ Roll of paper (for covering changing surface)

❑ Disposable gloves

Materials and Equipment
That Support Children's Movement

When children are . . .

Moving their limbs, turning themselves over, and rolling, they need

- ❑ Safe, soft spaces on the floor and ground for lying, turning over, rolling
- ❑ Interesting, graspable toys, materials, and people to reach for, hold on to, let go of

Sitting, they need

- ❑ Safe, comfortable places to sit, on a variety of physical levels, with a variety of vistas, both indoors and outdoors
- ❑ Very low tables to use while sitting on the floor
- ❑ Materials to explore, grasp, bang, and drop while sitting

Scooting and crawling, they need

- ❑ Safe open spaces and pathways for scooting and crawling on the floor and ground
- ❑ Ramps and steps for crawling to different levels
- ❑ Tunnels to crawl through
- ❑ Boxes or cartons, and other cozy spaces to crawl into
- ❑ A variety of appealing materials and vistas to crawl toward
- ❑ Balls to crawl after

Cruising, they need

- ❑ Sturdy, well-anchored equipment (to hold on to and lean against as they pull themselves up to stand (chairs, benches, tables, handrails, handholds)
- ❑ Sturdy push toys with long handles (to push, lean against, and help with balance)

Walking, riding, and rocking, they need

- ❑ Clear pathways with safe surfaces for walking both indoors and outdoors
- ❑ Ramps and steps with railings to practice walking up and down
- ❑ Pull-toys big enough to ride in (wagons, sleds)
- ❑ Rocking chairs, rocking boats, rocking horses, and low deep hammocks
- ❑ A variety of riding toys to sit on and propel by scooting with their feet

Climbing, jumping, and running, they need

- ❑ Safe spaces both indoors and out for climbing, jumping, running
- ❑ A variety of safe climbers, slides, steps, and ladders
- ❑ A variety of levels and padded landing areas for safe jumping
- ❑ Interesting things to run toward, around, up and down (trees, boulders, benches, bales of straw, ramps, hills)

Materials That Appeal to Children's Senses

Aromatic materials and experiences

- ❑ Large wooden balls and boxes
- ❑ Wool, felt, and leather balls
- ❑ Sturdy rubber balls and teething rings
- ❑ Tennis balls
- ❑ Sturdily constructed small cloth bags filled with common household spices
- ❑ Wicker baskets and woven mats
- ❑ Scented marking pens
- ❑ Bread dough, play dough, and clay
- ❑ Shaving cream
- ❑ Newspaper
- ❑ Flowering plants (nontoxic)
- ❑ Aroma therapy materials (heated cinnamon, apple, cedar, or wintergreen oils, above children's reach)
- ❑ Aromatic-herb ground cover in areas where children play
- ❑ Outdoor play where children can smell grass, dirt, leaves, bark, nuts, flowers, rain
- ❑ Smells of food being prepared and cooked
- ❑ A variety of foods to eat and smell

Sound-producing materials and experiences

- ❑ Toy rattles, dried gourds
- ❑ Firmly sealed film cans or tins containing beans, rice, pea gravel, water
- ❑ Rain sticks
- ❑ Castanets
- ❑ Bells
- ❑ Xylophones, metalophones
- ❑ Pan lids
- ❑ Metal juice-can lids, metal and wooden spoons and bowls
- ❑ Crinkly paper
- ❑ Wind chimes, ticking clocks, chiming clocks, music boxes
- ❑ Recordings
- ❑ Singing
- ❑ Outdoor play and sounds
- ❑ Banners, streamers that flap in the breeze
- ❑ Sound of rain on the roof and windows
- ❑ Jumping and rolling in piles of dry leaves

Materials to touch, taste, and look at

Objects from nature

- ❑ Pine cones (closed "petals")
- ❑ Small rocks
- ❑ Sturdy shells
- ❑ Dried gourds
- ❑ Large nuts (in shells)
- ❑ Big feathers
- ❑ Pumice stone
- ❑ Fresh avocado pits
- ❑ Natural sponge
- ❑ Pieces of loofah
- ❑ Lemons, apples

Objects made from natural materials

- ❑ Marble "eggs"
- ❑ Small baskets
- ❑ Bottle corks
- ❑ Small rafia mats
- ❑ Natural-bristle brushes with wooden handles (for nails, teeth, shaving, shoes, house painting, cosmetics)
- ❑ Prisms
- ❑ Stained-glass windows

➡

Materials That Appeal to Children's Senses, *continued*

Wooden objects

- ❑ Small boxes
- ❑ Small drum on wooden frame
- ❑ Rattles
- ❑ Castanets
- ❑ Clothespins (peg, not pinching type)
- ❑ Large, strung, colored beads
- ❑ Inch cubes
- ❑ Spools
- ❑ Spoons, spatulas
- ❑ Egg cups
- ❑ Small bowls

Metal objects

- ❑ Measuring spoons
- ❑ Spoons
- ❑ Small whisks
- ❑ Keys on a chain or ring
- ❑ Small tins
- ❑ Small pot-pie tins
- ❑ Lemon squeezer
- ❑ Small funnels
- ❑ Brass curtain rings
- ❑ Garlic press
- ❑ Whistle
- ❑ Slip-on bangle bracelets
- ❑ Bottle brush
- ❑ Small metal mirrors
- ❑ Key rings linked together
- ❑ Large bells, attached to wrap-around band (in musical instrument catalogs)
- ❑ Tea strainers
- ❑ Lengths of chain
- ❑ Bicycle bell
- ❑ Tea infuser
- ❑ Aluminum foil

Objects of leather, cloth, rubber, fur

- ❑ Leather purse
- ❑ Small leather bag or key case with zipper
- ❑ Leather eyeglass case
- ❑ High-bouncer balls
- ❑ Lengths of rubber tubing
- ❑ Bath/drain plugs with chains
- ❑ Velvet powder puffs
- ❑ Fur ball
- ❑ Pieces of felt in assorted colors, sizes, shapes
- ❑ Small rag dolls
- ❑ Small teddy bears
- ❑ Balls of yarn
- ❑ Potholders
- ❑ Bandanas
- ❑ Silk scarves
- ❑ Short lengths of blanket satin, lace
- ❑ Tennis balls
- ❑ Golf balls

Paper/cardboard items

- ❑ Small notebooks or note pads
- ❑ Wax paper
- ❑ Small boxes
- ❑ Paper towel/cardboard tubes
- ❑ Board books
- ❑ Postcards
- ❑ Foil paper

What You Need for Infants' Indoor Play

Pleasant reminders of home
❑ Comfort items (favorite "teddy," "blankie," pacifier)
❑ Family photographs (laminated)

Materials for sensory exploration and play
❑ Mirrors (unbreakable)
❑ Materials with aroma (wool, rubber, leather, cedar wood)
❑ Rattles, bells, sealed tins with noisy contents
❑ Other sound-producing materials (water, music recordings, chimes)
❑ Objects from nature (shells, rocks, cones, a lemon, a gourd)
❑ Objects made of natural materials (natural-bristle brushes, bottle corks, marble eggs)
❑ Wooden objects (spoons, inch cubes, clothespins, spools, large beads)
❑ Metal objects (keys on a chain, spoons, whisks, bangle bracelets, juice-can lids)
❑ Textile, leather items (scarves, powder puffs, leather eyeglass case)
❑ Soft dolls and stuffed animals
❑ Paper products (newspaper, boxes, towel tubes, food cartons)
❑ Open containers (juice cans, butter tubs, baskets)
❑ Lightweight blocks

Materials infants can set in motion
❑ Balls (cloth, fur, wool, leather, rubber, tennis balls, Wiffle balls)
❑ Hinged doors and boxes
❑ Small wheeled vehicles and animals

Movement equipment
❑ Ramps
❑ Steps
❑ Climbing platform
❑ Mattress
❑ Tunnels
❑ Boxes
❑ Full-sized chair, couch for pulling up to stand
❑ Handrails, handholds for pulling up
❑ Sturdy push toys to lean against while cruising

First picture books
❑ Cloth books
❑ Board books, for example,
   Blue Buggy by Janet and Allan Ahlberg
   Big Red Barn by Margaret Wise Brown
   Find the Duck by Stephen Cartwright
   Tomie's Little Mother Goose by Tomie dePaola
   Pat the Bunny by Dorothy Kunhardt
   Dressing by Helen Oxenbury

Storage
❑ Portable baskets, buckets, boxes, tins, cloth or mesh bags
❑ Low sturdy shelves (with clear plastic storage containers)
❑ Forward-facing bookrack, clear hanging book pockets

What You Need for the Toddlers' Movement Area

Things to climb on and jump off
- ❏ Steps
- ❏ Ramps
- ❏ Toddler loft
- ❏ Dowel climber
- ❏ Risers
- ❏ Sturdy wooden boxes
- ❏ Large hollow wooden blocks and planks
- ❏ Large vinyl-covered foam cubes and wedges
- ❏ Pillows and soft mats to jump onto

Things to get inside of
- ❏ Boxes, cartons
- ❏ Tunnels
- ❏ Small hollow risers that can be turned over to be boxes
- ❏ Space under toddler loft

Push- and pull-toys
- ❏ Wagons
- ❏ Pull-toys on strings
- ❏ Push-toys with long handles

Riding/Rocking toys
- ❏ Rocking toys (horse, boat)
- ❏ Riding toys (to sit on, scoot with feet, no steering mechanism) for younger toddlers
- ❏ Riding toys (to sit on, scoot with feet, simple steering) for older toddlers

Balls
- ❏ Cloth and foam balls
- ❏ Tennis balls
- ❏ Rubber balls
- ❏ Wiffle balls

Simple musical instruments/recordings
- ❏ Rattles, shakers
- ❏ Bells
- ❏ Xylophone and mallet
- ❏ Metalophone and mallet
- ❏ Sturdy bongo drum or floor drum
- ❏ Tambourine
- ❏ Small, sturdy rain stick
- ❏ Music recordings (see p. 363 for recordings of instrumental music with a distinct beat)
- ❏ CD or cassette player

What You Need for the
Toddlers' Sand and Water Area

Equipment
- ❑ Sand/water table(s), toddler height
- ❑ Baby bathtub or child's wading pool (inexpensive alternatives to sand and water table)
- ❑ Baskets, tubs for storage of sand/water playthings
- ❑ Washed playground sand
- ❑ Disinfectant and bucket for cleaning sand
- ❑ Low box/platform for shorter children
- ❑ Buckets for filling/draining water table

Things to fill and empty with
- ❑ Small plastic buckets, cups, ice cube trays
- ❑ Empty food containers (butter tubs, small milk cartons)
- ❑ Wide-mouth cloth bags
- ❑ Small plastic plant pots (one glued inside another)

- ❑ Basters and plastic squeeze bottles
- ❑ Metal shovels, scoops, spoons
- ❑ Funnels, sieves

Things to float
- ❑ Boats
- ❑ Corks
- ❑ Ping-Pong balls
- ❑ Sponges
- ❑ Loofah

Things to hide and find
- ❑ Shells
- ❑ Stones
- ❑ Feathers

Things to pretend with
- ❑ Rubber or plastic animal figures
- ❑ Rubber or plastic people figures

What You Need for the Toddlers' Book Area

Comfortable furnishings (some combination of the following)
- ❑ Mattress, quilt, pillows
- ❑ Low easy chairs
- ❑ Low couch
- ❑ Large carton (for book nook)
- ❑ Stuffed toys, toddler-sized puppets, representing story characters

Book storage
- ❑ Forward-facing bookrack
- ❑ Clear hanging book pockets
- ❑ Low shelf with tub(s) or basket(s)

Books
- ❑ Board books (see p. 363) with clear drawings or photos and simple text if any, such as,

    See the Rabbit by Janet and Allan Ahlberg

    Goodnight Moon by Margaret Wise Brown

    Bus by Chris L. Demarest

    All Fall Down by Helen Oxenbury

    I Can by Helen Oxenbury

    Shake Shake Shake by Andrea and Brian Pickney

- ❑ Picture books, for example

    My First Mother Goose illustrated by Rosemary Wells

    Play with Me by Marie Hall Ets

    Ask Mr. Bear by Marjorie Flack

    Flower Garden by Eve Bunting

- ❑ Wordless books, for example,

    The Snowman by Raymond Briggs

    Rosie's Walk by Pat Hutchins

Magazines, pictures, photos
- ❑ Small photo albums
- ❑ Postcard collection
- ❑ *Babybug*, a board book magazine for infants and toddlers (www.babybugmag.com)
- ❑ Magazines with pictures
- ❑ Catalogs

Fish (optional)
- ❑ Aquarium or fish tank
- ❑ Pebbles, stones for the bottom
- ❑ Goldfish or other low-maintenance fish
- ❑ Fish food

What You Need for the Toddlers' Art Area

Painting and drawing materials

- ❑ Finger paints (red, yellow, blue), commercial or homemade
- ❑ Tempera paints, liquid or powder (red, yellow, blue)
- ❑ Small, stable containers for paint (muffin tins; cut-down yogurt cups or tuna cans set in a cake tin; baby food jars set in a sponge; heavy, lidded plastic containers; paper or plastic plates)
- ❑ Short-handled brushes
- ❑ Small house-painting brushes (several widths)
- ❑ Brush alternatives (scrub brushes, dishwashing mops, feathers, sticks, cotton balls, sponges)
- ❑ Crayons
- ❑ Nontoxic water-based markers (like bingo markers)
- ❑ Chalk
- ❑ Small squeeze-bottles of dribble salt (equal parts flour, salt, water, with a few drops of paint)

Paper

- ❑ Newspaper, newsprint
- ❑ Roll of white butcher paper
- ❑ Kraft or construction paper
- ❑ Tissue paper
- ❑ Cellophane

Dough and clay materials

- ❑ Play dough
- ❑ Clay
- ❑ Poking and sticking materials (wooden pegs, popsicle sticks, shells, stones, jar lids, bottle caps, corks, unshelled walnuts, golf balls, metal keys)
- ❑ Airtight containers for dough and clay

Furnishings

- ❑ Sink or water supply
- ❑ Buckets, clear boxes, or racks to store brushes
- ❑ Holder for colored markers
- ❑ Labeled containers for crayons, chalk, similar items
- ❑ Bucket for transporting paintbrushes to sink
- ❑ Low shelves with wheels, low supply-cart
- ❑ Paper-storage rack
- ❑ Upright or horizontal holder for paper roll
- ❑ Table(s)
- ❑ Easel, freestanding or wall-mounted
- ❑ Plastic or vinyl smocks, wooden pegs to hang them on

What You Need for the Toddlers' Block Area

Blocks

❑ Large plastic, foam, or cardboard "brick" blocks (at least 20)

❑ Wooden unit blocks (including half units, basic units, double units, see p. 363)

Vehicles, people, animals

❑ Sturdy wooden or plastic dump trucks

❑ Sturdy wooden or plastic bulldozers

❑ Small cars (easy for child to hold in one hand, see p. 363)

❑ Small vehicles that can hold peg people or animals

❑ Wooden, rubber, or plastic people and animal figures

Furnishings

❑ Low storage shelves

❑ Labeled baskets, bins, or clear plastic containers

What You Need for the Toddlers' House Area

Dolls and accessories
- ❑ Baby dolls (soft-bodied, reflecting the racial and ethnic identities of the children in the program)
- ❑ Simple doll clothes (with Velcro closings)
- ❑ Baby bottles
- ❑ Baby blankets
- ❑ Doll bed (large and strong enough to hold a toddler)
- ❑ Doll carriage (large and strong enough to hold a toddler)

Kitchen furnishings
- ❑ Toddler-sized stove
- ❑ Toddler-sized sink
- ❑ Toddler-sized refrigerator
- ❑ Toddler-sized table and chairs
- ❑ Telephones (toy and/or real)

Dishes and utensils (real, not toy)
- ❑ Small pots and pans
- ❑ Utensils: spatula, whisk, tea strainer, wooden spoons, metal measuring cups and spoons, bottle brush
- ❑ Plastic cups, bowls, plates
- ❑ Spoons
- ❑ Empty food containers (milk cartons, cereal boxes)
- ❑ Corks and shells for food

Dress-up clothes and accessories
- ❑ Hats
- ❑ Shoes
- ❑ Vests, jackets, short dresses
- ❑ Scarves, bandanas
- ❑ Purses (with handles or short straps), change purses
- ❑ Briefcases
- ❑ Keys on chains
- ❑ Lunch boxes
- ❑ Bangle bracelets without clasps
- ❑ Full-length mirror (unbreakable)

Nontoxic plants
- ❑ Hardy house plants (philodendron, Christmas cactus, grape ivy)
- ❑ Traditional garden plants (nasturtiums, lettuce, herbs, grass)

Storage
- ❑ Low shelves
- ❑ Large open containers, baskets, tubs
- ❑ Wooden pegs and shower-curtain rings (to hang pots and pans)

What You Need for the Toddlers' Toy Area

Things to fit together and take apart

- ❑ Sturdy puzzles (3 to 5 pieces; any knobs should be firmly attached)
- ❑ Shape-sorter and shapes
- ❑ Graduated-size nesting objects: cans, tins, boxes, cups, spoons, people or animal shapes
- ❑ Large interlocking blocks (LEGO, Duplos, bristle, magnetic)
- ❑ Wooden pounding-bench, pegs, and mallet
- ❑ Large plastic pop-together, pull-apart beads

Off/on, open/close materials

- ❑ Flashlights (easy-to-operate switches or buttons, child-safe battery compartments)
- ❑ Zippered bags, pouches, cosmetic cases
- ❑ Wooden and metal boxes with hinged lids, easy-to-work latches or locks

Things for filling and emptying

- ❑ Small colored wooden blocks
- ❑ Wooden counting cubes
- ❑ Large wooden beads, short lengths of lacing or plastic-coated wire
- ❑ Lengths of metal chain
- ❑ Large pegs and pegboards
- ❑ Collections of strong shells, smooth stones; unshelled nuts; pine cones; wooden peg-style clothespins, spools, balls/blocks; fabric pieces
- ❑ Containers to fill and empty (oatmeal boxes, tins, baskets)

Things for pretend play

- ❑ Small people figures
- ❑ Small animal figures
- ❑ Small, sturdy vehicles: cars, trucks, buses, campers
- ❑ Simple train
- ❑ Small, soft puppets, toddler-sized

Furnishings

- ❑ Low storage shelf
- ❑ Open baskets and containers (labeled) for small items

What You Need in the Outdoor Play Yard for Infants and Toddlers

Natural features
- ❑ Shade trees
- ❑ Shrubs, grasses, flowers
- ❑ Raised vegetable/herb garden
- ❑ Hill
- ❑ Shallow water course
- ❑ Stepping stones
- ❑ Soft surfaces (sand or rubber matting) under climbers and swings

Movement materials (infants)
- ❑ Gentle slope
- ❑ Tree stump rounds
- ❑ Logs
- ❑ Railroad ties or landscape timbers
- ❑ Flat rocks
- ❑ Steps
- ❑ Large, inflated inner tube
- ❑ Low platform
- ❑ Canvas- or vinyl-covered mattress
- ❑ Bench or wagon (to pull up to stand)
- ❑ Boxes, cartons
- ❑ Tunnels
- ❑ Tents
- ❑ Infant swing-seat

Things that move in the wind
- ❑ Banners, streamers
- ❑ Foil pie tins
- ❑ Wind chimes

Crawling surfaces
- ❑ Grass
- ❑ Aromatic-herb ground cover
- ❑ Sand
- ❑ Leaves
- ❑ Decking
- ❑ Pathways of flagstone, clay, concrete, wood

Water play materials (mobile infants)
- ❑ Small pails, pans for water
- ❑ Floating objects

Things to climb (toddlers)
- ❑ Toddler climbing structure (over soft surface)
- ❑ Slide

Things to get inside of (toddlers)
- ❑ Sturdy corrugated boxes, cartons
- ❑ Tunnels
- ❑ Low-hanging trees or shrubs

Things to balance on (toddlers)
- ❑ Tree stump rounds
- ❑ Flat rocks
- ❑ Planks, flat boards (1" x 12")
- ❑ Balance beam on or very close to the ground

Swings (toddlers)
- ❑ Soft-seated swings (over soft surface)
- ❑ Very low cloth hammocks (over soft surface)

Materials for sand play and water play (toddlers)
- ❑ Large sandbox
- ❑ Buckets and other containers
- ❑ Shovels, scoops, funnels, sieves
- ❑ Plastic dump trucks
- ❑ Shells, sticks, stones
- ❑ Water source

Balls (toddlers)
- ❑ Beach balls
- ❑ Rubber playground balls, 10" and 12"
- ❑ Tennis balls
- ❑ Small rubber balls toddlers can hold in one hand

➡

What You Need in the Outdoor Play Yard for Infants and Toddlers, *continued*

Riding/rocking toys (toddlers)
- ❑ Rocking toys (rocking horse, rocking boat)
- ❑ Riding toys (to sit on, scoot with feet, no steering mechanism) for younger toddlers
- ❑ Riding toys (to sit on, scoot with feet, simple steering) for older toddlers
- ❑ Horns and bells for riding toys
- ❑ Small tricycles (10" wheels) for toddlers approaching age 3

Push- and pull-toys (toddlers)
- ❑ Wagons
- ❑ Lightweight wheelbarrows, garden carts, shopping carts, baby buggies
- ❑ Plastic toboggans

Loose materials (toddlers)
- ❑ Paints and paper
- ❑ Colored chalk
- ❑ Bubble-blowing materials
- ❑ Beanbags
- ❑ Blankets for tents

Storage
- ❑ Shed
- ❑ Watertight storage box
- ❑ Carts/baskets, bags, buckets with handles for transporting materials from indoors

Transport vehicles (infants)
- ❑ Wagons
- ❑ Strollers

Surfaces/play space boundaries (infants)
- ❑ Blankets or mats to lie on
- ❑ Low fence or wall of wood, stone, brick
- ❑ Low shrubs
- ❑ Large bolsters (canvas- or vinyl-covered)

References

Allison, Dorothy, and J. Allen Watson. 1994. "The Significance of Adult Storybook Reading Styles on the Development of Young Children's Emergent Reading." *Reading Research and Instruction* (34): 57–72.

Bergen, Doris, Kenneth Smith, and Stephanie O'Neill. 1988. "Designing Play Environments for Infants and Toddlers." In *Play as a Medium for Learning and Development: A Handbook of Theory and Practice,* ed. Doris Bergen, 187–207. Portsmouth, NH: Heinemann.

Evans, Judith, and Ellen Ilfeld. 1982. *Good Beginnings: Parenting in the Early Years.* Ypsilanti, MI: High/Scope Press.

Gerber, Magda. 1996. *Understanding Infants: What Makes It So Difficult!* National Association for the Education of Young Children Conference presentation, Dallas, TX, November.

Gerber, Magda, and Allison Johnson. 1998. *Your Self-Confident Baby: How to Encourage Your Child's Natural Abilities—From the Very Start.* New York: Wiley.

Goldschmied, Elinor, and Sonia Jackson. 1994. *People Under Three: Young Children in Day Care.* New York: Routledge.

Gonzalez-Mena, Janet. 1995. "Cultural Sensitivity in Routine Caregiving Tasks." In *Infant and Toddler Caregiving: A Guide to Culturally Sensitive Care,* ed. Peter Mangione, 12–19. Sacramento, CA: California Department of Education.

Greenman, Jim. 1988. *Caring Spaces, Learning Places: Children's Environments That Work.* Redmond, WA: Exchange Press.

Harms, Thelma. 1994. "Humanizing Infant Environments for Group Care." In *Children's Environments* 11(2): 155–67.

Hohmann, Charles. 1998. "Software for Toddlers—Too Much, Too Soon?" In *High/Scope Extensions* (May/June): 5.

Lally, J. Ronald, and Jay Stewart. 1990. *Infant and Toddler Caregiving: A Guide to Setting Up Environments.* Sacramento, CA: California Department of Education.

Miller, Karen. 1984. *Things to Do With Toddlers and Twos.* Chelsea, MA: Telshare.

Soundy, Cathleen S. 1997. "Nurturing Literacy With Infants and Toddlers in Group Settings." In *Childhood Education* 73(3): 149–53.

Theemes, Tracy. 1999. *Let's Go Outside! Designing the Early Childhood Playground.* Ypsilanti, MI: High/Scope Press.

Thorndike, Robert L. 1973. *Reading Comprehension, Education in Fifteen Countries: An Empirical Study.* New York: Wiley.

Torelli, Louis. 1992. "The Developmentally Designed Group Care Setting: A Supportive Environment for Infants, Toddlers, and Caregivers." In *Zero to Three Child Care Classics: 7 Articles on Infant/Toddler Development,* ed. Emily Fenichel, 37–40. Arlington, VA: Zero to Three/National Center for Clinical Infant Programs.

Torelli, Louis, and Charles Durrett. 1998. *Landscapes for Learning: Designing Group Care Environments for Infants, Toddlers, and Two-Year-Olds.* Berkeley, CA: Torelli/Durrett.

Wells, Gordon. 1986. *The Meaning Makers: Children Learning Language and Using Language to Learn.* Portsmouth, NH: Heinemann Educational Books.

Related Reading

Bredekamp, Sue. 1997. "Developmentally Appropriate Practice for Infants and Toddlers." Chapter 2 in *Developmentally Appropriate Practice in Early Childhood Programs,* rev. ed., eds. Sue Bredekamp and Carol Copple. Washington, DC: National Association for the Education of Young Children.

Bronson, Martha B. 1995. *The Right Stuff for Children Birth to 8: Selecting Play Materials to Support Development.* Washington, DC: National Association for the Education of Young Children.

Derman-Sparks, Louise. 1995. "Creating an Inclusive, Nonstereotypical Environment for Infants and Toddlers." In *Infant and Toddler Caregiving: A Guide to Culturally Sensitive Care,* ed. Peter L. Mangione, 64–68. Sacramento, CA: California Department of Education.

Dombro, Amy L., Laura J. Colker, and Diane Trister Dodge. 1997. "Creating a Welcoming Environment." Chapter 2 in *The Creative Curriculum for Infants and Toddlers.* Washington, DC: Teaching Strategies.

Gordon, Linda, Ellen Khokha, Lorraine Schrag, and Ellen Weeks. 1996. "Setting Up the Environment for Infants." In *Setting Up for Infant/Toddler Care: Guidelines for Centers and Family Child Care Homes,* rev. ed., eds. Annabelle Godwin and Lorraine Schrag, 55–65. Washington, DC: National Association for the Education of Young Children.

Greenman, Jim, and Alice Stonehouse. 1996. *Prime Times: A Handbook for Excellence in Infant and Toddler Care,* Chapters 6, 11, and 12. St. Paul, MN: Redleaf Press.

Harms, Thelma, Debby Cryer, and Richard M. Clifford. 1990. *Infant/Toddler Environment Rating Scale.* New York: Teachers College Press.

Hirsch, Elizabeth S., ed. 1984. *The Block Book,* rev. ed. Washington, DC: National Association for the Education of Young Children.

Honig, Alice Sterling. 1981. "Recent Infancy Research." In *Infants: Their Social Environments,* eds. Bernice Weissbourd and Judith Musick, 5–46. Washington, DC: National Association for the Education of Young Children.

Lally, J. Ronald, Abby Griffin, Emily Fenichel, Marilyn Segal, Eleanor Szanton, and Bernice Weissbourd. 1995. *Caring for Infants and Toddlers in Groups,* 64–76. Washington, DC: Zero to Three.

Malaguzzi, Loris. 1996. *The Little Ones of the Silent Movies: Make-Believe With Children and Fish at the Infant-Toddler Center.* Reggio Emilia: Reggio Children.

Moore, Gary T. 1998. "Child Care Facility Design: Image and Scale." In *Child Care Information Exchange* (March): 97–101.

Readdick, Christine A. 1993. "Solitary Pursuits: Supporting Children's Privacy Needs in Early Childhood Settings." *Young Children* 49(1): 60–64.

Wachs, Theodore D. 1995. "The Physical Environment and Its Role in Influencing the Development of Infants and Toddlers." In *Infant and Toddler Caregiving: A Guide to Cognitive Development and Learning,* ed. Peter L. Mangione, 34–54. Sacramento, CA: California Department of Education.

White, Burton L. 1975. *The First Three Years of Life.* Englewood Cliffs, NJ: Prentice-Hall.

A child-sized table accommodates these toddlers. (Note the child-friendly pan-hanging method—shower curtain rings through the pan handle holes!)

Related Videos

First Moves: Welcoming a Child to a New Caregiving Setting. 1988. Color videotape, 27 min. Sacramento, CA: California State Department of Education.

Space to Grow: Creating a Child Care Environment for Infants and Toddlers. 1988. Color videotape, 22 min. Sacramento, CA: California Department of Education.

Infants and toddlers need to climb. A well-arranged environment allows them to do so.

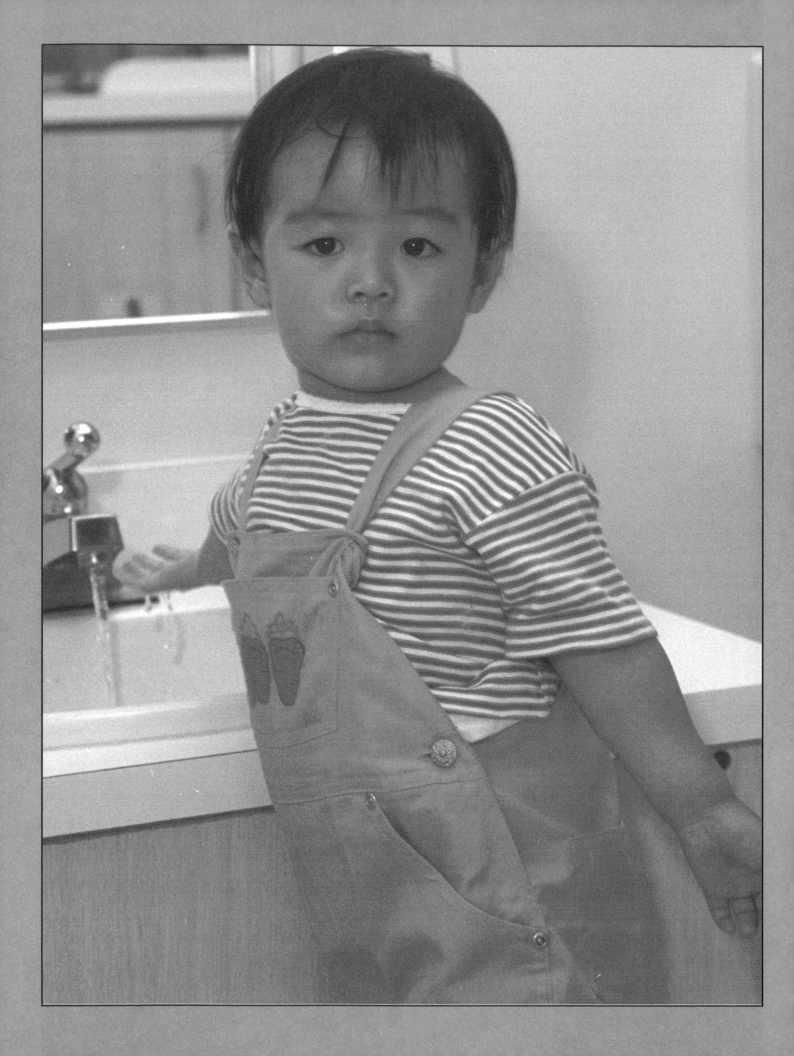

4
Establishing Schedules and Routines for Infants and Toddlers

A routine is more than knowing the time the baby will eat, nap, have a bath, and go to bed. It is also how *these things are done. . . . your child's* day to day *experiences are the raw materials of [his or] her growth.*

—Judith Evans and Ellen Ilfeld (1982b)

Providing a predictable daily schedule and unhurried caregiving routines in an infant-toddler care setting assures children of many opportunities to try out their actions and ideas. The following scenarios illustrate the dynamics in a center with a day organized for active learning:

Three older infants—Jacob, Jesse, and Eva—play on the floor at midmorning choice time. Shannon, their primary caregiver, sits on the floor with them. Jesse crawls up and down a slightly inclined ramp. Eva, sitting in a large carton tipped on its side, explores a collection of tins and oatmeal boxes. Jacob explores two big rubber balls, several tennis balls, and a Wiffle ball. He holds them, mouths them, drops them into a hole at the top of a large plastic cube, takes them out through a hole in the side of the cube, and crawls after them as they roll across the floor. At one point, he crawls to Shannon, puts his head in her lap, and rubs his eyes. "Jacob," she says while stroking his head, "you look sleepy. I'm going to pick you up." When she picks him up, Jacob nestles close, lays his head on her shoulder, and closes his eyes. "It looks like it's time for your nap," she says, gently rubbing his back. She carries Jacob to his crib, lays him down, checks to make sure he doesn't need a diaper change, and covers him with his favorite bunny blanket. "Have a nice sleep," she says as Jacob at first fights to keep his eyes open and then quickly falls asleep. Shannon returns to Jesse and Eva, who continue with their play.

∽

Six toddlers sit at a low table, eating lunch. Their caregivers, Rudy and Ann, sit with them at the table. As the children finish, they put their cups and plates into a dish tub, leave the table, and return to the riding toys they were playing with before lunchtime. Rudy stays at the table with the children who are still eating, while Ann sits on the floor near the children who are using riding toys. When all the children have finished eating, Rudy removes the dish tub and wipes the table. Ann then takes the children, individually or by twos, into the bathroom for the caregiving routines that precede nap time. After that, she returns them to play with the riding toys until naps. Until each child has been to the bathroom and it's time for stories and naps, Rudy takes Ann's place on the floor with the children who are using riding toys.

A consistent overall daily schedule gives children a sense of continuity and control.

These scenarios typify the daily occurrences in a High/Scope active learning infant-toddler program. In the first scenario, the three infants have selected materials of particular interest to play with during choice time. When Jacob shows signs of sleepiness, his caregiver responds to his cues by putting him into his crib for a nap. Eva and Jesse continue to play and, like Jacob, will nap when they are ready. The six toddlers in the second scenario are engaged in a sequence of activities—lunch, riding toys, bodily care routines, riding toys, stories, and naps. They move with assurance from one part of their day to the next. Using the riding toys serves as an enjoyable transition from lunch and bodily care to stories and naps. The children also experience certain predictable elements within each activity. For example, every day as they finish lunch, the toddlers put their dishes into the dish tub.

Caregivers learn and respond to each infant's or toddler's *personalized* daily schedule and at the same time develop an *overall* daily schedule that accommodates as closely as possible all children in the group. Coordinating multiple infants' and toddlers' schedules can be a challenge. This is one reason that infant-toddler care groups are small and there is one caregiver for every two to four children. The complexity of dealing with multiple schedules also makes it critically important for the caregiver teams to spend time each day discussing their observations of children and planning around them. (See Chapter 5 for more about the caregiver team's planning process.)

Though it is challenging to organize a program around a number of children, the benefits to those in your care are great. When daily schedules and caregiving routines are predictable and well-coordinated rather than frequently in flux, infants and toddlers are more likely to feel safe and secure. Knowing what will happen next when they wake up from a nap, for example, helps children become attuned to the rhythm of their own body and the

Coordinating children's personal schedules can be a challenge. That's why infant-toddler care groups are small, with one caregiver for every two to four children.

rhythm of the day. When the day moves along on a known course, children can signal their individual needs to eat, sleep, wash, change into dry clothes, or use the toilet, and after participating in these care routines, they can rejoin the ongoing flow of events. At the beginning of the day, if children know what they will be doing after their parents leave, separating from parents and joining caregivers and peers is easier for them. As they experience the rituals and repetitions of a consistent daily schedule, infants and toddlers gain a sense of continuity and control.

Guidelines for Organizing Daily Schedules and Caregiving Routines

This chapter deals with specific ways to establish and carry out daily events and caregiving routines in an active learning setting. It begins with a discussion of these two basic guidelines:

- Create an overall daily schedule that is *predictable yet flexible.*

- Incorporate *active learning, including adult support,* into each event and caregiving routine.

Create an overall daily schedule that is predictable yet flexible

Infant-toddler caregiver teams strive for an overall daily schedule that is predictable—organized and consistent—and still flexible enough to accommodate the needs of individual children. Caregivers and children alike need the reassurance of knowing the general shape of the day (what event will happen next) and of having the ability to bend the overall schedule of events to suit various sleeping, eating, and bodily care needs. So, while predictability and flexibility may seem contradictory, in fact, in an infant-toddler center, they go hand-in-hand to create an unhurried, child-centered day. Some strategies for combining predictability and flexibility are these:

✦ *Organize the day around regular daily events and caregiving routines*

In an active learning program, the infants' and toddlers' day includes certain *regular daily events:* arrival and departure, one or more choice times, outside time, and (for older infants and toddlers) one or more group times. Interspersed among these daily events are *individual caregiving routines:* the supportive, child-focused adult-child interactions that occur during eating, napping, and bodily care (including diapering, using the toilet, washing, and dressing).

✦ *Follow the overall daily schedule consistently*

In a typical caregiver team's group of children, each child has a daily schedule based on his or her particular needs. This means that a number of individualized daily schedules occur simultaneously, calling for both flexibility and organization on the part of caregiving staff. Fortunately, there are common elements among infants' and toddlers' individual daily schedules that often overlap. This overlap makes it possible for caregivers to create an overall daily schedule that is stable and yet responsive to individual children. For samples of three individualized daily schedules (for Bobby, Carlos, and Latisha) and the overall schedule that evolved from them, see "Sample Daily Schedules for an Infant-Toddler Program," pp. 196–197.

One task of the caregiver team is to arrange the elements of the day in an order that makes sense for them and their children. For example, in the sample daily schedules shown here, caregivers Yvonne, Kim, and Leanne have organized the events of their center's day into the following sequence: arrival, choice time, breakfast, choice time, group time, outside time, lunch, nap, group time, snack, outside time, choice time, and departure. Whereas they consistently follow this schedule with most of the children on most days, they integrate each child's personal caregiving routines—eating, bodily care, napping—into this overall schedule as needed. Young infant Bobby, for

Sample Daily Schedules for an Infant-Toddler Program

Overall	Bobby (Young Infant)	Carlos (Young Toddler)	Latisha (Older Toddler)
Arrival (7:30–8:30 a.m.)	7:45 a.m. Bobby's mom holds him as she talks with Yvonne, his primary caregiver. Mom gives Bobby to Yvonne. He smiles from Yvonne's arms as his mom leaves.	8:05 a.m. Carlos leans against Leanne, one of his secondary caregivers, and waves to his mom from the window as she walks to her car.	7:35 a.m. Latisha says "Bye-bye" to her dad as she sits in Yvonne's lap (Yvonne is her secondary caregiver). Latisha shows Yvonne her new hat.
Choice time	Bobby lies on a blanket, exploring balls and scarves with his whole body.	In the house area, Carlos plays with corks, shells, pots, and pans.	In the house area, Latisha puts on bangle bracelets and wraps baby dolls in scarves.
Breakfast	Bobby drinks from a bottle while Yvonne holds him. Bobby gazes, smiles, and coos with Yvonne as she changes his diaper.	Carlos eats toast and cereal, drinks juice from a spouted cup, pauses often to watch other children at the table. He greets Kim, his primary caregiver, when she arrives. Carlos climbs up the steps to the changing table. He gives Kim the dry diaper.	Latisha eats toast and cereal. She pours her own and Carlos's juice. She hugs Kim, her primary caregiver, when Kim arrives. Latisha uses the toilet and washes her hands by herself. "I do it!" she tells Kim.
Choice time	Bobby stretches and rolls. He reaches for, grasps, and explores a rattle, a small tin, a cloth bear, and a small paper bag. Bobby cries and rubs his eyes. Yvonne puts him in his crib for a nap.	Carlos carries and stacks blocks. He brings a book to Kim for her to look at with him.	Latisha loads blocks into the doll buggy, wheels them to the dolls, builds an enclosure, and puts the dolls inside it. She wheels the blocks back to the block shelf at the end of choice time. She and Kim put blocks back on the shelf.
Group time Today caregivers Yvonne and Kim have planned an experience around exploring rhythm instruments.	When Bobby wakes, Yvonne takes him to the changing table. Bobby sucks his thumb and places his other hand on Yvonne's hand as she changes his diaper. Bobby drinks briefly from his bottle while Yvonne holds him. He watches children at group time shaking bells.	Carlos shakes bells with his caregivers and the other children, then returns to the book area and looks at books by himself.	Latisha shakes bells, then plays the drum with her caregivers and the other children.
Outside time	Bobby lies on a blanket, wiggles, stretches, and watches children on the climber.	Carrying a book, Carlos climbs up the steps to the changing table. He looks at the book while Kim changes his diaper. Carlos uses a shovel and a rake in the sandbox.	Latisha rolls balls down the slide and also under the climber. She brings a ball to Bobby. Latisha uses the toilet and washes her hands. She plays for a bit with the stream of water from the faucet.
Lunch (begins at noon)	Bobby coos as Yvonne talks to him about how she is changing his diaper. 12:30 Bobby drinks from his bottle in Yvonne's arms.	Noon. At Kim's table, Carlos eats spaghetti with a spoon and with his fingers.	Noon. Latisha eats spaghetti and pours her own milk. After lunch she wipes off the lunch table with a cloth. "I do it!" she tells Kim.

Sample Daily Schedules for an Infant-Toddler Program, *continued*

Overall	Bobby (Young Infant)	Carlos (Young Toddler)	Latisha (Older Toddler)
Nap	Bobby rolls, stretches, and explores balls on the mattress next to the window. Bobby holds a dry diaper as Yvonne changes him. Bobby trades the dry diaper he has been holding for his striped blanket as Yvonne settles him in his crib for a nap.	Carlos climbs up to the changing table. He looks out the window and shows Kim a dog he sees outside. Carlos brings a rubber dog and a picture book to nap time. Kim tucks his blanket around him. Carlos climbs up to the changing table. He is still a bit groggy from his nap.	Latisha takes books to her cot. Kim tucks a blanket around her. After looking at books, she sleeps briefly.
Group time Today, Kim and Yvonne have planned an opportunity for children to explore and play with containers, paint-brushes, stones, and a tub of water.	Bobby sleeps in his crib.	With Kim and the other children in his group, Carlos fills and empties containers with water.	With Kim, Carlos, and the other child in her group, Latisha uses water and a paintbrush to "paint" stones. Latisha uses the toilet, washes her hands and her stones. "Clean," she tells Kim.
Snack	Bobby plays peek-a-boo with his secondary caregiver, Kim, as she changes his diaper after his nap.	Carlos smooshes some banana pieces and licks them off his fingers. Carlos brings a diaper from his cubby when Kim asks him to.	Latisha tells Kim, "I do it" and peels her own banana half.
Outside time	Since the other children are outside, Bobby has his bottle outdoors in Yvonne's arms. When he is finished, he lies on a blanket, watching and kicking at dandelions. Bobby continues to kick his legs as Yvonne changes his diaper.	Carlos rides a wheeled toy, pushes a small grocery cart, and fills it with balls and leaves.	Latisha puts her stones in a wagon and pulls it about looking for "more stones."
Choice time	Bobby plays peek-a-boo with Kim. He lies on a blanket on the floor and babbles to Mallory, another infant, lying next to him.	Carlos looks at books. He brings Kim over to the bookrack and tells her to "sit" and "read." Carlos climbs up to the changing table. He looks out the window for the dog.	Latisha washes her stones, puts them in her cubby, and rides a wheeled toy. Latisha uses the toilet, washes her hands, and then changes into a clean pair of socks.
Departure (4:00–5:00 p.m.)	3:35 p.m. Bobby's aunt arrives. Bobby wiggles all over with pleasure. His aunt holds Bobby, snuggles him, and chats with Yvonne about Bobby's day. Then they leave for home.	4:40 p.m. Giving Kim a hug, Carlos leaves with his grandmother after taking her to the window and saying "doggy."	4:15 p.m. Latisha's mom arrives. Latisha shows her mom her stones, gives Kim a hug, and leaves with her mom.

One task of the caregiving team is to arrange the elements of the day in an order that makes sense for them and their children. For example,

(2) breakfast,

(3) choice time,

(1) arrival,

(5) group time,

(6) lunch,

(4) outside time,

(7) nap,

(8) group time,

(9) choice time,

and (10) departure.

example, generally naps through part or all of the morning and afternoon group times and through most of the afternoon outside time, although he often has his bottle outdoors, when he wakes up from his afternoon nap. Carlos and Latisha, both toddlers, participate in the entire sequence of morning events and then lie down for naps after lunch. Carlos tends to sleep soundly and sometimes naps through afternoon group time. Latisha generally plays on her cot and is always up and ready for afternoon group time!

By creating a consistent overall schedule, caregivers enable children to drop in and out of various events according to their personal needs and to still be able to anticipate what happens next. Bobby, Carlos, and Latisha do not know that lunchtime occurs at noon every day, but they do know that every day after morning outside time they have lunch and that after lunch come naps. (See "Using Photographs of the Daily Events," p. 200.) While the daily overall schedule remains the same, the duration of any given event may change from day to day. On the day the children play on the new climber, for example, they nap a little longer than usual, so caregivers shorten afternoon choice time.

✦ Accommodate children's natural rhythms and temperaments

As caregivers spend time with children, they begin to see the day through the children's eyes. With a comfortable overall daily schedule in place, they can approach it in an unhurried manner, giving children time to deal with daily events and caregiving routines according to individual temperament. You will see this approach in the following examples.

> *At choice time, Travis, an older infant, takes one thing after another out of a basket of household objects. He examines each object briefly, then discards it for something new. On the other side of the basket, Daemon, also an older infant, selects one wooden spoon, which he mouths and explores with great interest, often pausing to watch Travis, then turning his full attention again to the spoon. After 20 minutes or so, Daemon rubs his eyes, yawns, and looks drowsy. He readily goes to sleep when his caregiver places him and his favorite stuffed rabbit in his crib. Travis, however, continues to explore the objects in the basket throughout choice time. Next, he joins the group singing activity, then heads out the door when it is outside time. He skips his morning nap altogether, even though yesterday he napped through group time and most of outside time.*

Because Daemon's caregivers understand temperamental differences, they see his fairly calm and persistent play and predictable sleeping patterns, as well as Travis's high-energy play and irregular sleeping habits, as normal variations within the boys' daily schedules.

Using Photographs of the Daily Events

Older infants and toddlers enjoy looking at themselves in photographs. To give children a sense of their daily schedule, take a series of photographs of children involved in regular daily events and caregiving routines. Mount the photographs in order along a wall at children's eye level or in a small photograph album. Over a period of time, it is possible to assemble a personal daily-event photo sequence featuring each child. Providing and looking at these photos with children is one way to help them begin to identify and talk about the parts of their day at the center. The photos also provide a good way to share the children's daily experiences with their parents.

Throughout the day, children take time out—alone and with others—to look at photographs of daily events.

At the end of afternoon nap time in a toddler program, Matt takes great pleasure and care in putting on his socks and shoes. By the time he's completed the task, however, the other children have finished snack and are on their way to outside time. Instead of attempting to hurry Matt with his shoes so he can eat with the other children, Matt's caregivers take his snack outside. He eats it while sitting on the steps, then looks for a tricycle to ride.

It may be, reason Matt's caregivers, that he takes a long time with his shoes after nap because, after a very sociable morning, he is not yet ready to be sociable at snack time. Other children, they notice, sometimes choose to watch rather than join group singing and movement experiences, or they choose to leave the group to spend time by themselves sitting under the climber or in the pillows with a book. Because Matt's caregivers understand that children in group care need time alone, they are flexible in anticipating and supporting the choices children make about watching, joining, or leaving the group experiences embedded in the overall daily schedule.

Flexibility was also the key in another toddler program in which children routinely fussed before the morning outside time. When their caregivers discovered that some of the children were hungry at this time, they made a midmorning snack available as part of the overall daily schedule.

◆ Provide a smooth flow from one interesting experience to the next

Caregivers try to ease children's transitions from one major part of the day to the next. One way they do this is through short, predictable transitional activities. A typical transitional activity is planned carefully to avoid disrupting children's chosen exploration and play, and it is consistent from day to day so children know what to expect. To help children retain a sense of control, the transitional activity is simple and active—for example, toddlers regularly using riding toys between lunch and bodily care. Giving

As individual children finish breakfast, they leave the table and begin choice time while other children continue to eat. In this way, regular daily events overlap somewhat to accommodate children's personal rhythms.

children some choices about the coming activity is another way to ease a transition. ("What would you like to bring to nap time?") Caregivers also help children to anticipate what will happen next. ("Stories and nap are next.")

It is important to avoid having children line up or sit waiting for the next event without anything to do. Take cues from children (rather than from the clock) about the beginnings and endings of events. This may mean beginning the next event with some children who are ready while the other children are still engaged in or completing an earlier activity. When, for example, toddler Cassie wakes up early from her nap and begins to play with her doll, her caregiver gets a doll and plays along next to her. As other children wake up, they watch or come over with their dolls. Gradually nap time ends, and group time begins. In the process, the dolls *and* the children get their diapers changed!

In general, caregivers provide time and support for children as they shift gears to move from one regular daily event to another. Even when children must leave the child care home or center at the end of the day but are reluctant to stop what they are doing, caregivers give children choices along with the reason for stopping: "We have to leave the sandbox, Martin, because your mommy's here. You can get in the wagon for a ride to the gate, or you can pull the wagon to the gate."

Incorporate active learning, including adult support, into each part of the day

Instead of setting aside a special time of the day for active learning, caregivers in a High/Scope infant-toddler setting include the ingredients of active learning in each daily event and caregiving routine. This means that throughout the day, they support and interact with children as they work with materials, make choices, and communicate or talk, and that they interpret and build on children's actions and communications in terms of the key experiences. The specific strategies caregivers use are these:

✦ *Be patient with children's intense interest in things around them*

Infants and toddlers are curious about anything that moves, makes a noise, smells, or touches their skin or mouth—an ant, a blade of grass, an orange, a shoe, a person's hand, a ticking clock, a stair tread, a stick, a piece of newspaper. Materials adults may view as commonplace and uninteresting can fascinate young children. Running water and even the water faucets themselves, for example, may fascinate a toddler washing up before lunch. Though caregivers might wish that toddlers would spend less time at the sink, they are patient. They understand that for toddlers, hand washing is not the mundane experience it is for adults.

✦ *Value children's need for sensory-motor exploration in each event and routine*

Throughout the day, infants and toddlers manipulate and mouth materials. At snack and meal times, many children explore their food as they eat, because food to them is simply another irresistibly attractive material. They do not yet make distinctions between materials to play with, materials to eat, and materials to look at but not touch. Therefore, caregivers in active learning settings assume that some exploration is

Water fountains are for play, not just for drinking!

part of children's eating, and they plan accordingly. As another example, interacting with a baby in a game of peek-a-boo with the clean diaper adds to the time it takes to change a diaper. At the same time, it does lend interest and thus often enhances the child's willingness to take part in this inescapable caregiving routine.

✦ *Share control of the day with children by giving them choices*

Infants and toddlers in group care have no choice about being in child care. Each part of the day, however, presents opportunities for choices and decisions they *can* make: They can choose how and when to make contact with caregivers and parents at the beginning and end of the day; where to go, how to move, what and how to explore at choice time and outside time; what, how much, and how to eat; what to hold, look at, or put on during diaper changes; whether to use the potty or the toilet; whether, how, and how long to participate in an activity; what child to sit next to at group time; what comfort items and quiet toys to take along to nap time. Making these choices and decisions on a daily basis and being able to change their mind from one day to the next tends to give children a sense of control over their day.

✦ *Be alert to children's communications and talk throughout the day*

Each part of the day is ripe for communication and language from children. A bottle-feeding infant, for example, may communicate with a caregiver by

steadily maintaining eye contact, smiling, playing games with the bottle, turning away, and pausing to watch other children. A hungry toddler may give full attention to eating and turn to conversation only later, when he or she feels full and satisfied. A toddler may talk or sing to a favorite stuffed animal at nap time, recalling an experience or telling a story. Children often communicate very little when they are thoroughly engaged with materials. Other times they have a lot to communicate and say when you least expect it—while walking outdoors, while sitting on the toilet, or while wiping the table after lunch.

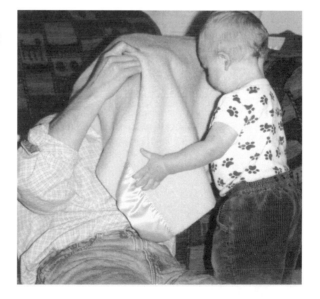

Each time of the day is ripe for communication, even when the caregiver gets covered up with a big "blankie" for a game of peek-a-boo!

✦ Work as a team to provide ongoing support to each child throughout the day

Adult support should remain constant from the time a child enters the care setting until the child leaves. The members of a caregiver team do not have the option of switching from having supportive interactions with a child at choice time, for example, to having directive interactions with that child at group time, to letting that child cry in his crib at nap time. They instead work together to acknowledge children's feelings and maintain a problem-solving approach to conflict throughout the entire day. This includes not taking a punitive approach to biting, not sending children away from the lunch table when they play with food, and not taking toys away from children when they tussle over them in the sandbox. Throughout the day, caregivers use the support strategies discussed in Chapter 2 to build a sense of a community where children can feel safe, secure, and free to explore and to enjoy the company of their peers.

✦ Look at children's actions and communications through the lens of the key experiences

Caregivers in a High/Scope active learning setting watch and listen to whatever children are doing throughout the day. They gather information about children's interests, strengths, and development by relating these observations to the key experiences for infants and toddlers. These scenarios, for example, all involve key experiences:

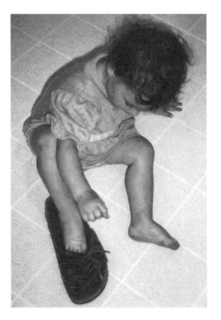

> *At lunch, Michael swats at his spouted cup to make it rock back and forth. When it stops rocking, he says "Again!" and gives it another push. (**Time** key experience: Repeating an action to make something happen again, experiencing cause and effect)*

> ∾

> *At choice time, Emma sits on the floor, holding and rocking a doll, then lays the doll in the cradle. When Malek, another child, approaches, Emma holds her finger to her mouth and says "Shhh!" (**Creative representation** key experience: Imitating and pretending)*

*As she tries on her caregiver's shoe, this toddler engages in the **creative representation** key experience imitating and pretending and the **space key experience** filling and emptying, putting in and taking out.*

⌒

*At group time, Evan stands up and spins around in circles. Periodically he says "Down," and plops to the floor on his bottom. (***Movement and music** key experience: *Moving the whole body*)

⌒

*At outside time, Seanna sits in her caregiver's lap, fills one plastic bottle with small rocks and another plastic bottle with small sticks and grass. She shakes both bottles, then gives the stick-and-grass-filled bottle to her caregiver, indicating that she wants the caregiver to shake it. (***Space** key experience: *Filling and emptying, putting in and taking out;* **Exploring objects** key experience: *Exploring and noticing how things are the same or different.)*

Using the key experiences to interpret children's communications and actions serves as the basis for the next day's plans and provides caregivers with a daily bank of detailed stories and anecdotes to share with parents and guardians. Each daily event and caregiving routine thus provides an opportunity to enjoy, learn about, and understand individual children.

Guidelines for Organizing Daily Schedules and Caregiving Routines: A Summary

Create an overall daily schedule that is predictable yet flexible.

❑ Organize the day around regular daily events and caregiving routines.

❑ Follow the overall daily schedule consistently.

❑ Accommodate children's natural rhythms and temperaments.

❑ Provide a smooth flow from one interesting experience to the next.

Incorporate active learning, including adult support, into each event and caregiving routine.

❑ Be patient with children's intense interest in things around them.

❑ Value children's need for sensory-motor exploration in each event and routine.

❑ Share control of the day with children by giving them choices.

❑ Be alert to children's communications and talk throughout the day.

❑ Work as a team to provide ongoing support to each child throughout the day.

❑ Look at children's actions and communications through the lens of the key experiences.

Understanding Arrival and Departure

"Good morning, Martha and Monique," says Chantall, a caregiver, to Monique and her mom. Monique, a young nonmobile infant, has been coming to the child care center for 5 weeks. She arrives in her mother's arms and smiles at Chantall, who is her primary caregiver. After her mom and Chantall chat for a bit about Monique's new interest in watching and laughing at the family cat, Monique's mom snuggles and kisses her, then gives her to Chantall, who hugs her, smiles, and says, "It's nice to see you, Monique!" They walk with Mom to the door. "Bye, bye, Monique," says her mom. "I'll be back this afternoon." "Bye, bye, Mommy—see you later," Chantall says for Monique.

At the end of the day, Monique lies on her back on a quilt next to Sasha, another infant. Monique holds and mouths a wooden ball. When she hears her mom arriving and greeting Chantall, Monique drops her ball, smiles, and wiggles all over in anticipation. Her mom sits down next to her, and after picking her up for a kiss, a hug, and a snuggle, she holds her close and says, "You've been playing next to Sasha again!" Monique smiles and coos in her mom's arms as her mom walks over to Chantall to catch up on the day's events and round up Monique's bottles and supplies. At the end of their chat, Chantall strokes Monique's arm and says, "Bye, Monique! See you tomorrow!" Monique and her mom depart.

∽

Evan, a young toddler, arrives with Veana, his mom, for his third day at the center. "Good morning, Veana and Evan," says Chantall. Evan holds his mom's hand and watches another toddler, Athi, at the sand table while Mom and Chantall exchange information about the day. Observing Evan's tight grip on his mom and his focus on the sand play, Chantall joins Athi at the sand table with the thought that Evan might come there, enabling her to gradually make contact with him through a mutual interest in sand toys. She doesn't address or approach Evan at this point, because he is so clearly avoiding her.

Eventually, Evan and his mom make their way to the sand table. When his mom squats down by the table, Evan stands between her knees and scoops up sand with his hands. From her place on the other side of the sand table, next to Athi, Chantall moves a bucket and shovel within Evan's reach. He takes the shovel and begins to fill the bucket. Chantall, continuing to interact with Athi, says gently, "Athi, you're digging a pretty big hole!"—whereupon Athi gives her a spoon so she can dig a hole like his. Throughout this time, Chantall talks now and then with Evan's mom about how and why she is following Evan's cues in the getting-acquainted process. Eventually, when she sees Evan eyeing her spoon, she gives it to him, saying "Maybe you would like a spoon, too, Evan." He takes the spoon and begins to dig. As he enlarges his hole, he leaves the safety of his mom's knees and moves to the end of the sand table, between his mom and Chantall. When Athi begins to drive a dump truck around the sand table, Chantall backs away from the table so Athi and his truck can drive in front of her. When Athi gets to where Evan is playing in the sand, Evan puts his hand on the truck, and Athi stops. "Looks like Evan wants your truck to back up!" Chantall says. Athi laughs at this idea and begins backing his truck around the table. Looking up at Chantall briefly, Evan smiles and then returns to his play.

When it's time for Evan's mom to leave, she gives him a hug and tells him she'll be back after nap. He watches her sadly as she walks toward the door but remains at the sand table with

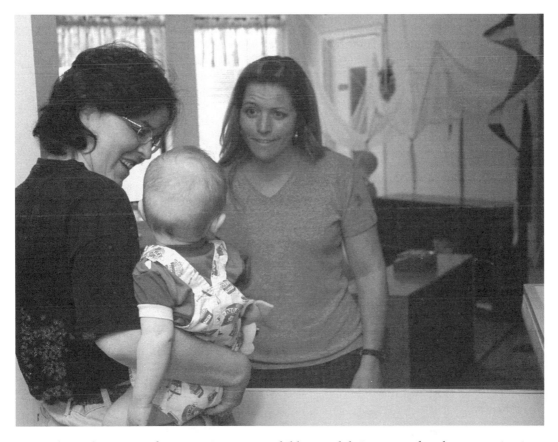

Warm, leisurely greetings from caregivers assure children and their parents that the care setting is a safe and friendly home-away-from-home.

Chantall and Athi. "Mommy go," he says to Chantall, pressing himself against her side. "It's sad for you to see Mommy go— she'll come back after nap," Chantall says, slipping her arm around his shoulders.

At the end of the day, Evan is just waking up from his nap when he sees his mom come through the door. He runs into her arms, and as she talks with Chantall, he strokes her face. After gathering Evan's things, his mom says goodbye to Chantall. Lightly touching Evan's back, Chantall tells him, "See you to-morrow!" He smiles at her from the safety of his mom's arms.

Arrivals and departures like the ones in these scenarios involve the rituals that set the tone for the child's away-from-home experience. At arrival time, warm, leisurely greetings from caregivers help to assure infants and toddlers that even though their parents must leave, they are in the hands of trustworthy people who will respect them and keep them safe until their parents return. At departure time, the caregivers' pleasant, friendly goodbyes and warm wishes for return allow children to reunite with their parents but to be free of concerns about their sense of belonging at the center; they are

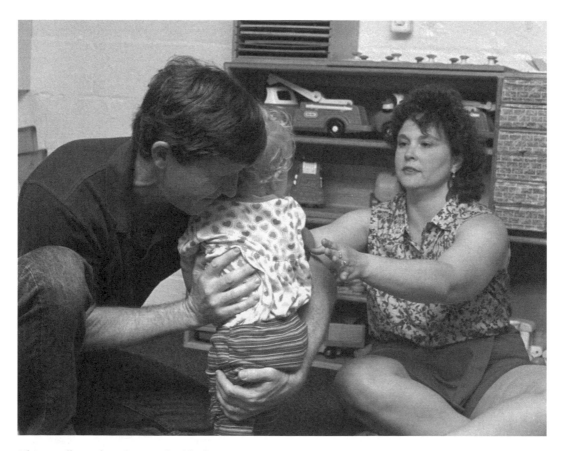

This goodbye takes place in the block area.

relieved to see their parents, and at the same time, they know that the adults saying goodbye do care for them. In the short run, learning to deal with the daily greetings and goodbyes at arrival and departure times allows children to enlarge the scope of their trust from parents and family at home to caregivers and peers at the center. In the long run, coping successfully with these rituals gives children a solid basis for coping with the comings and goings of relatives and friends for the rest of their lives.

Even when a care setting has a reception area, there is no definite place in the care setting where greetings and goodbyes must take place. Where they occur depends on the needs and preferences of the child and parent. One mom may sit in a comfortable chair, nurse her infant, chat with the caregiver, and give her child to the caregiver without ever leaving the reception area. Other parents will come into the play space and say their goodbye or hello wherever their child is comfortable that day—at the sand table, on the mattress next to the books, or outside in the play yard. At one center, when Nolan grew to be an older toddler and had been going to the same center for 2 years, he and his mom developed a fairly elaborate goodbye ritual that took him to the top of the indoor climber. He would first give his mom a goodbye kiss near the door, then hurry across the room and climb rapidly up to what everyone called the crow's-nest. When he got to the top, he would say "Okay, mommy!" to signal that it was okay for his mom to go out the door. Once outside, she turned and waved at him, and from his high perch, he waved back at her through the window.

As infants and toddlers separate from their parents to join the child care community at the beginning of the day, they typically engage in a variety of behaviors. These may range from crying, screaming, flailing, clinging, thumb sucking, avoiding eye contact, or simply ignoring the parent or caregiver involved, to smiling, cooing, picking up an interesting plaything, watching other children with interest, waving goodbye to the parent, or joining an activity in progress. Their responses to rejoining a parent at the end of the day may vary just as widely. Furthermore, these responses may change from day to day and from one stage of development to the next, with islands of predictability in between!

Nonmobile (very young) infants generally respond to separations and reunions with relative ease. At this age, an infant is apt to greet a familiar primary caregiver with a smile, settle peacefully into her arms, and gaze into her face. At the end of the day, the infant will often alert to the sound and sight of a returning parent and begin to wiggle, smile, and vocalize with pleasure.

As they learn to creep and crawl, infants develop a sense of themselves as separate beings distinct from their parents. Realizing that parents can disappear, they fear they may not return! At arrival time, therefore, it is not uncommon for these mobile infants to cling to their parents, cry, avoid eye contact with the caregiver, and head for (maybe even try to open) the door through which their parents have just taken leave.

Young toddlers enjoy their newfound walking ability and the freedom it allows them to explore and carry all kinds of interesting objects. While they remain concerned about losing sight of their parents, they are usually irresistibly drawn to examine whatever they can get their hands on. They may still protest a parent's leave-taking, but they can also make connections with caregivers and peers through objects and playthings of particular interest. At the end of the day, young toddlers may simply continue their explorations and play when their parents arrive, or they may throw themselves into their parents' arms and cry with relief!

At the end of the day, father and son are happily reunited!

Older toddlers are developing the ability to hold in mind mental images of absent people and past events. They remember their parents leaving them at the center on previous mornings and anticipate that it will happen again today. At the same time, they are developing a strong sense of independence and initiative and an increasing ability to communicate with such powerful phrases as "Mommy stay!" and "No!" At the beginning of the day, their objections to a parent's departure can be loud and physical. They need to sense some control over how they ease themselves into the setting and how long it takes to do so. Fortunately, they are usually increasingly interested in the people and materials in the child care setting and eager to make choices about what they are going to do after their parents leave. At the end of the day, older toddlers may resist leaving the center until they have finished a particular activity. They may be perfectly cheerful as they reunite with their parents, or they may be tearful, whiney, and demanding.

How Caregivers Support Children at Arrival and Departure

During arrival and departure times, it is important for caregivers to give children and parents warm welcomes and goodbyes and to support their separation and reunion processes. The following strategies can help in carrying out this caregiver role:

- Carry out your greetings and goodbyes calmly to reassure the child and parent.

- Acknowledge the child's and the parent's feelings about separation and reunion.

- Follow the child's signals about entering and leaving the activity of the care setting.

- Communicate openly with the child about the parent's comings and goings.

- Exchange information and child observations with the parent.

Carry out your greetings and goodbyes calmly to reassure the child and parent

Separating and reuniting can be difficult for children and their parents. Given the potential for family distress at the beginning and end of the day, it is important that caregivers approach these times calmly and optimistically. By remaining attuned to yet outside of the emotional fray, caregivers make themselves available to offer reassurance and support. Although some caregivers may recall their own less-than-happy separations and reunions, it is important that they refrain from reliving them at these times so they can focus instead on the immediate needs of the children and parents before them. The presence of a calm, friendly caregiver can help to reassure anxious children and parents. A caregiver's calmness can also reassure the other children who are present, who have already separated from their parents for the day.

Acknowledge the child's and the parent's feelings about separation and reunion

An infant or toddler may feel especially vulnerable when left by a parent in a place that is not home, with people who are not familiar. Having no conventional sense of time, the child cannot distinguish between being left for 6 hours and being left forever. Thus, young children's emotions at the

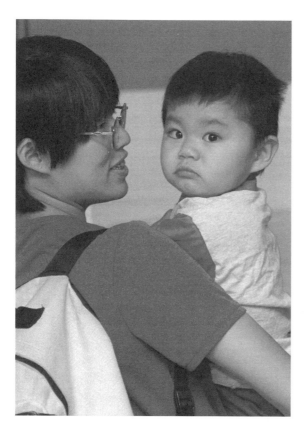

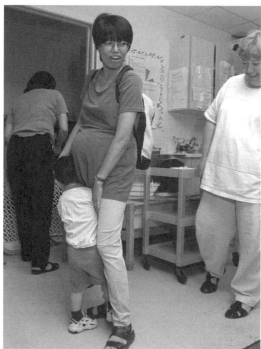

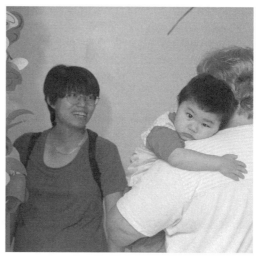

Letting go of Mommy and accepting a trusted caregiver in her place for the day takes time, courage, and lots of support.

beginning of the day in group care may range from discomfort, anxiety, fear, or terror to sorrow, loneliness, grief, or despair over abandonment. At the end of the day, it is not unusual for children to express conflicting emotions—residual anger at being left by their parent, increasing fear they may be abandoned by their parent as they watch other children being picked up before them, and finally, joy at their parent's return and relief that at last, in their parent's arms, they can safely fall apart from the stresses and strains of their day.

When parents leave their child at the child care center or child care home, they may feel sad about missing their child, guilty about leaving him or her in someone else's care, and anxious about getting to work on time. Later, at the end of the day, they may look forward to reclaiming their child, feel hurt and perhaps jealous when the child ignores them or resists leaving the caregiver, and tense about fitting in all the household tasks that need doing before bedtime.

Caregivers can help reduce the emotional intensity of separations and reunions by gently and matter-of-factly describing the emotions they are witnessing. Here are several examples of ways you might describe a child's feelings at a parent's departure:

- "It's sad for you to see your mommy go, Terry."

- "You're crying so hard that your eyes are closed, Jamal. You don't like to see Mommy leave for work."

- "You're holding on to me so tightly, Angelina! It's scary for you to see Mommy go, isn't it? Let's sit in the cozy chair together."

You might also try to describe a parent's feelings. Here are some examples:

- "It looks like you want to stay with Verdell *and* leave in time for work, Ms. Smith. It's hard to be pulled in opposite directions."

- "It must be upsetting to have Mickey cry when you're so glad to see him, Ms. Greene. Maybe it's his way of telling you how relieved he is to see you at the end of the day. Now he really feels free to express himself."

Letting children and parents know that you recognize and are trying to understand their feelings actually helps them begin to regain emotional balance. By putting words to children's and parents' feelings, you help their emotions to recede, clearing the way for them to think about moving on to the next part of the day.

Occasionally a child seems inconsolable when a parent leaves. The child may be new to the center, returning from a long absence, tired, coming down with an illness, or entering a new stage of self-awareness. At these times, it is important for the caregiver who always greets the child to remain calm, to describe the child's feelings, and to stay with the child to provide comfort and physical contact (holding, stroking, rocking, carrying) until the child recovers.

Sometimes, as they prepare to leave their child in a child care setting, parents have more difficulty with separation than their children have. Again, caregivers can support anxious parents by remaining calm, acknowledging their feelings, and encouraging them to take plenty of time and stay at the center as long as they are able to. Eventually, over time, with caregivers displaying patience and giving attention to the feelings involved, both children and parents will gain trust in the center staff and confidence in themselves and will be able to enter and leave the center with a sense of hope and ease.

Follow the child's signals about entering and leaving the activity of the care setting

Parents, of course, make the decision about placing their infant or toddler in a particular care setting. However, when adults follow the child's signals or cues about how he or she prefers to enter or leave the activities of that care setting each day, this gives the child as much control as possible in the larger situation of having to be in that setting. Each child copes with making the transition from home to care setting and back again in a particular and personal way. One way many infants and toddlers soothe themselves during this emotional time is by clinging to some item that connects them in a tangible way to home—a special blanket, a dolly or stuffed animal, a pacifier, a photo of a family member (see p. 110). If a child hangs on to such a comfort item during arrival and departure, it is important for caregivers to respect this choice as an assertion of self and an important step in the development of self-help skills.

Older infants and toddlers who can move about on their own may cope with the transition from home to care setting in a variety of ways. For example, they may at first cling to their parent, then turn to a toy or select some plaything and come back to their parent, showing no desire for physical or eye contact with any caregiver. When ready, however, such children will gradually ease their way into caregiver contact in the presence of their parent, or after the parent departs. For example, when Evan (p. 206) arrives with his mom for his third day at the center, Chantall (his caregiver) respects Evan's initial avoidance of her, knowing that he will make contact with her when *he* is ready. She also knows that if she imposes herself on him, she will only heighten his concerns about his new setting. Instead, she makes herself available for gradual approach by kneeling down on the far side of the sand table, using the table both as a buffer against too much contact too quickly and as something mutually interesting that they can both play at without direct interaction.

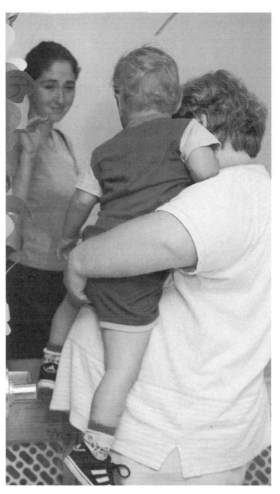

After saying goodbye to Mommy, this toddler takes an interest in the pet parakeet.

Communicate openly with the child about the parent's comings and goings

To foster trust and communication, let children know when their parents leave and return to the center. Although occasionally a parent may wish to leave quickly and quietly while his or her child is engaged in play, it is important for the child to know where the parent is, rather than to look up and discover that Daddy or Mommy has left without saying goodbye. In the long run, for the child, the pain of hearing a parent's "Goodbye, see you after nap" is less than the pain of actually feeling betrayed by a parent who leaves with no notice.

One way to make the parent's comings and goings no mystery is to encourage the child and parent to establish a ritual for separation and re-union. The scenarios presented on pp. 206–208 contain several examples of these types of rituals. In these examples, each time a parent says good-bye, she also lets the child know when she will be coming back. Although very young children may not comprehend what such statements actually mean or precisely how long it will be until Mom returns, at some level, the children understand and are comforted by the parent's reassuring promise of reunion.

Parent-child separations and reunions have a relationship to the end-less games of peek-a-boo and hide-and-seek that caregivers play with in-fants and toddlers. Hiding behind the sofa and then popping out, or hiding the stuffed bunny under the blanket and then revealing the bunny with a flourish and an exclamation of "peek-a-boo," is a way for children to act out and begin to understand that people come and go, that parents leave in the morning and return at the end of the day.

Exchange information and child observations with the parent

Seeing parents at arrival and departure times provides an opportunity for caregivers to exchange information about the child's life at the center and at home. Caregivers can fill parents in on children's actions and com-munications at the center: "Today, Evan spent all of choice time with Emma at the sand table, digging holes and driving dump trucks." Parents can let caregivers know what children did at home: "I couldn't believe my eyes this morning. Monique was standing up holding on to the side of her crib. She's never done that before!" (See Chapter 5 for further discussion of settling into the center and exchanging information with parents.)

Understanding Feeding and Mealtime

Molly, a young infant, lies cradled in her caregiver's arms and drinks from a bottle. When Molly stops sucking for a moment, her caregiver says, "My, Molly, you sure are hungry today!" Molly gazes intently at her caregiver's face for several seconds, then returns to her bottle and resumes sucking.

∾

Shannon, an older infant, sits on the floor, eating at a small tray-table. She holds a cracker in one hand as she tries with her other hand to eat with a spoon. After several attempts to get some green beans onto the spoon, she drops the spoon and eats the beans, one at a time, with her fingers, still holding the cracker in her other hand.

∾

At snack time, toddler Steven accidentally bumps his arm into his spouted cup, tipping it over on the table. He watches a little milk dribble out, then picks up the cup, takes a drink, and sets the cup upright again. After a slight pause, he repeats this action sequence a couple more times before drinking the rest of his milk.

∾

In George and Nanette's home child care program, each toddler brings lunch from home. Just before lunch, while Nanette plays with the children and helps them put toys away, George gets the lunches and finishes any necessary preparations, such as warming, cutting, or combining ingredients. When George begins to bring the food to the table, Nanette starts the children with hand washing. Once the children sit down around a small table with their lunches, George and Nanette get out their lunches and join the children's table as the children are comparing with one another what drinks they brought from home. Toddler Sarah takes a spoonful of a cup of yogurt, then decides to put her grapes in the yogurt before continuing to eat it. Nanette comments that she too sometimes likes to dip fruit into her yogurt. Throughout the meal, children and care-

givers continue to eat and converse together about topics raised by the children, such as drinking with straws and cups, and dipping things in yogurt.

Babies' feedings and children's mealtimes go beyond fulfilling a basic need for nourishing food. For infants, feedings or mealtimes provide close physical contact with an attentive adult. When a young infant's cries of hunger are met with a full bottle and the comforting arms of a pleasant caregiver, that child is able to grow and thrive because he or she learns to trust the world as a place where people recognize and respond to an infant's needs. For the older infant, mealtime is a time to eat but also to explore new tastes, smells, and textures and to try self-feeding with fingers, a spoon, or a cup. For the toddler, mealtime becomes increasingly sociable. As toddlers eat, they usually enjoy interacting with others and being part of the mealtime conversation. They also continue to explore and try new foods and gain skill at feeding themselves. As infant educator Peter Mangione (1990) has said, "Young children are in the process of developing lifelong attitudes toward food and the experience of eating. In a relaxed setting they form positive attitudes and learn vital social skills" (p. 11). In short, feedings and mealtimes are social interludes based around eating and enjoying food.

Where a feeding or a mealtime takes place depends on the stage of the child involved. A primary caregiver of young infants lovingly holds each child and attends to his or her bottle-feeding while sitting in some comfort-

Even for toddlers, mealtimes are social interludes based around eating and enjoying food.

able place. Some infants, content with this close contact and attention, focus intently on their bottle and caregiver, with little or no regard for where they are and whatever is going on around them. Other infants, who are easily distracted and continually turning away from the bottle to watch other children and adults, may best be fed in a fairly secluded place.

As discussed in detail in Chapter 3 (pp. 120–121), infants who are sitting and beginning to try solid foods are generally propped up in some way while the caregiver offers food on a spoon. Older infants who are interested in picking up finger foods, guiding the spoon to their mouth, and exploring food with their hands usually sit on low chairs or on the floor to eat at low one-person tables. Toddlers eat together with their caregivers in small groups at low tables. Both infants and toddlers can enjoy mealtimes outdoors in pleasant weather.

The scenarios at the beginning of this section illustrate typical behaviors very young children engage in during feeding or mealtime. Molly, in the first scenario, is like many young infants in that she enjoys her bottle, satisfies her hunger, and pauses from time to time to gaze at something that catches her attention—her caregiver's face, another child, the movement of a curtain. In the security of their caregiver's arms, bottle-feeding infants are free to set their own pace, dividing their energies between drinking and examining the world through their eyes.

Older infants, like Shannon, bring new physical skills to eating. They can sit unassisted, so they have greater control of their arms and hands and can easily put things in their mouths! Shannon enjoys figuring out the best

Each step in the process of learning to feed yourself is a satisfying accomplishment!

way to get the green beans into her mouth. When the spoon doesn't work, she uses her fingers to feed herself. Just as she explores materials during the rest of the day—fitting blocks into a shape-sorter, nesting graduated cups inside one another, or putting a bottle into a baby doll's mouth—Shannon uses mealtime for problem solving, exploring, and developing physical skills.

Toddlers continue to explore food and materials during mealtime. For several minutes, Steven, for example, is more interested in the reactions of his cup and milk than in eating. *What happens to the milk in the spouted cup when it tips over? Why doesn't more of the milk spill out? Is there any more milk left in the cup?* We don't know, for sure, if these or similar questions are going through his mind as he experiments with his cup, but we can observe his fascination with tipping and dribbling. Toddlers also tend to enjoy socializing and interacting with others as they eat.

As caregivers become accustomed to the exploratory feeding and mealtime practices of infants and toddlers, they find, much to their relief, that most children also do actually *eat* their food—in adequate quantities and at a pace that meets their personal needs—and thus they receive the benefits of good nutrition. At the same time, caregivers know that fingering food and dribbling milk are normal behaviors at feeding or mealtime in an infant-toddler care setting. Infants and toddlers do not refrain from active learning as they eat. They simply transfer their attention and actions to things edible! While they are not yet ready to practice formal table manners, they do engage in an experience that eventually leads to manners—the pleasure of eating and conversing in a warm, supportive setting.

How Caregivers Support Children During Feeding and Mealtime

During feeding or mealtime, caregivers provide a pleasant, relaxed atmosphere so children can eat and enjoy their food in the company of others. The following strategies help them carry out this role:

- Hold and pay close attention to the bottle-feeding infant.

- Support the older infant's interest in feeding him- or herself.

- Join toddlers at the table during meals.

- Include older toddlers in mealtime setup and cleanup.

Hold and pay close attention to the bottle-feeding infant

Because bottle-feeding babies cannot feed themselves, they depend entirely on caregivers to hold and feed them when they are hungry. "Feeding time," developmental psychologist Judith Evans (1982a) has said, "is an important time for the caregiver and the infant to establish bonds. It is an intimate time,

This caregiver gives her major attention to the baby she is feeding.

physically and emotionally. By holding and cuddling the child . . . and communicating with her, you are giving her a warmth which helps her develop trust and a sense of security" (p. 2). We also know from brain research (Schiller, 1997) that touch during bottle-feeding increases infants' digestive abilities and decreases stress. By holding bottle-feeding babies, caregivers try to re-create the familiar closeness and security infants feel in their parents' arms when they are nursing or drinking from a bottle at home.

During the feeding, the caregiver gives her major attention to the infant. Though she does not disturb the child's active engagement with the bottle, she is ready to interact whenever the baby shows an interest in doing so. For example, during pauses when the child takes a rest from sucking, the caregiver may smile, make faces, chat softly, or stroke the infant's head; the infant may grasp the caregiver's fingers, face, hands, or clothing. Through these exchanges, the caregiver and baby build a personal relationship through which the child learns, on a very basic level, that he or she can rely on this nonparental adult for physical and emotional needs.

Propping babies up to drink from their bottles unattended may be efficient, especially in a group-care setting. However, we know from the work of Rene Spitz (see p. 32) that children fed consistently in this manner fail to thrive not from a lack of food, but from the absence of loving human attention and physical contact. Fortunately, holding bottle-feeding babies comes quite naturally to most caregivers! Also, when each primary caregiver is responsible for at most three infants, there *are* enough arms to hold babies while they eat.

Support the older infant's interest in feeding him- or herself

As children learn to creep and crawl and sit by themselves, they generally become interested in the eating habits of older children and adults. They watch "big" people eat crackers, use spoons, and drink from cups or glasses, and they attempt to imitate these actions. While caregivers take pleasure in holding and feeding infants, it is important to allow infants to change and grow. Be alert to the signals that they are ready to take over parts of the meal themselves. Children generally begin self-feeding by using their fingers, because this is easier for them than using a spoon—they are usually adept at putting their fingers in their mouth. It will take them more time to master the use of a simple utensil, like a spoon, to convey food from a plate or bowl to their mouth. Understanding these facts of child development, caregivers give older infants some foods they can easily pick up and eat with their fingers along with some runny foods (applesauce, yogurt, cooked cereal) that work better with a spoon.

Toddlers are adept at putting their fingers in their mouth, so fingers are often a welcome respite from the complexities of using a spoon!

Using fingers to eat has these two distinct advantages for the very young active learners, according to Goldschmied and Jackson (1994): "(1) They are not obliged to wait entirely on the adult's help and control; and (2) handling food directly provides varied tactile experiences" (p. 105). Young children are interested in spoons; they are equally interested in how food feels in their hands. When you serve them spoon food, provide one spoon for the child and another for yourself. This way, the child can practice using the spoon, along with his or her fingers, and you can help with feeding without taking away the child's spoon. Before a child gains skill with a spoon, "it will help, as we offer a loaded spoon, to give him a spoon to hold and brandish also. This is our message to him, that we acknowledge that later on he will handle the spoon for himself" (Goldschmied and Jackson, 1994, p. 77).

Just as older infants mix finger and spoon use, so they might drink some milk from a spouted cup and some milk from their bottle. When a bottle-feeding child begins to show interest in drinking from a cup, share this observation with parents so you can coordinate your mealtime practice and theirs (regarding cup versus bottle use). If, for example, the parents are gradually cutting back on bottles at home as the child uses a cup more and more often, caregivers can support this new undertaking so that children's dual needs—for milk and for practicing self-help—are acknowledged in the same manner at home and at the center. Again, during the time infants drink from both cups and bottles, do not leave them to drink from their bottle unattended.

Remember, too, that children's abilities to feed themselves can change abruptly. For example, one day Amanda drops her spoon over and over again, not getting any food to her mouth, and the next, she is scooping spoonful after spoonful of applesauce into her mouth with great gusto!

Join toddlers at the table during meals

In the scenario on page 217, George and Nanette join their toddlers for lunch to create a pleasant setting in which to enjoy food and one another's company. Caregivers in High/Scope programs approach mealtimes as daily opportunities to build relationships with children by supporting their conversation, exploration, and repetition and by providing assistance as needed as children continue their journey toward independent eating within a social context. By taking part in meals with children, caregivers send a positive message not only about eating but also about social relationships at the child care center: *We can do all sorts of enjoyable things together—play, take walks, read books, talk, and share food and food experiences!*

Toddler-initiated mealtime conversation tends to focus around children's observations and musings about the materials at hand—"Who make [lunch]?" "You like eggs?" "Oranges at our house, too!" "Look! Bread broke!" "Dripping!" "More milky!" "No 'nanas. No!" "Dog cookie!" "He gots more!" Because caregivers come to know each child, they can help carry on the conversation by filling in the missing parts of children's often very brief statements, as this example shows:

Zach: (Addresses Rachel.) *Who make?*

Caregiver: *Rachel, Zach is wondering who made your lunch.*

Rachel: *Daddy.*

Zach: (He watches Rachel take a bite of her sandwich.) *Daddy make.* (He picks up his own sandwich.) *Mommy make. Make Todd's.*

Caregiver: *I understand, Zach. Your mommy made your sandwich, and she made your brother Todd's sandwich, too.*

Zach: (Chewing a bite of his sandwich, nods his head and smiles.)

At the table with George and Nanette, where Sarah has added her grapes to her yogurt, and Nanette has commented that she sometimes does the same thing, this is what ensues:

> *Watching Sarah and hearing Nanette's comment, Elijah*
> *holds a cracker in his hand and looks around for something he*
> *can dip it into. The closest thing he can see is Henry's yogurt,*
> *but when he dips his cracker into it, Henry says "No!" and*
> *pushes his hand away. Nanette says, "You want something to*

Conversations at mealtime occur during the pauses, when children take a break from eating.

dip your cracker into, Elijah, but Henry doesn't want you to dip into his yogurt. Let's get you some yogurt from the refrigerator." Elijah's face clears, and he nods yes. Nanette brings a large container of yogurt, a serving spoon, and a small bowl. Elijah serves himself some dipping yogurt and begins to dip.

For snack, Denise, a caregiver, has given her four toddlers each a half of a banana with the peel still on (she knows her children like to do the peeling themselves):

Leon removes his peel entirely and flaps it about with one hand as he holds and eats his banana half with the other. Minyon peels her banana, puts it on her napkin, and breaks it into bits with her spoon. She lifts each banana piece to her mouth with her fingers. Clea watches Minyon, then peels her banana half, mashes it with her spoon, and spoons it up to her mouth. Max peels his banana half and squeezes it in his hand, then licks it off his hand.

Although Denise prefers to eat her banana in a more conventional manner, she understands that the children's explorations are a normal part of their ongoing curiosity about objects and how their actions affect them.

Caregivers eating with toddlers can also support their need for the repetition that allows them to eventually master a variety of self-help skills—pulling out the stool or chair to sit on and pushing it in again at the end of the meal; unwrapping a sandwich; peeling a banana; pouring a cup of milk; wiping up their spills.

Include older toddlers in mealtime setup and cleanup

Mealtimes present routine tasks older toddlers can easily carry out and take great satisfaction from—passing out plates, bowls, cups, and napkins; pouring their own juice and milk from small pitchers; serving themselves food from plates and serving dishes; throwing napkins into the wastebasket; scraping

After lunch, this toddler uses her spoon to scrape the remains of her lunch into the waste can.

leftover food from plates; putting used dishes in dish tubs for clearing; and wiping the table with soapy water and a sponge. As Goldschmied and Jackson (1994) have stated,

> Involving the older children in tidying and cleaning up can mean more effort for the staff as it is usually quicker for the adults to do it themselves. But if we look on everything that happens in the nursery as part of the children's learning, this [preference for doing it quickly] is a short-sighted approach. There will be some occasions when time pressure is too great, but it is usually possible to organize some of the helping so that both adults and children enjoy it and feel a sense of achievement. (p. 24)

Understanding Time for Bodily Care

Josh, a young infant, intently watches his caregiver, Isobel, as she changes his diaper and sings these words to the tune of "Here We Go 'Round the Mulberry Bush": "Josh is getting his diaper changed, his diaper changed, his diaper changed. Josh is getting his diaper changed, early in the morning."

∽

Sydney, an older infant, wiggles his toes and kicks his legs as Melissa, his caregiver, changes his diaper. At one point, he holds one foot with both hands and guides his foot into his mouth. "Oh, Sydney," says Melissa, pausing to admire his flexibility, "you've put your 'toesies' into your mouth!" She tickles his free foot. He then lets go of the foot he already has in his mouth, grabs his other foot, and puts that into his mouth. "Now you've put your other toesies into your mouth!" says Melissa. He and Melissa repeat this game several times before completing his diaper change.

∽

Maria, a young toddler, reaches for the washcloth that Toni, her caregiver, is about to use on Maria's face. "So, Maria," says Toni, "you want to wash your own face!" Maria takes the washcloth from Toni and uses it to pat her cheeks. "You really know how to wash your cheeks, Maria!" says Toni. "Let's see if you can wipe your mouth, too." Maria moves her hand toward her mouth, then rubs the cloth back and forth across her lips.

∽

Zar, a toddler, notices a bunch of balloons suspended from the ceiling above him while Annie, his caregiver, changes his diaper. "Balloon?" he says. "Yes, you see balloons, Zar," says Annie, "lots of balloons!" Zar repeats the word "balloon" over and over again. After each repetition, he pauses and looks at Annie, who repeats "Lots of balloons!" and laughs.

❧

After lunch, Joan and Pam's six toddlers look at books and work with puzzles before they take their nap. As they play, Pam tells them, "You have time for a few more books and puzzles. Then I'm going to help you change diapers." While Joan remains on the floor with the children, looking at books and helping with puzzles, Pam approaches and speaks to Aura, who is holding a book in her lap and rubbing her eyes: "You're looking at the book about farm animals, Aura," (Aura nods) "and you're rubbing your eyes!" Aura replies "Sleepy." "Come with me for a diaper change, then nap," says Pam, leading her to the changing table. As Pam changes Aura's diaper, Aura wipes her own hands and face with a warm, moist paper towel that Pam has handed her. After changing Aura's diaper, Pam approaches each of the remaining children in a similar manner—commenting on their play, taking them to the changing table, offering them a warm, moist towel, and continuing the conversation with children who are not too sleepy. Two of the older toddlers, Jason and Misty, are in the process of learning to use the toilet. She asks them, in turn, if they need to sit on the potty. Jason says no, but Misty says yes and takes a turn on the potty before getting her fresh diaper.

❧

Misha, an older toddler, is learning to use the potty chair. His caregiver, Carla, and his parents are working together to support this new interest. Today when Misha gets up from his nap, Carla checks his diaper. "Your diaper is still dry, Misha!" she says. "Would you like to sit on the potty chair?" He sleepily rubs his eyes and shakes his head no. The other children are not awake yet, so Carla holds Misha in her lap in the rocking chair and reads him a storybook. When they're finished, Carla asks again if he'd like to use the potty chair. This time he says yes and removes his own diaper. "You took off your own diaper, Misha," says Carla. Misha heads for the potty chair, clutching the storybook they have just read.

For infants and toddlers, the brief routines of bodily care—diaper changes, dressing, washing, and using the potty or toilet—occur frequently and fairly regularly throughout the day. This means whenever children are wet or soiled, before and/or after eating and napping—generally every hour or so, depending on the age, health, and habits of the child. At the most basic level, these routines promote cleanliness, physical comfort, and health by minimizing children's exposure to infection and diaper rash, but they can also contribute to children's emotional well-being. Through the gentle, one-to-one interactions involved in bodily care, children have an opportunity to build trusting relationships with caregivers and gain a sense of security in the care setting. Also, during the process of washing, diapering, dressing, and

Through the gentle, one-to-one interactions involved in bodily care, children have the opportunity to build trusting relationships with caregivers.

undressing, infants and toddlers begin to sense how their own bodies can bend and move. They eventually use this knowledge to accomplish such self-help tasks as holding and handing over their diaper or washcloth or pulling up and pulling down their own pants. They also learn that while the inevitable care routines often interrupt their exploration and play, they can almost always return fairly quickly to the situation they left.

In a group-care setting, bodily care consistently takes place in the diapering and dressing areas and the child-oriented bathrooms described in some detail on pp. 128–132. In short, the diapering and dressing areas and bathrooms should be easily cleaned, reasonably located, convenient for

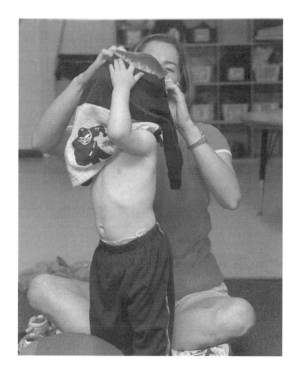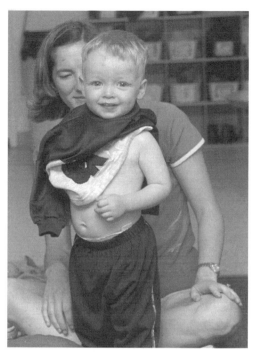

This toddler takes an active role in putting on a dry shirt after playing outside under the water faucet.

adults, and pleasant for children. To support the development of children's self-help skills and their "me do it" approach to life, sinks and toilets need to be low; faucets, as well as soap and towel dispensers, need to be child-friendly. For toddlers, there should be steps leading up to the changing table and child-access to clean clothes.

As adults help younger children with their bodily care routines, the children will continue to explore, play, fuss, babble, talk, cling, laugh, giggle, wiggle, drop things on the floor, ask questions, grumble, put things in their mouth, cry, smile. In other words, they remain sensory-motor learners even when engaged in an activity that is largely adult-controlled. As they grow from infants to toddlers, however, children can begin to take an increasingly active role in their own care routines.

Nonmobile infants are apt to lie fairly still for the diapering and washing process. As they lie there, they are often content to simply gaze at their caregiver's face or some nearby interesting object. They may also smile, imitate simple sounds the caregiver makes, grasp her finger, or hold some easily grasped object, such as a rattle or a small wooden spoon. Infants, like Josh (p. 226), enjoy hearing a simple diaper-changing song about themselves.

Enjoying their newfound mobility, older infants tend to move around a lot during their bodily care routines. They may roll back and forth, kick their legs, or put their toes in their mouth as Sydney does (p. 226). They may reach for and try to grasp their caregiver's hair, glasses, or shirt—or any appealing thing within reach. Given a clean washcloth or a clean diaper to hold, an older infant may drop it over his or her own face, then pull it away, initiating a game of peek-a-boo. During diapering and washing, children at this stage also take great pleasure in interacting with their caregiver in other simple games, such as playing "This little piggy . . ." on the toes, tickling, dropping the diaper or any other handy object, or pointing to body parts ("Where's Sydney's nose? . . . There it is!")

By the time they can walk, young toddlers often actively resist the idea of lying still on their back for any length of time, especially just for a diaper change! Climbing up and down the steps of the changing table seems to make up for some of this temporary constraint. To have *some* control over their own diapering-washing-dressing process, young toddlers need to take as much action on their own behalf as possible—using their own washcloth or towel and picking out which diaper, diaper cover, or clean clothing to wear. They enjoy communicating in a give-and-take manner, as Zar does when he and his caregiver take turns saying "Balloon!" and "Lots of balloons!" (p. 227) and playing hiding games. As a further example, during Zar's diaper change on another day, he holds a baby wipe tightly in his fist and says "Gone" to caregiver Annie. "Oh, dear," Annie replies, "Zar's wipe is all gone!" Zar opens his fist and, with a big smile, reveals the missing baby wipe. "There it is!" exclaims Annie. Again, Zar closes his fist around the wipe, and they repeat the same action sequence and interchange several more times.

Older toddlers are quite involved in their own bodily care routines and often refuse help: "Me do it!" They can take off their own diapers, shoes, socks, pants, and shirt; wash their own hands and face by themselves at the sink; and fetch their own clean clothes and diapers. Toward the end of their second year, many older toddlers, like Misha and Misty (p. 227), take an interest in sitting on the potty or toilet and passing the time there with an interesting picture book or magazine.

How Caregivers Support Children During Bodily Care Routines

While going through the routines of children's bodily care, caregivers try to share control with children as much as possible by following child cues and finding ways for the infant or toddler to take an active part in the task at hand. Being mindful of the following specific strategies is helpful in carrying out this role:

- Fit bodily care around the child's exploration and play.

- Focus on the child at hand during the care routine.

- Give the child choices about parts of the routine.

- Encourage the child to do things for her- or himself.

Fit bodily care around the child's exploration and play

In an active learning setting, caregivers approach bodily care routines from a child's perspective. This means first of all respecting whatever the child is already doing at the time bodily care becomes necessary. Instead of swooping down and briskly carrying a child off to the changing table for an efficient diaper change and hand washing, for example, first try to enter the child's

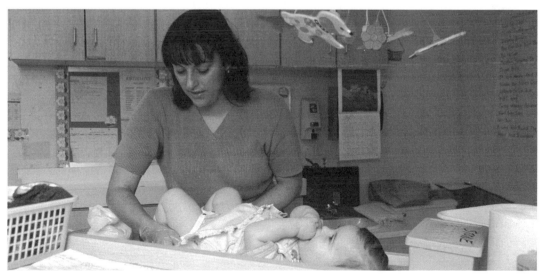

This caregiver waits for a natural pause in the child's play before carrying him off for a diaper change.

current experience. Although bodily care will disrupt that experience, it is possible to lessen the impact of this disruption by giving children some advance indication of their need for a diaper change or potty break and then giving them some time to come to a stopping point in their play.

Young infants busily exploring materials may not understand what you are saying to them about an upcoming diaper change, but how you act and speak may make a difference:

> *"Josh, I see you holding that silk scarf and watching it move," says caregiver Isobel. She watches him wave the scarf and follow it with his eyes. "I'm going to take your scarf so I can pick you up," she says, to let him know what is going to happen next. "Then we'll go to the changing table for a diaper change." Although Josh is reluctant to give up his scarf, he nestles comfortably into Isobel's arms, reassured by her interest in his actions, warm tone of voice, and gentle touch. After his diaper change, Isobel brings Josh back to his blanket on the floor. "Here you are with a clean diaper, and there's your scarf," Isobel says as Josh reaches for the scarf.*

Older infants and toddlers at play begin to understand what you are saying:

> *"Zar, I can see that you are stacking up the blocks," says Annie as she watches him balance a column of small, colored wooden blocks. "After a few more blocks, we need to go to the changing table to change your diaper." Zar looks up toward the changing table and back to his blocks. "You can come back to the blocks after your diaper change," she reassures him. Zar adds several more blocks to his stack, then, while holding a block in one hand, he reaches for Annie's hand with the other and heads with her to the changing table. After Zar, still holding his block, climbs down from the changing table in his clean diaper, Annie says, "There you go, Zar, back to the blocks!"*

Gradually, children begin to fully realize that although they have to interrupt their play, they can play a bit more before stopping, and after their care routines, they can return to what they were doing. Some children, like Zar with his block, carry a toy along to the changing table as a solid reminder of the play they wish to continue.

Focus on the child at hand during the care routine

Although infants and toddlers cannot read words, they can read people. They distinguish between caregivers who regard bodily care as distasteful or a drudgery and those who take pleasure in interacting with them during bodily care. When caregivers understand the impact of their interactions with children, they give their major attention to the child they are diapering, dressing, washing, or assisting in the bathroom. They know that this genuine interest in the child strengthens the child-caregiver bond and the child's feelings of trust and security.

One way to focus on the child during bodily care is for the two of you to *make lots of eye contact*. This allows you to make sense of what the child is communicating through every expression, action, or gesture. It also lets the child see and read your face and have the sense of commanding and holding your attention. When Sydney puts his toes in his mouth, he is aware that caregiver Melissa sees him do it (p. 226). She watches his actions closely instead of continually gazing out over the rest of the room as her hands go through the motions of diapering. Because she watches and responds to his actions, Sydney knows he has her attention and energetically plays "This little piggy . . ." with her during his diaper change.

Focusing on the child includes *responding to child cues*. Infants and toddlers rely greatly on nonverbal communication and depend on caregivers to understand what they are saying, as caregiver Melissa does in this scenario:

Before a diaper change, it's fun to play a mirror game!

One morning during his diaper change, Sydney feels like playing the game of putting toes in the mouth and having his other foot tickled by Melissa. Later that day, however, he's really sleepy and lies quietly with his hand on Melissa's as she changes his diaper. Even though they both enjoyed playing the "toesie" game earlier in the day, Melissa sees that Sydney's mood has changed and that what he really wants now is to fall asleep in his crib. As she changes his diaper, she softly sings him a lullaby.

A similar example would be this one involving Zar who, on one day (see p. 227), plays the balloon game with Annie, his caregiver, as she changes his diaper:

The next day, Zar lets Annie know that he really wants to get back to the sand table as quickly as possible. He wiggles around so he can see the sand table, points in that direction, and says "Down! Down!" "Let's get this diaper changed quickly," Annie says as she removes his soiled diaper, "so you can get back to the sand!"

And in another example, some days, Misha (p. 227), who is learning to use the potty, lets caregiver Carla know that he wants her to stay near him in the bathroom. Other days he tells her, "Go there!"—so she moves away from him to stand in the bathroom doorway. (See "When Toddlers Use the Potty or Toilet: Tips for Caregivers" on the facing page.)

Focusing on the child also involves *talking about what you and the child are doing*. Caregivers can comment on what they see and understand about the child they are changing, washing, or dressing. ("Oh, Sydney, you've put your 'toesies' in your mouth!" "You really know how to wash your cheeks, Maria!" "Yes, you see balloons, Zar, lots of balloons!" "You're looking at the book about farm animals, Aura!" "Your diaper is still dry, Misha!" "You took off your own diaper, Misha!") Older children understand these comments and know that their caregivers are interested in them. Very young children may not understand exactly what their caregiver is saying, but they know that her actions and words are concerned with them.

Give the child choices about parts of the routine

With the help of supportive caregivers, children can make choices within each bodily care routine. For example, a child wearing cloth diapers can choose which type of diaper pins to use—the ones with the yellow bunnies on the end or the ones with the green frogs—and whether to wear the purple or the orange protective pants. A child in disposable diapers can hold a clean diaper in each hand and decide which one to give to the caregiver to put on. Children can choose which washcloth to use, or whether they want to use a cloth or a disposable wipe on their face and hands. Like the older toddlers in Joan and Pam's group (p. 227), children can decide whether or not to sit on the potty and whether to sit on the potty or the toilet. Such simple decisions may seem insignificant to adults, but they involve infants and toddlers as active players rather than passive recipients and give them a sense of being in charge of their own bodily care.

Another way to give children choices during bodily care is through the physical environment. How you set up the dressing and diapering area and bathroom determines what choices children have about what to look at or watch during bodily care. A strategically located mirror, a window, or a rotating display of family photographs, pictures, art reproductions, plants, or weavings, for example, can provide children with a range of choices about what to look at when they are not gazing at their caregiver or putting their toes in their mouth. For example,

> *Sean, a young infant, lies on his back on the changing table, sees his reflection in the mirror on the wall next to him, and makes cooing noises at his own image. "There you are in the mirror, Sean," his caregiver says during a pause between coos, "getting your diaper changed!"*

Since infants and toddlers are sensory-motor learners, even during bodily care routines they like to have something in their hands to see up close, feel, mouth, smell, or listen to. Provide infants with some choice about what to hold: You might offer a choice between holding a clean diaper or a small clean washcloth for example, or you can provide a basket of small objects to choose from (a set of metal measuring spoons, a rubber squeaker toy, a rattle, a small board book). The objects should be compact so children can hold on to them with one hand without putting them in contact with bodily waste. If contact does occur, however, simply put the object aside for a thorough sanitizing before returning it to the basket. Provide these same kinds of choices for toddlers, though they may also decide to bring some toy from their play along with them to the changing

When Toddlers Use the Potty or Toilet: Tips for Caregivers

1. **Follow children's cues.**
   Children will let you know by their words and actions when they are interested in sitting on the potty or toilet or trying to wear underpants in place of diapers. Be alert to each child so you can support his or her efforts when the time is right.

2. **Coordinate with parents.**
   When you see that a child is interested in using the bathroom, share your observations with parents. Together, come up with a way to proceed that is as consistent as possible from home to child care setting.

3. **Be patient with children.**
   Children take their time learning any new skill, and using the toilet is a fairly complex one. Remember that each child will learn this skill at a personally comfortable pace. Pressure from adults can actually slow down the whole process. When accidental soiling occurs, treat it matter-of-factly, as you would any other problem children encounter during the day: "Looks like your pants are wet, Jacob. Let's go find your dry ones to put on."

table. As they are making their selection of an item to bring with them, help them find something that is not too big and will not easily be soiled. The small block Zar brings to the changing table, for example, fits in his one hand. And on the potty, Misha reads a book he can easily hold by himself. Remember, too, that the objects children see and hold during bodily care may spark conversation:

> *"Twee," says Jill, pointing to a postcard she is holding during her diaper change. "You see a tree on your postcard," replies Shannon, her caregiver. "Birdy," continues Jill. "There's a birdy in the tree," comments Shannon.*

Encourage the child to do things for her- or himself

As they move toward independence, children assert their desire to do things for themselves. While their early attempts at bodily care are time-consuming and inefficient by adult standards, caregivers patiently support these attempts, just as they patiently support children in learning to feed themselves, stack their own blocks, and walk unassisted.

Bodily care routines provide ongoing opportunities for infants and toddlers to try out and practice self-help skills. Older infants can hold their clean diapers, washcloths, and small articles of clothing for the caregiver. Young toddlers enjoy using a washcloth to wipe their face and hands and climbing up the steps to the changing table. Many older toddlers will naturally insist on washing their own face and hands, brushing their teeth, pulling their own pants down and up again when they use the potty, putting their own arms in sleeves and legs in pants, pulling off their own socks and working at putting them on, getting their own clean clothes from their cubby or tub, putting on their own hats, and zipping their own zippers (with a little help in getting them started).

As children do more and more things for themselves, caregivers are freer to watch them in action and to appreciate and comment on their emerging skills: "I see you pushed your hand all the way through your coat sleeve, Misha," says his caregiver, Carla, as she holds his coat for him.

As children do more and more things for themselves, caregivers are freer to watch them in action and to appreciate and comment on their emerging skills.

Understanding Nap Time

Sue and Rosie's eight toddlers are busily engaged in their personal before-nap rituals: Lydia and Sam each pull off their socks, put them carefully under their cot, and then lie down, whereupon caregiver Sue sits down between their cots and lightly rubs each child's back. Sam sucks his thumb, and Lydia clasps her favorite stuffed bunny—both lie quietly on their cots. Jonah gets his pacifier from his cubbie, puts it in his mouth, and curls up on his cot for sleep. Colin lies holding his stuffed monkey and singing quietly to himself "Monkey, monkey, monkee! Monkey, monkey, mon-kee!" Colleen and Ida search the room for their "dollies." When they find them in their cubbies, they return with them to their cots. Colleen covers herself with her blanket, keeping her doll outside the blanket. Ida asks caregiver Rosie's help in covering herself and her doll. Lex, lying on his side, drives a small truck across his pillow. Teresa brings a basket of books to her cot and selects one to look at. Ten minutes later, all the toddlers are asleep but Teresa—she lies on her cot looking at books.

∾

Shawna, an older infant, rubs her eyes after midmorning snack and looks very sleepy. Pam, her caregiver, puts Shawna in her crib for a nap even though recently she hasn't been taking a morning nap. On this particular day, however, Pam is alert to Shawna's signs of tiredness, because Shawna has just returned to the center after a few days at home with a bad cold.

∾

This is Lamont's first day at the child care center. An older toddler, he plays energetically until midmorning, when he falls asleep on the floor in the block area. Although the other toddlers in the group no longer take a morning nap, caregiver Bonnie sets up a cot close to where Lamont is sleeping and gently lifts him onto it. There he sleeps soundly for about 45 minutes while the rest of the children continue to play around him. "Why he sleeping?" another toddler, Malika, asks Bonnie, pointing to Lamont on his cot. "This is Lamont's first day," she says, "and he's worn out!" "Night, night," says Malika, patting him softly on the back. Lamont does not stir. After lunch, Lamont naps again along with the rest of his peers.

∾

It is midafternoon. Four of the six young infants in Jenna and Barbara's care are still napping in their cribs. Lena, one of the infants awake, is having a bottle in caregiver Barbara's arms. As Hannah, one of the sleeping infants, begins to wake up, she fingers the edge of her favorite yellow "blankie" and catches the eye of her caregiver, Jenna, who smiles back at her. Hannah quickly covers her face with her blankie, then pulls it away. "Peek-a-boo" says Jenna every time Hannah's smiling face emerges from under the blanket. After several rounds of peek-a-boo, Jenna says to Hannah, "Okay, one more peek-a-boo, then it's time for a diaper change and a bottle!"

In the meantime, Lena finishes her bottle, and Barbara settles her on a blanket spread out on the floor and offers her a basket of interesting things to play with. Just then Zeke wakes up and starts crying furiously in his crib. Leaving Lena, who has chosen a wooden clothespin from her basket, Barbara moves to pick up Zeke and hold him in her arms, saying "I bet you're ready for your bottle right now!" She takes his bottle from the warmer, and he eagerly takes it with both hands and begins to suck on it.

Nap time occurs both on demand, when children tire, and as a regularly scheduled part of the day. This child has fallen asleep on her caregiver's lap. After a bit, her caregiver will gently move her to a crib to continue napping undisturbed.

Nap time in an infant-toddler program occurs both on demand, when children tire, and as a regularly scheduled part of the day. Naps provide the sleep and rest that are necessary for children's growth and development. Physiologically, sleep permits the brain to work at consolidating the maturational changes of the central nervous system (Kagan, Kearsley, and Zelazo, 1978). Like adults, tired children are often cranky and irritable; sleep helps restore their good nature. It also provides a quiet retreat from the intensely social demands of the group-care setting. In short, napping allows children to reenergize physically and emotionally for the next part of the day.

Although an infant or toddler may fall asleep anywhere in the center—in a caregiver's arms, in a cozy armchair, under the climber—caregivers usually move the child to continue and complete the nap in a cradle, basket, crib, or cot. In a group-care setting, this practice frees caregivers to attend to other wakeful children, protects the sleeping child from being stepped on by peers at play, and consistently provides each child with a personal, familiar sleeping place. (For a complete discussion of children's sleeping and napping places, see pp. 124–128.)

Toddlers, as they gain a stronger sense of self and a familiarity with the care setting, often express a particular preference about where to sleep. For example, a toddler may wish his cot to be close to a light source (for look-

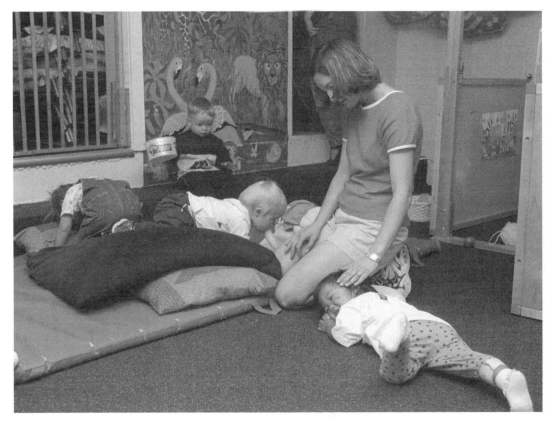

Sometimes, a brief rest in the midst of play is essential.

ing at books), near a particular caregiver, or alongside the cot of a special friend. Caregivers may also decide to use one area of the room for the cots of the children who tend to sleep longer and another area of the room for the cots of those who wake up first. The "early risers" might sleep closer, for example, to the bathroom, the book area, or the exit to outdoors.

For the most part, children in an infant-toddler program fall asleep at nap time. And if they do not sleep, they rest. Most infants take from two to three sleeping naps a day, whereas for older toddlers, one nap after lunch generally is enough. While most toddlers take either a long or a short sleeping nap, some get the rest they need by lying awake on their cots for some or all of their nap time, looking at books or busying themselves quietly with some chosen plaything.

How Caregivers Support Children During Nap Time

Caregivers respect and accommodate each child's need to sleep or rest when tired and to wake up on his or her own when rested. They use these specific strategies in doing so:

- Schedule nap time around each child's individual needs.
- Help children settle down to nap.
- Provide quiet alternatives for nonsleepers.
- Provide for children's various styles of waking up.

Schedule nap time around each child's individual needs

When children are involved throughout the morning in interesting and vigorous exploration both indoors and out, it makes sense to schedule an after-lunch nap time as part of the overall daily routine. However, with this predictable nap time in place, it is also very important to accommodate children's personal napping schedules, recognizing that a child's need for naps changes with age and personal circumstances. For example, when Shawna (p. 237) returns to the center after an illness, her caregivers anticipate her continued need for extra sleep, and Pam is not surprised to see Shawna rubbing her eyes in the middle of the morning. "You're still working on getting over that cold," she says to Shawna. "I'm going to tuck you into your crib for a nap so you'll feel better." Nor is Bonnie (p. 237) surprised that Lamont, though one of the older toddlers, falls asleep before lunch on his first day at the center. Instead of expecting him to conform to the routine that works for the other toddlers, she accepts his tiredness as an indication of the energy he is pouring into his new venture.

Talk with and listen to parents when they arrive with their children. They will let you know when to anticipate a change in children's sleep patterns: "Ola was up late last night with his cousins. He may need an extra nap today!" "Seraya fussed all through the night. I think it's her teeth." "I had a hard time getting Lukas up this morning. He wanted to stay asleep, then he fell asleep in the car on the way here."

Help children settle down to nap

Once it is clear to them that it is nap time, infants and toddlers develop their own rituals for falling asleep. Some infants fall asleep as soon as they are in their own familiar crib or cradle. Some fuss, and to settle into sleep, they may need their caregiver to rock, stroke, or pat them and perhaps sing them a little song. Other infants suck their thumb or pacifier, clutch a blanket or stuffed pet, or wiggle and squirm until they find a comfortable sleeping

Children have individual ways of settling down for a nap. Soon, however, everyone is in conventional sleeping position.

position. Toddlers continue to need personal attention as they settle down for naps. Some toddlers may request a back-rub or a song. Others may need help or simply acknowledgment as they choose a book to look at on their cot, locate the special blanket or toy they want to sleep with, or get a drink of water. Over time, through observation, trial and error, and tips from parents, you can discover how to help each child settle down to nap.

Provide quiet alternatives for nonsleepers

During their regularly scheduled after-lunch nap time, some toddlers may occasionally or routinely remain awake for some or all of the time. This presents another opportunity for choice. Caregivers Sue and Rosie, for example, expect their children to rest on their cots during the nap time, but they can choose a book or a toy to use as they rest. On the day described on p. 237, each of the toddlers except Sam has brought something to bed—a favorite stuffed bunny, a pacifier, a stuffed monkey, a "dolly," a small truck, a basket of books. After 10 minutes, all the children are asleep except Teresa, who looks at books. And on some days, even Teresa sleeps.

In another center, caregivers Lynne and Elba have four toddlers who routinely sleep for about 2 hours and four who rest or sleep for only an hour or less. Upon waking, the four "short nappers" have the choice of playing in the book area, the toy area, or the art area—all areas of quiet activity, located the farthest away from the "long nappers." And on some days, after all the short nappers are awake, they go outdoors with one of the caregivers.

Here are two alternatives to actually sleeping at nap time—"reading" books, or playing with toys next to the toy shelf!

Provide for children's various styles of waking up

Some children awake from a nap happy and ready to get on with their day. Some are fussy, unsure of where they are, and in need of physical contact and comfort—being rocked in the rocking chair, taking a trip in a caregiver's arms to look out the window. Others wake slowly and are content to lie on their cot or in their crib for a few minutes, just watching the afternoon unfold and reorienting themselves to their surroundings.

Caregivers provide comfort and contact as needed, interact with children during after-nap bodily care, and begin the next part of the day—snack, outside time, choice time, for example—in such a way that children are free to join in gradually as they awake and feel ready.

Understanding Choice Time

Ike, a young nonmobile infant, lies on his back on a blanket. He kicks his legs and waves his arms, then stills and reaches for a small cloth ball that lies near him. He grasps the ball, brings it to his mouth, chews on it for a bit, and lets it go. He sees a wooden spoon on his blanket, grasps it in his hand, then lets it go. He turns his head back toward the ball, which has rolled just out of his reach, and he reaches toward it. El, his caregiver, is seated near him on the floor and gently pushes the ball in his direction. Ike grasps it and brings it to his mouth, where he holds it with both hands. He turns for several minutes to watch Aisha, the baby on the blanket next to his, then turns back to his ball.

∾

At choice time, Shelley and Nick, two infants in the creeper-crawler stage, sit on the floor on either side of a basket. The basket contains small rocks, balls of yarn, postcards and greeting cards with colorful pictures, pieces of lightweight metal chain, a set of metal measuring cups, and an empty oatmeal box. Nick pulls out a ball of yarn, drops it, watches it roll away from him, then crawls after it. Shelly dips a length of chain in and out of a measuring cup, then tries the same thing with the chain and the oatmeal box.

∾

During choice time, T.C., an older infant, crawls toward a "platform" that is actually a large, low, corrugated carton covered in red Con-Tact paper. As T.C. crawls along, the small

Throughout choice time, no matter where she is, this toddler shows a preference for playing with connecting blocks.

wooden block he holds in one hand makes a bumping sound each time it hits the carpet. When he reaches the red platform, he crawls onto it, arranges himself in a sitting position, and with a big smile on his face, bangs his wooden block against the box-platform to make a hollow thumping sound. "You're banging the box with your block, T.C.!" says Anne, his caregiver. T.C. laughs and keeps banging. She moves three similar blocks over next to his platform so they are within his reach. "Maybe you would like to have a block for your other hand," she comments. T.C. pauses, looks at the additional blocks, selects one, and bangs both blocks on the platform.

At the water table, two young toddlers, Sarah and Micah, stand side by side dropping stones and shells into sieves. Sandy, a caregiver, joins the children at the table. Kneeling down, she too begins to drop objects into a sieve, selecting only shells and looking at each shell carefully as she does so. "Shell!" Micah says, handing a shell to Sandy. "Thanks for the shell, Micah!" she says, adding it to the others in her sieve. Observing this interaction, Sarah digs down into the shells at the bottom of the table, comes up with one, and offers it to Sandy, saying "S'ell." "Thanks for the shell, Sarah," says Sandy.

Matt, a toddler, and Joan, his caregiver, sit on the floor facing each other. Matt rolls three balls toward Joan, who rolls them back to him. After 10 minutes or so, Matt leaves the balls and heads for the dress-up clothes in the house area. He selects a shirt and takes it to Joan for help with putting it on. As Joan holds the shirt while Matt slips his arms into the sleeves, she asks, "Where you are going in your shirt, Matt?" In reply, Matt goes to the water table, where toddlers Sarah and Micah (from the preceding scenario) are playing with shells. He watches them, then puts a shell in Micah's sieve. Micah takes it out of the sieve, looks at it, puts it back, then looks up and smiles at Matt.

During choice time, Magali sits on the floor in sight of Sharelle, Kevin, Maurice, and Dierdre, the four toddlers in her care. Sharelle scrambles up the ladder climber, pauses to look at herself in the mirror mounted on the wall behind the climber,

This child selects a variety of materials to explore and play with at choice time—a lidded food container, a book, a pan and spatula, a toy workbench.

then scoots back down again. Then she calls out Magali's name ("Gali"), climbs up the ladder again, and turns at the top to make sure Magali sees what she is doing. "Sharelle, you climbed up the ladder, and now you're at the top!" Magali observes. Over in the book corner, Kevin looks at the big book about cars and trucks. Maurice, who is at the table in the art area, scribbles with a red crayon on a big sheet of paper. Dierdre takes all the food out of the house area's refrigerator and arranges it on the table, then sits on a stool beside the table and pretends to eat. In the meantime, Kevin brings his book over to Magali, plops down in her lap, and says "Read!" As Magali reads, Dierdre leaves the house area and also climbs onto Magali's lap to hear the story. "So, you want to hear the story, too, Dierdre!" says Magali.

Choice time is a sustained block of time when infants and toddlers can investigate and explore materials and actions and interact with their peers and caregivers. In a supportive and safe environment that affords interesting materials and opportunities as well as space to move in various ways, each child chooses what to do based on personal interests, inclinations, and level of development. Choice time provides children with a virtually uninterrupted period of exploration and play.

A great deal of learning occurs at choice time. Through their self-chosen sensory-motor explorations, infants and toddlers engage in key learning experiences: filling and emptying, putting in and taking out, discovering that objects still exist when out of sight, repeating an action to make something happen again, and so forth. As they interact with people and materials, children construct knowledge about representation, movement, communication, objects, early quantity and number, space, and time. In group care, choice time takes place within a rich social context, so children have the opportunity to watch others at exploration and play, imitate their actions, and build relationships with others. They can also communicate their frustrations and triumphs to attentive, interactive caregivers.

Caregivers familiar with the High/Scope preschool approach may recognize choice time as the infant-toddler version of work time, when High/Scope preschoolers pursue activities

"Uh-oh! Now what?" In a very basic way, choice time promotes children's sense of themselves as doers, decision-makers, and problem solvers.

of their own choosing. Unlike the preschool work time, choice time for infants and young toddlers is not flanked by a time for planning and a time for recalling. However, older toddlers may begin to plan and recall once they are able to hold mental images and thus think about what they want to do or have done. In a very basic way,

Nonmobile infants make their choices from an array of materials they can reach. They are also interested in the actions of the older children!

choice time promotes infants' and toddlers' sense of themselves as doers, decision-makers, and problem solvers. By carrying out their own initiatives, they learn how to make things happen. They discover they can choose where to crawl; what to climb; what to mouth, stack, or carry; and whose hand to hold. This time of being fully in charge of these decisions forms the heart of the infant's or toddler's day in a High/Scope program.

The segment of the day called choice time takes place in the thoughtfully equipped and arranged infant and toddler indoor play spaces described in Chapter 3, on pp. 132–139 and 141–158. (As we discuss later in this chapter, outside time is also a children's choice time, but in an outdoor setting.)

Throughout choice time, infants and toddlers move about, explore materials and actions, and play near and with peers and caregivers. They do all of this at their own pace, according to their individual interests and abilities.

Nonmobile infants make their choices from an array of appealing materials caregivers place within their reach. They grasp, wave, mouth, drop, coo, or babble at whatever they have chosen—a wooden rattle, a woolen ball, a silk scarf. They try out and explore such physical actions as stretching, kicking, rolling, turning over, and looking at themselves in a mirror. They also sometimes stop to watch other infants and older children and to perhaps babble or gesture toward them or cry (if, for example, they see another child crying).

The choices and possibilities for exploration and play are greater for mobile infants. They may sit next to and explore baskets containing commonplace treasures (for example, a lemon, a wooden spoon, metal keys on a ring, a tennis ball). They may crawl or creep to a shelf of books or toys and choose one to examine. They may carry things in their mouth or hand as they crawl, or they might sit beside a shallow pan and dabble in water or pat sand. They may decide to crawl up and down a gently sloping ramp or to pull up to a standing position by taking hold of various fixtures or furnishings. As they move about the play space, they may seek another child to sit or stand next to, watch, or play beside. They might choose to interact with a caregiver in a simple game of peek-a-boo, drop the spool, or bang the blocks.

Toddlers engage in increasingly complex exploration and play. For example, they look at books and identify familiar people, animals, and objects in pictures; stack, topple, and carry blocks; maneuver toy trucks, cars, motorcycles, and animals; work with puzzles and pegboards; scribble, tear, and paint; dress up, play house, and push their baby dolls in buggies or carts; throw balls, climb, slide, and crawl into cartons and tunnels. As they grow in awareness of themselves and others, younger toddlers begin to initiate social behaviors, such as hugging and patting another child to show affection, bringing a toy or comfort item to another child, or playing a game of peeking at another child through the window in the climber. Older toddlers can address one another by name and make simple requests of peers: "Ben, me [want] car." They try out the actions of a child playing nearby. For example, when Marie fits pegs in a pegboard, Alana joins her with another pegboard. As Alana starts to sing "Row, Row, Row Your Boat" while putting pegs into *her* board, Marie sings along with her. The two girls enjoy doing things together—going down adjacent slides, playing together in the rocking boat, scaling the climber side by side, painting next to each other, using telephones together. As they begin to have a strong sense of "me" and "mine," toddlers also tend to engage in social conflict. And, as they begin to be able to hold mental images, some toddlers may, when asked, indicate what they plan to do: They may point to the art area when they want to explore with play dough, for example, or say "balls" before they run to find some balls to play with.

How Caregivers Support Children During Choice Time

During children's choice time, caregivers make themselves physically and emotionally available to observe and interact with them. At the same time, they respect children's need to explore and play at their own pace with people and materials of particular interest to them. The following strategies are all part of this role:

- Pay close attention to children as they explore and play.

- Tailor your actions and responses to follow children's leads and ideas.

- Engage in communication give-and-take with children.

- Support children's interactions with peers.

- Use a problem-solving approach to children's social conflicts.

- Offer older toddlers opportunities to plan and recall.

- Encourage toddlers to put materials away after choice time.

Pay close attention to children as they explore and play

As they venture out to explore the physical and social world, infants and toddlers depend on caregivers to see and understand what they are doing and to provide the support, encouragement, and assurance they need. A caregiver's attentive, responsive presence during choice time assures infants and toddlers of the immediate availability of a known and trusted adult. Caregivers also benefit when they pay attention to children. It allows them to enter the child's world; see each child's strengths, interests, and temperament; attune themselves to each child's pace and interests; and collect anecdotal information that guides the way they support, plan, and advocate for the children in their care.

Literally joining children at their level in the play space lends an important physical dimension to paying them "close attention." In High/Scope active learning settings, caregivers find themselves crawling along on hands

In the presence of a trusted adult, this child is free to explore. Her caregiver, in turn, has the opportunity to enter the child's world and witness her persistence with these small blocks.

and knees with the creeper-crawler, kneeling next to the cruiser, lying on the floor near the baby who is stretched out on a blanket, peeking into a tunnel as toddlers crawl through it, squatting next to toddlers playing at the sand table. A caregiver might sit on the floor with a lapful of children, sit on a small chair at a low table as children scribble and mold play dough, or serve as a leaning post for a child who is learning to sit or stand or cruise.

If you assume vantage points such as these, you will find that you can readily see, hear, and touch the children in your care. Once you are down on the floor and physically close to children, watch and listen carefully in an attempt to understand what individual children are doing and communicating. Carefully consider each child's choices and intentions so you can interact and respond in a meaningful way. This is better than swooping down on a child with new and possibly unrelated ideas, which may actually be disruptive to what the child is doing. Anne (p. 243), for example, watches T.C. crawl and climb onto the platform with his block in hand, but she doesn't understand what he has in mind until he proudly starts to bang the hollow platform with his block.

Watching exploration and play unfold allows an accessible caregiver to be ready with any needed comfort and contact. For example, from time to time, as very young children explore and play at choice time, they momentarily lose their nerve and may search out a touch, hug, or cuddle or a lap to sit on before returning to their chosen activity. Caregivers have often witnessed, for example, the event of a creeper-crawler climbing into his or her caregiver's lap for refuge when a loud toddler pushing a big truck huffs by. Or consider this scenario of a child in need of contact and reassurance:

> *Jason, a toddler, is sucking his thumb while he has his other arm wrapped around his caregiver's leg. He is watching two children molding clay at the art table. His caregiver kneels down, slips her arm around him, and says, "Jason, it looks like you're watching the kids with the clay." He nods in agreement. "Shall we go to the art table and work with some clay too?" she asks. He nods yes, takes her hand, and leads her to the art table.*

Tailor your actions and responses to follow children's leads and ideas

Throughout choice time, children make a series of spontaneous choices and decisions. By tailoring your actions and responses to follow children's cues, you acknowledge and respect children's intentions, which shift and change over the course of their explorations and play. When their caregivers heed, respond to, and build on children's communications and actions—instead of ignoring or overriding them—children retain a sense of control over what is happening. By taking this nondirective but participatory approach, you also have the opportunity to gain insight into children's thinking and reasoning.

When caregivers heed and respond to children's communications and actions, children retain a sense of control over what is happening.

Often, the cues infants and toddlers offer are expressed not in words, but in actions, gestures, or facial expressions. For example, when Ike's ball rolls away from him (p. 243), he is too young to crawl after it or to say "Hey, I want my ball back!" Instead, he conveys this message to El, his caregiver, by turning his head and reaching toward the ball. From her attentive position next to him, El reads his gestures, gets the message, and rolls the ball back within his reach.

In another situation, caregiver Sandy joins toddlers Sarah and Micah at the water table (p. 245). Watching the children put rocks and shells into their sieves, Sandy follows their lead by imitating their actions—with a slight variation. When Sandy begins to select *only shells* for her sieve, the toddlers find this of interest and spontaneously begin to say "shell" each time they offer her another shell. Sarah and Micah continue their play and include Sandy in it, because instead of attempting to redirect or restructure their play, Sandy follows their idea and builds on what they are already doing. At the same time, Sandy learns about Sarah's and Micah's ability to distinguish shells from stones and to name objects they have chosen. She recognizes this ability as the **exploring objects** key experience *exploring and noticing how things are the same or different*.

Older toddlers often indicate that they want to do things for themselves. At choice time, it is not unusual for them to push away a helping hand or to say "Me do it!" as they try to fit puzzle pieces together, take the top off a container, wrap a baby doll in a blanket, stack objects that repeatedly topple over, fit shapes into a sorting box, or try to climb into a low carton and get stuck with one leg hanging over the side. In these situations, caregivers respect children's initiatives and their desire to figure things out on their own. They simply remain attentively present and offer the children encouragement by describing what they see. ("You're turning that block a lot of different ways to try to fit it in the slot, Chris.") If the child is becoming too frustrated, a caregiver might offer a suggestion ("Sometimes when I wrap a baby doll, I put her on the floor") or might offer some physical support, for example, holding a bottle still while the child unscrews its cap. Although toddlers' problem-solving attempts are often awkward, time-consuming, and difficult for caregivers to witness, it is clear that most children take great pleasure in solving these toddler-sized problems on their own with a minimum of help.

Following children's leads and ideas calls for you to be observant, patient, flexible, and open to the child's viewpoint. It also calls for resisting the urge to jump in with a set agenda based on preconceived ideas of what an infant or toddler of a specific age does or should be doing.

Engage in communication give-and-take with children

At choice time, caregivers in a High/Scope active learning setting communicate in an even give-and-take manner with infants and toddlers in both conversation and play. This means encouraging the child to set the pace and to freely contribute to each interchange, and it means matching, not ignoring or overriding, the child's contributions. This allows them to share control with the children and to model the partnership of everyday social exchange.

Before they learn to talk, infants and toddlers keep up their end of the conversation with sounds, gestures, and actions. Caregivers, in turn, incorporate children's nonverbal contributions into their part of the conversation. The following examples illustrate some exchanges between caregivers and nonverbal children at choice time:

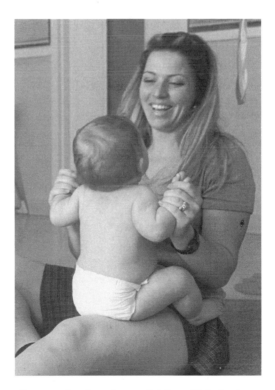

Communication give-and-take with infants involves the exchange of sounds, gestures, and actions.

> *Aneesha, a young infant, lies on her back, touching her stuffed lamb and cooing to it. Still touching her lamb, she turns to smile at Elba, her caregiver, and then smacks her lips at Elba. In return, Elba smiles at Aneesha, imitates her lip-smacking, and says, "I see you, Aneesha!" Aneesha wiggles and smacks her lips again. Elba, in turn, smacks her own lips and says to Aneesha, "You like to smack your lips!" Aneesha wiggles, then turns her attention back to her lamb.*

Bryce sits on the floor, dropping chestnuts into one of two empty tin buckets. At one point he stops and, catching the eye of Cora, his caregiver, drops another chestnut into the bucket with a clatter; then he laughs. In return, Cora picks up a chestnut and drops it into the other bucket. They repeat this chestnut-dropping exchange until Bryce finally turns away from Cora and focuses his attention on patting down his bucket full of chestnuts.

∾

From his perch at the top of the climber, toddler Ethan drops a rubber ball over the rail. He watches where the ball finally comes to rest on the floor, then climbs down to retrieve it, and scrambles back up the climber with it. He then throws it down again, this time looking at caregiver Brandon and making the sound "ffwiiisssss" as he throws it. "Ffwiissss," says Brandon, "there goes the ball!" They repeat this exchange several times as Ethan goes through the same action sequence over and over again until he finally tires.

Older toddlers like Sarah and Micah (p. 245) incorporate words into their exchanges. Note that each time Sarah or Micah says the single word "shell," Sandy, their caregiver, makes a reply that is relatively short as well ("Thanks for the shell"). By making a short reply, Sandy matches the child's contribution instead of burying Sarah or Micah in a barrage of words. Consider another situation at choice time:

Caregiver Sylvia watches Jamie paint on a large sheet of paper on the art area table. Jamie stabs his brush at the paper over and over again. As he pauses to examine the resulting splotches of color, he says "Feets!" "It looks like you made feet on your paper," observes Sylvia. "More feets!" Jamie says, as he selects a new brush and a new color and resumes making splotches. "You're making more feet," says Sylvia. Jamie is too engrossed in painting to respond to this second observation, and Sylvia does not press him to do so.

While these conversational exchanges may seem brief and mundane, they are examples of how adults respect the style and pace of the children involved. Notice that Jamie's caregiver does not try to press her point or prolong the conversation with such questions as "Do you like playing with paint?" and "Are you having fun?" and "What color are you using?" Toddlers need time to find the language that fits with their actions. Questions often pressure children to respond to subjects they may not be inclined toward at the moment and tend to disrupt children's actions or thought processes. Con-

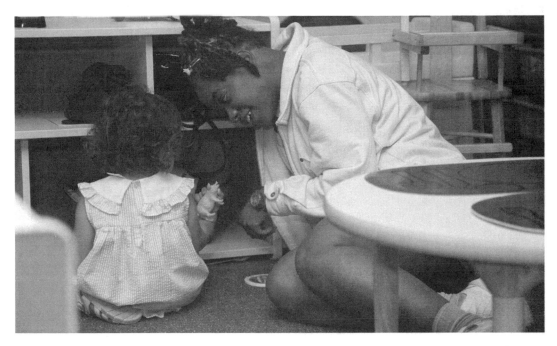

Toddlers need time to find the language that fits with their actions, so caregivers spend a lot of time patiently listening—in this case, the conversation is about pigs!

sequently, when questioned by an adult, children many times ignore the question or even leave what they are doing (perhaps to get away from the questions and the questioner). In fact, caregiver questions can interfere with communication give-and-take, whereas caregiver comments, observations, and acknowledgments tend to keep conversational exchanges going. (For research that supports these findings, see Wood, McMahon, and Cranstoun, 1980, pp. 71–81.)

Support children's interactions with peers

In group care, choice time takes place within a social context. Though infants and toddlers often choose to engage in solitary pursuits, they also take the opportunity to observe, play alongside, and imitate their peers. By thoughtfully supporting these early bids at social interaction, you can help children to form positive peer relationships and to see themselves and others as members of a community.

Caregivers in infant-toddler settings find that given the opportunity, even very young children may exhibit interest in one another. For example, putting a pair of nonmobile infants on their back close together on the floor at choice time allows them to enjoy each other's company. The two infants will often communicate their interest in each other through wiggling; turning their heads toward each other; and exchanging gazes, smiles, coos, and babbles. If one cries, the other cries. One of the pair may become less animated or even sad when his or her special "blanket-mate" is out of sight or at home for the day. As caregivers pay close attention to certain pairs of infants, they gently comment on the social interactions they see: "Meagan, you're watching Lu." "I'll bet you miss Rabb today, Jack. He's home with a cold."

In group care, choice time takes place within a social context. Though infants and toddlers often choose to engage in solitary pursuits, they also like to observe, play alongside, and imitate their peers.

Caregivers continue to watch for and acknowledge peer preferences as infants begin to creep and crawl and to pull themselves up to stand. At choice time, these infants will often use their newfound mobility to seek the company of a particular child, as in this scenario:

> *Toddler James deliberately chooses to sit on the floor and explore materials next to another toddler, Tab, and he even makes a friendly but unsuccessful attempt to touch the wire whisk Tab is examining with his hands and mouth. When Tab finally gives up his whisk, crawls over to the sofa, and pulls himself up to a standing position, James abandons his basket of household items, crawls after Tab, and pulls himself up to stand at the other end of the sofa. After a struggle, Tab climbs onto the sofa. James works very hard to climb onto the sofa, too. During a moment of rest, he looks over his shoulder at his caregiver, Marsha. "James," she says, recognizing his action and its social implications, "you're working very hard to climb onto the sofa with Tab."*

Caregivers support toddlers' peer interactions by providing equipment that allows children to play side by side: wide slides, climbers, and stairs; lots of table, floor, and easel space; rocking boats; cozy chairs and nooks with room for two. They provide two or more similar wheel toys, shovels, buckets, so children can play with such toys together and try out one another's actions with the toys. Finally, they provide play materials that two or three toddlers can gather around and still retain individual control of, such as play dough, sand and water, and finger paints.

When a toddler's attempt to connect with a peer goes unnoticed by the other child, an attentive caregiver can help bridge the gap by describing the child's attempt, as this scenario with toddlers Sasha and Nells illustrates:

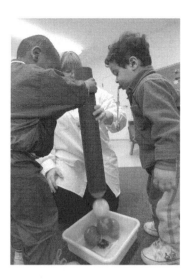

Caregivers support toddlers' peer interactions by providing materials several children can gather around and still individually control—like this large, lightweight tube and the balls that fit through it!

>   *Sasha is stacking the large cardboard blocks. Nells sees what Sasha is doing, gets two more blocks from the shelf, and puts them down in front of Sasha. When Sasha does not notice the blocks, caregiver Mona comments, "Nells, you brought some blocks for Sasha to use." At this, Sasha looks up, sees the blocks, and adds them to his stack. Nells goes back to the shelf for two more blocks. This time, as Nells approaches Sasha, he says "Blocks," puts them down, and adds one to the stack himself. Sasha looks up and adds the remaining block to the stack.*

By thoughtfully describing children's intentions toward their peers, caregivers can help to facilitate toddlers' attempts at social play.

Use a problem-solving approach to children's social conflicts

Toddlers are primed for social conflict! They are strong, mobile, and adept. They have a growing sense of possession ("Mine!") and a fixed belief in their own point of view. During the most peaceful choice time in a well-stocked setting, toddlers, with their gusto, emerging communication skills, and social inexperience, are bound to engage in disputes with peers over claims to space, materials, and even caregivers. At the same time, with adult support, they are usually capable of quickly settling their own disputes—possibly because they are so focused on the immediate present. Conflicts and disputes at choice time are opportunities to help toddlers find sociable alternatives to such negative behaviors as biting and grabbing. As described in Chapter 2 (pp. 87–90), calmly approach toddlers in conflict, stop hurtful actions,

This caregiver calmly works through the problem-solving process with two toddlers who want the same little plastic peg-figure. In the end, the children decide on having two figures apiece!

acknowledge children's feelings, gather information, engage toddlers in describing the problem and finding a solution, and offer follow-up support. Here is an example of these problem-solving strategies in action:

> *Colin and Justin, two older toddlers, stand in the block area. Colin holds a plastic figure of a firefighter that Justin is trying to take away from him. They struggle, becoming increasingly upset. Nancy, their caregiver, approaches calmly and kneels on the floor beside them. They stop struggling to look at her. "You look upset!" she says to the two children, stroking each one gently. Colin nods in agreement. "I **angry!**" Justin announces loudly. "So, you're **angry**," Nancy says to Justin, "and you're upset," she says to Colin. "You both want the firefighter," she continues, stating the problem as she sees it. Colin and Justin nod yes. "Let me hold the firefighter," she says to Colin, who then opens his hand, releasing his grip on the figure. Nancy takes it gently from him and holds it in her hand so both children can concentrate on the problem rather than the toy itself. "What can we do about this?" she asks the boys, seeking their ideas rather than offering her own. She wants them to think, and she knows that they will be far more interested in carrying out their own idea, rather than hers, for a solution. At first they look at her blankly, but after a minute or so, Colin says "Bambulance ban!" and heads off toward the toy shelf. He returns shortly with a figure of an ambulance driver (belonging to the same toy set as the firefighter). He hands his "ambulance man" to Justin, who takes it with a smile. "So, now Justin has the ambulance man," states Nancy. "I can give the firefighter back to Colin." Neither child disputes this. She hands the firefighter to Colin, and the two boys toddle off in different directions, each clutching his own toy figure. With their caregiver as mediator, they have solved the problem themselves.*

Offer older toddlers opportunities to plan and recall

Planning (thinking about what you are going to do before you do it) and recalling (remembering and reflecting on what you did after you did it) are intellectual processes that depend on the ability to imagine, to form mental images of materials, places, or actions. From High/Scope's work with older children, we know that 3-, 4-, and 5-year-olds are increasingly able to plan and recall—to think about their own future and past doings and to talk about and describe these thoughts. As older toddlers approach age 3, they are beginning to have ideas about what they want to do in the future and are developing the capacity to remember what they have done in the past. They communicate these intentions and recollections through a streamlined combination of gestures, actions, and key words.

Simple, brief times of planning and recalling with older toddlers help them to call up mental pictures of themselves in action, to connect their ideas with actions, to communicate their intentions to others, and to begin to organize their past actions into a simple narrative. This planning before children have started their exploration or play and recalling when they have come to a stopping point gives caregivers a chance to support children's emerging ability to think about future and past events.

Caregivers using the support strategies for choice time that are listed on pp. 249–250 are already supporting toddlers' planning and recalling as they describe what they see and hear children doing:

- "You're banging the box with your block, T.C.!"

- "Sharelle, you climbed up the ladder, and now you're at the top!"

- "You're turning that block a lot of different ways to try to fit it in the slot, Chris!"

- "Meagan, you're watching Lu."

- "James, you're working very hard to climb onto the sofa with Tab."

These descriptive statements help toddlers build the language to refer to their own actions and playthings. Eventually, with his caregiver providing a wide array of climbing choices and patiently describing what he is doing when he climbs, James, for example, as an older infant, begins to understand what it means to "climb." By the time he reaches later toddlerhood, based on his

One way to support older toddlers who may be starting to plan and recall is to briefly describe what you see them doing—"You're putting dinosaurs on blocks!"

broad range of experiences, James may well be able to picture himself climbing something before actually doing so. When his caregiver says at the beginning of choice time, "James, show me what you will play with at choice time today," he may point to the climber and say "Cwimb!" before heading off to put this simple, toddler-appropriate plan into action.

Caregivers plan and recall with individual toddlers when they see some signs that a child might be ready for and interested in this process. One sign is the child's ability to form mental images. In an active learning setting, infants and young toddlers accumulate a wealth of sensory-motor experience. Eventually, as older toddlers, they begin to be able to hold in mind pictures of these experiences. For example, Teri, a toddler, realizes when settling down for nap time that she does not have her favorite blanket with her. From her position lying on her cot, she cannot see the blanket, but she has a mental picture of it laying on the floor between the couch and the wall in the book area, where she last used it at choice time. Seeing that Teri can retrieve an unseen object by remembering its location,[9] Teri's caregiver knows that the toddler can hold an experience in mind and therefore may be ready to indicate a simple plan before going into action at choice time.

Other signs that a toddler may be ready to plan are the child's spontaneous actions and pronouncements. In the anecdote on p. 247, for example, Kevin brings his caregiver a book he has selected, plops down in her lap, and says "Read!" Through his actions and words, he lets her know that he has a pretty clear picture of what he (and she!) are about to do. In another situation, Jamie (p. 254) pauses to look at his painting, names his splotches "feets," then declares "more feets" before continuing to work on his idea with a new brush and new color. Saying "more feets" and selecting a new brush and color is his toddler shorthand for *Now I'm going to make some more feet using a different color.*

When a toddler like Teri, Kevin, or Jamie seems ready to plan, ask that child at the beginning of choice time (or perhaps during choice time—at the point of an activity change) a simple question about his or her intentions. It should be a question the child can answer with an action, gesture, or word. Here are examples of ways to begin:

> *"What will you play with, Jody?" Jody leans against her caregiver and looks around. "Can you show me something you'd like to play with?" asks her caregiver. Jody goes to the doll buggy, grabs the handle, and looks back at her caregiver, who nods and says, "You're going to play with the buggy." Jody pushes the buggy toward the house area.*

∽

---

[9] See the 1999 field test edition of the *High/Scope Child Observation Record (COR) for Infants and Toddlers,* item AA, level 5: "Child retrieves an unseen object by remembering its location."

Like planning, recalling is a brief, intimate caregiver-toddler exchange: "Something happened!" comments the caregiver. "Popped!" says the toddler to her caregiver, pointing to the pop-up box.

"Can you show me where you will play, Deno?" Deno points toward the block area. *"Oh, you're going to play in the block area,"* says his caregiver. Deno nods and heads for the shelf of wooden unit blocks.

～

"What will you do at choice time, Mimi?" Mimi sits in her caregiver's lap, removes her thumb from her mouth, points to a child drawing with markers on a large sheet of white paper, and says, *"Do that!"* *"Oh, you're going to draw with markers, like Elana,"* interprets her caregiver. Mimi nods and repeats, *"Do that!"* *"That's what you're going to do,"* affirms her caregiver. Mimi heads for the art area, selects a sheet of paper and a marker, and begins.

Note that planning with toddlers is a brief, intimate, one-to-one interaction. The caregiver kneels or sits on the floor next to the child, often putting an arm around the child or in some way offering comfortable physical contact. The child communicates a plan by using actions (pointing, nodding, looking at, or going to an object or place) and sometimes by saying a key word or two. When the caregiver translates the toddler's plan into a short verbal statement, it is a way of checking to make sure the child's intentions are understood. It's a good idea to ask toddlers about their plans for choice time when they are in a relatively open part of the play space, where it is easy for them to look around to see what their choices are.

Recalling with toddlers often begins quite spontaneously, like this, as children share home stories with their caregivers:

> *When he arrives in the morning, Kamari runs to his care-giver, saying "Puppy, puppy!" "Oh, Kamari," exclaims his care-giver, "you saw a puppy?" "Puppy Nama's," he explains. His mom nods, backing up his story. "You saw a puppy at your Nama's house?" asks his caregiver. "Lick me!" says Kamari. "And the puppy licked you!" responds his caregiver.*

This puppy story illustrates how recalling occurs because children, like adults, want to share the important things that happen to them with the im-portant people in their lives. The recalling about a toddler's activity might occur *during* choice time, as Jody leaves playing with the doll buggy to play with puzzles, for example. Or the recalling might occur *at the end of* choice time, as Deno is putting away some blocks. A caregiver may encourage a child to recall with a simple statement or question:

> *"I saw you pushing this doll buggy over to the climber, Jody," says her caregiver. She has joined Jody, who is now stand-ing next to the buggy but gazing across the room. Jody nods. "What did you do with the buggy?" asks her caregiver. "Babies," says Jody, patting the babies in the buggy. "You put babies in the buggy?" asks her caregiver. Jody nods yes. Then Jody takes her caregiver's hand, leads her across the room to the puzzle shelf, and says "Puzzles!" She is announcing her next plan. "Oh, so now you plan to play with puzzles," her caregiver says, interpreting Jody's new plan. Jody dumps out the three-piece duck puzzle and begins to move the pieces about.*

∾

> *"What did you do with the blocks, Deno?" his caregiver asks, as she and Deno stack the blocks on the shelf at the end of choice time. Deno raises his arm over his head and says "Up." "You stacked the blocks up. I remember—I saw you!" interprets his caregiver. "Up, up, up!" says Deno. "You stacked the blocks up, up, up!" his caregiver affirms.*

Like planning, recalling is a brief, intimate caregiver-toddler exchange. Either one—planning or recalling—may occur at almost any time of the day. At nap time, for example, Mimi sits on her cot, taking off her shoes and socks. She looks up and sees her drawing hanging on the wall. "Me do!" she says. When her caregiver sees what Mimi is looking at, she tries filling in the context for her story. "That's the picture you drew in the art area today." "Me draw!" agrees Mimi, making drawing motions with her arm. "You moved your arm back and forth just like that to draw," comments her caregiver.

The idea behind planning and recalling with older toddlers is to provide them the opportunity to think about what they are going to do and what they have done and to express these thoughts in their own particular blend of actions and words. To do so, each child needs individual support from an attentive caregiver and freedom to get started on his or her plan right away. (For some toddlers who are approaching 3 years of age and playing in small groups, planning and recalling might take place with a group of two or three.)

Encourage toddlers to put materials away after choice time

Toddlers exhibit a number of developmental characteristics that enable them to participate in the process of putting things away at the end of choice time. Because they like water and are interested in imitating adults and using adult tools, they see washing the paint off the art table as an enjoyable activity, not a chore. Also, toddlers like to fill and empty containers, so putting balls back into the ball tub or shells into the shell basket is as satisfying as taking them out! Because toddlers notice similarities and differences, they can see that the books on the couch belong back on the rack with the other books, whereas the blocks on the couch belong back on the shelf with the other blocks. At the same time, toddlers have no need to be thorough, efficient, or exact. Even in a well-organized and labeled play space, toddlers participate in putting toys away in their own particular manner ("Me do it!") and at their own pace, as the following anecdotes illustrate:

> *At the end of choice time, Mario's caregiver suggests, "Let's put these books back on the shelf, Mario." Mario picks up an armload of books from the pile of cushions where he and several other children have been looking at them, carries them over to the low bookshelf, and places the whole armful in a pile on the shelf.*

∽

> *John picks up the empty food containers, plates, and utensils he has spread out on the table in the house area, puts them into the wooden refrigerator, closes the door, and looks with satisfaction at the now-empty table. "Aw gone!" he says.*

∽

Putting toys away works best when caregivers take part with children and accept toddlers' ideas about how to do it, whether it is returning blocks to the shelf or putting plastic caps in the bag.

Lydia stands at the sink with several paintbrushes. She holds each brush under the running water for quite some time, watches the colors swirl down the drain, then "paints" the counter next to the sink with water.

∽

Blake loads into a wagon some blocks he has been playing with, pulls the wagon to the block shelf, dumps the wagon over to unload these blocks next to the shelf, rights the wagon, and heads back to load some more blocks into his wagon.

Putting toys away works best when caregivers put toys away along with the children and are willing to accept toddlers' ideas about how to do things. Remain calm and positive, and do not expect toddlers to handle the cleanup process all on their own or even to completely pick up any one area or group of items. With patient support and encouragement, toddlers can participate in the *process* of cleanup and enjoy the contact, interaction, and satisfaction it affords. After a good effort on everyone's part, caregivers move on to the next part of the day. After all, they can always complete cleanup while children nap or after they have left for the day.

Understanding Outside Time

At outside time, two nonmobile infants, Tabor and Lizzy, are wiggling and cooing as they lie on a blanket. Sheila, their caregiver, sits next to them on the grass holding a third infant, Crescent, who is sucking her thumb and gazing at Tabor and Lizzy. "Here we are outside, looking all around," Sheila sings to all three babies as she gently rocks Crescent.

∽

Hans and Thomas, who are both at the creeper-crawler stage, sit on a blanket spread under a tree on the playground. From a basket of objects beside them, Hans chooses a large pine cone to hold, and Thomas picks out two hand-sized rocks to hold and bang together. Sandy, their caregiver, sits next to them, watching as they explore. She also watches Annie, a nonmobile infant who is lying on the blanket and looking up at the leaves on a low-hanging branch. "You see the leaves, Annie," she says softly. Annie waves her arms and kicks her legs.

∽

Sarah, an older infant, crawls over to the chain link fence that surrounds the play yard. She sits next to it, grasps one of the links, and wiggles the fence back and forth as she watches the preschool children playing in the tree house in the adjacent play yard. In the meantime, infant Amanda crawls to Robin, her caregiver, sits in Robin's lap, and watches Sarah at the fence. Looking up at Robin, Amanda points in Sarah's direction. "You see Sarah over at the fence," Robin comments. Amanda leaves Robin's lap to crawl across the grass toward Sarah. Close by, Jason, another infant, crawls up the two low steps of the deck, sits on the deck for a bit, crawls back down the steps, and crawls back up again. As he pauses again on the deck, Robin says, "Jason, you've been crawling up and down the steps!"

Outside time allows infants and toddlers to extend their exploration and play to an outdoor setting.

⌒

At outside time, Tessa, a young toddler, throws balls into an empty plastic wading pool. When all the balls are in the pool, she climbs into the pool with the balls, sits down, and throws the balls out. She bangs on the empty pool with her hands and her heels, climbs out, retrieves each ball and throws it into the pool again.

⌒

At the sandbox, Riley, a young toddler, scoops handfuls of sand into a bucket while Carole, his caregiver, holds the bucket steady. When Carole puts one hand into the bucket, Riley laughs as he pours sand over her hand. Joel, an older toddler, sits on the edge of the sandbox near Carole, shoveling sand into a small bucket he has placed between his feet. When the bucket is full, he dumps out the sand and starts over again.

⌒

*Crane and L.J., two toddlers, travel back and forth between the foot of the beech tree, where they have discovered some stones, and Carole, their caregiver, who is perched on the edge of the sandbox holding Riley's bucket. On each of their trips, they bring Carole a stone. "Big," says Crane, handing her a stone. "This **is** a big stone," Carole agrees. "My big," says L.J. "Your stone is big, too, L.J.," she says. The children pile their stones in front of Carole, then head back to the beech tree for more.*

∽

Toddlers Maria and Samuel each climb into one of the two child-sized cartons they have helped their caregiver carry outside. They laugh as they first squat down in their carton, then jump up, and then climb out. They repeat the same action sequence several more times.

∽

Nanette, a caregiver, and two of her toddlers, Lindy and Peter, spread out a long sheet of white butcher paper on the grass. Nanette puts a rock at each corner of the paper to help hold it in place. Then Peter pulls the "paint wagon" over to a spot near the paper (the wagon holds some containers of tempera paint, a bucket of water, and several kinds of brushes). Peter and Lindy each select a brush, dip it into one of the paint containers, squat next to the paper on either side of the paint wagon, and paint. They use whole-arm motions to make large painting strokes.

Outside time allows infants and toddlers to extend their exploration and play to an outdoor setting. As at choice time indoors, children make choices about what to do outdoors. Children find the outdoors rich in sensory-motor experiences for constructing new knowledge. They can feel the texture of lawns, leaves, pine needles, snow, sand, dirt, wood, bark, brick, and stone. They hear the sounds of wind, birds, traffic, sirens, airplanes, older children at play. They smell flowers, earth, grass, rain, animals, good aromas wafting from kitchens or bakeries. And they see the many shades of green, the seasonal changes, light and shade, the play of shadows, the movement of branches and clouds. At outside time, infants and toddlers begin to gain a sense of distance as they experience what is up close—spiders, worms, grass—and what is far away—the treetops, the house next door, the clouds. They have the rare opportunity to be big compared to ants, grasshoppers,

When you are this age, outside time is a good time to pull yourself up to stand and figure out how the playhouse shutters work!

birds, squirrels, and dandelions. They can freely move, throw things, and play in water and snow. They gather and collect leaves, twigs, rocks, walnuts, and seed pods. In the sunlight, they soak up the vitamin D they need to absorb calcium for strong bones and teeth. Overall, spending daily time outdoors in all seasons positively affects the way even very young children eat, sleep, and feel.

Outdoor play spaces appropriately designed and equipped for infants' and toddlers' outside time were described in Chapter 3, on pp. 158–165. To sum up, for infants the play space includes materials and equipment that encourage movement, things that flutter in the wind, a variety of crawling surfaces, water-play materials, and things that are visually interesting. For toddlers the play space includes natural features like hills and boulders; things to climb and swing on; things to get inside of, crawl through, and balance on; sand and water; toys to rock, ride, push, and pull; and items like balls, beanbags, chalk, painting materials. Occasionally at outside time, caregivers, infants, and toddlers take a walk around the block, to a nearby park, a neighbor's garden, or a local shop.

During outside time, infants and toddlers observe, explore, and play on their own or with others at their own pace and level of interest and development. Depending on temperament, some children cautiously approach outdoor sounds, textures, sights, and sensations, while others take to outdoor play with energy and curiosity about every new creature and experience.

Nonmobile infants like Tabor, Lizzy, Crescent, and Annie (p. 266) spend most of their outside time lying on their backs while gazing at nearby sights, wiggling, stretching, and reaching for or grasping at objects. They enjoy feeling the warmth of the sun and the movement of the air. They also move from place to place in their caregiver's arms or in a stroller.

Mobile infants like Hans, Thomas, Sarah, and Jason (pp. 266–267) sit and explore objects or materials and examine growing things. They crawl across the grass, up and down steps, over small hills, and into large boxes. They pull themselves up to stand by holding on to a low bench, a picnic table, or the edge of the sandbox. With help, they swing in a swing or go for gentle wagon rides.

Young toddlers use the clear expanses of the outdoor play area for walking, carrying, pushing, climbing, throwing, and exploring. While their movements may be awkward, outside they have lots of space for maneuvering, falling down, and picking themselves up. Older toddlers, who have become pretty steady on their feet, take advantage of the outdoor space to run, ride, climb, swing, slide, throw, dig, paint, play in water, fill and empty, collect stones, make up simple games, and grapple with problems—how to cover the picnic table with a sheet to make a house, how to get the riding toy back up the hill, what to do when two toddlers want to fill the same dump truck with walnuts.

How Caregivers Support Children at Outside Time

Caregivers pay close attention to children's outdoor exploration and play, offer children physical and emotional support, and interact with children in enjoying all the features of the outdoor environment. The following specific strategies help them carry out this role:

- Provide loose materials for children's comfort and play.

- Provide a variety of experiences for nonmobile infants.

- Use the support strategies appropriate at choice time.

- Observe nature with children.

- Bring outside time to a gentle close.

Provide loose materials for children's comfort and play

Nonmobile infants spend most of their time outdoors lying on blankets spread on the ground, so caregivers keep some clean blankets in a basket or diaper bag that they can easily grab on their way out to the play yard. Be-

"Loose materials" in this play yard include these apples just gathered up from under the apple tree!

cause some older, mobile infants may at first be hesitant to crawl or cruise around outdoors, they often appreciate being given a basket of interesting objects to explore while sitting on a blanket, working up their courage to move across the grass, up the steps, or over the stone walkway to find their own things to explore. The baskets of playthings for mobile infants can also be kept ready by the door to the play yard.

Caregivers can place other loose playthings or materials in wagons so toddlers at the "Me do it!" stage can help to transport them outside, as Peter does when he pulls the paint wagon outside (p. 268). Caregivers can also provide small buckets, baskets, or cloth bags with handles, and toddlers can use these to carry out their sand toys, tennis balls, streamers, bubble-blowing equipment, and playground chalk.

Provide a variety of experiences for nonmobile infants

While mobile infants and toddlers generally find lots of things to explore and play with outside in the presence of their trusted caregivers, nonmobile infants depend on caregivers to put them in some location where they can easily stretch and wiggle and watch interesting things. This means putting infants down in a safe place and varying that place from time to time. Then they can see a variety of sights—blooming flowers, tree bark, dried leaves on the lawn, branches overhead, sky and clouds, children crawling, stems of grass, stones, banners waving, stirring wind chimes. On warm days, place babies near the edge of a blanket so they can feel the grass with their feet or hands. As you carry them outside and back inside again, stop so they can have an up-close look at the pine tree, the toddlers playing next door, or the rabbit in his cage. If you wheel infants in strollers, choose a route that provides interesting things for them to see.

Use the support strategies appropriate at choice time

In many ways, outside time is choice time moved outdoors. Therefore, once you have gotten infants and toddlers and their materials safely outdoors, use the strategies described on pp. 249–266 for supporting children at choice time: Pay close attention as they explore and play, follow their leads and ideas, engage in play and conversational give-and-take with them, support their peer interactions, and help them take a problem-solving approach to any social conflicts. Listen for older toddlers to talk about their intentions and about what they have done (their planning and recalling). And at the end of outside time, encourage toddlers to help put away playthings and carry materials back indoors.

Here's one of the simple pleasures of outside time—filling a bowl with grass, sitting at the picnic table, taking the grass out of the bowl, and letting it fall to the ground!

Observe nature with children

One of the special pleasures of being outside with very young children is witnessing their wonderment as they roll in snow, splash in puddles, squat to watch ants move a crumb toward their anthill, find an intricate spider web on the fence, point to birds flying overhead, or gather their own pile of stones. Even though infants and toddlers say relatively little during these experiences ("Big," "My big"), they are gaining an essential understanding of the natural world through their actions and sensory intake. Caregivers do not need to overwhelm very young children with a barrage of words and lengthy explanations about what they are seeing and doing, but they do need to appreciate children's actions and interests, comment on or acknowledge them when it is natural to do so, and allow children plenty of time to stop and smell the flowers, watch the worms in the dirt, shuffle through the leaves, and pick up yet another stick.

Bring outside time to a gentle close

Five minutes or so before the end of outside time, tell children that the time outdoors is almost over. Nanette, for example, going from child to child, sings, "Five more minutes of outside time, then we'll go inside for lunch." Even though children may not know exactly what you are saying or singing, eventually they associate the same ritual phrase or song with rounding up the toys and going back inside, going home, or whatever happens next in the routine. Even with infants, it is important to let them know why you are picking them up, folding up their blanket, and carrying them inside. "I'm going to pick you up, Annie," says Sandy, her caregiver. "It's time for us to go back inside."

Understanding Group Time

> *At group time, caregiver Sonja places a dishpan on the floor between Maggie and Sean, mobile infants. The dishpan contains about an inch of water and some yellow rubber ducks. "Here is some water and some ducks," Sonja says to the children, joining them on the floor. Maggie leans over and splashes her hands in the water. Sean pushes a duck along, then picks it up by the head and brings it to his mouth. Watching him, Maggie puts the fingers of one hand into her mouth, makes a face, then returns to splashing.*

> ~

> *At group time, toddlers Conner, Nick, Cher, and Jo and their caregiver, Jenna, spread newspapers on the art table. When the table is covered, Jenna sets down a tray of small plastic squeeze*

These four children and their caregiver gather around the table to make play dough.

Once the play dough begins to take shape, two other children crowd in to take a look!

bottles that the children have been using at the water table. "Here are some bottles of dribble salt (p. 151) for you to squeeze," she says to the children. Conner selects a bottle, shakes it, turns it upside down, and squeezes it with both hands, Jenna tries the same actions with a bottle she selects, and Nick watches Conner. Noticing Nick watching him, Conner takes another bottle, sets it down in front of Nick, and says "Bottle?" Nick simply looks at the bottle. "Nick, it looks like Conner is giving you a bottle to squeeze," Jenna interprets. Taking the bottle, Nick squeezes it as Conner did, then sticks a finger into the resulting pool of dribble, licks his finger, and makes a face. Jenna follows suit, sticking her finger into the dribble she has squeezed out and then tasting it. She comments to Nick, "It tastes salty." Cher and Jo squeeze their bottles while moving their arms back and forth in front of them to dribble their salt. Jenna tries moving her arms back and forth the same way. As Conner and Nick continue to squeeze and muck about, Cher and Jo leave the table, wash their hands at the sink, then take their empty squeeze bottles to the house area. Jenna continues to squeeze bottles of dribble salt with Conner and Nick. When Conner and Nick have emptied all the squeeze bottles and have saturated the newspaper, they help Jenna push the sodden newspaper into the wastebasket. "Aw gone!" says Conner.

Debbie, a caregiver, and her four toddlers, Miranda, Timmy, Sean, and Sarah, sit on the floor in the toy area. They have between them three containers of plastic stacking pegs, one with red, one with blue, and one with yellow pegs. Each person has a pegboard. "Here are some new pegs and pegboards," Debbie says. "Let's see what we can do with them!" Sean immediately selects one peg after another and pushes them into the holes on his pegboard. After watching Sean, Timmy also puts a few pegs in his board, then fits a peg on top of one that is already in the board. "Oh, Sean," comments Debbie," you're stacking one peg on top of another! I think I'll try that," and she does. Sean tries out Timmy's stacking idea and laughs as some of his stacks tumble over. In the meantime, Miranda and Sarah, ignoring the pegboards, make chains by fastening several pegs together in a line on the floor. At one point, Sarah dumps out the container of red pegs and picks out several red pegs that she adds to the end of her chain. Then she goes to the book area, selects a book, and looks at the pictures, talking softly to herself.

❧

Mike and Shawna, a caregiver team for eight toddlers, have a morning group time for all their children. As Mike helps children remove and hang up their coats (since their group time follows outside time), Shawna begins to play a CD of lively recorded instrumental music she knows the children like[10] and puts a basket of rhythm instruments on the floor in the movement area. Shawna sits down next to the basket, selects a set of sand blocks, and begins to play her blocks along with the music. As the children (and eventually Mike also) join her in the movement area, they begin to select other instruments and also play along with the music. Toddlers Rene and Eddie, however, simply watch the instrument players for a bit, then settle down in the toy area to play with some toy cars and animals. Shawna and Mike use their instruments to try out actions they see the children using. When the first musical selection ends, Shawna selects another, slower piece of music. When that piece ends, Shawna sings, "Time to put your instruments away, your instruments away. Time to put your instruments away, and wash your hands for lunch." The children drop their instruments back into the basket and head for the low sinks in the bathroom. Mike, in the meantime, wheels the lunch cart to the eating area.

During a typical group time, one or two caregivers gather with the older infants and toddlers in their care to explore and play with a particular set of materials or to take part in some common activity. The group is small—generally with no more than four children per caregiver and no more than eight children altogether. This allows children to have close physical contact with their caregiver, and it allows the caregiver to pay close attention to each child. It is a daily opportunity for children and caregivers to share or use common materials and to communicate in an intimate social setting.

Caregivers gather the group together and introduce the materials or activity for group time, but children are the doers and choice-makers, actively shaping what happens as the group time unfolds. Children also determine the length of group time. Some children, for example, may squeeze dribble salt for 10 minutes, whereas others may spend several minutes watching the activity, then turn to play with other materials around the room. To suit the nature of older infants and toddlers, group times are fluid and dynamic, varying in length and content, depending on the actions, ideas, and interests of the children involved.

---

[10]For examples of recordings suitable for a toddlers' movement activity like this one, see the *Rhythmically Moving 1–4* recordings listed under "Related Media" on p. 293.

Group times help children build a repertoire of shared experiences they can turn to in their play and in communication give-and-take at other times of the day. Caregivers will notice that over time, children grow in their ability to communicate and interact with one another during group time; also, the time they remain together in common pursuits gradually increases.

Group time can also serve as a time when children check in for reassurance and support from others after venturing out into the play space during choice time and outside time. For caregivers, group time serves as a unique opportunity to offer children materials and challenges that reflect the key experiences and to observe the various ways different children think of using the materials or solving any problems they meet along the way.

Group time needn't occur at the same place every day. Where the group gathers depends on the materials called for and the nature of the activity. In

This group of children and their caregiver gather on the floor to find out what they can do with clothespins and a series of boxes.

the scenarios beginning on p. 274, for example, group time takes place in the infants' play space, in the art area, in the toy area, and in the movement area. At other times, the group might gather for their activity in a tent, on the deck of the climber, around the sand and water table, on the steps, under the low-hanging branches of a pine tree, or in the garden. Children and their caregiver might sit on the floor, on the ground, at a table—wherever the chosen activity dictates. Group times involving singing and movement generally take place in the movement area or outdoors, where there is plenty of space for children to move freely.

Caregivers do not plan group times for the youngest, nonmobile infants. In settings with mixed-age groups, however, these very young infants, when awake, may watch the group activity of the older children from a safe vantage point (as Bobby does while drinking from his bottle, p. 196). Watching allows infants to be part of the communal action, and they often will be eager to join group time once they can sit up and use both hands for exploration.

Older infants and toddlers explore and play with materials at group time much as they do at choice time (see p. 276). Mobile infants, like Maggie and Sean (p. 274), enjoy very simple group experiences, such as splashing in water. During music and movement activities with older children, they are apt to watch from a distance or from the safety of a caregiver's lap. Young toddlers may drift in and out of group time, while older toddlers, with their increasing sociability and sense of self, are both likely to engage in social conflict *and* likely to sense the needs of their peers as they go about a group-time activity.

How Caregivers Support Children During Group Time

During group time, caregivers present children with a specific set of materials or some experience that may be new or of particular interest to them. Caregivers then support the choices children make as they explore, try out their own ideas, and solve problems in connection with the materials or experience presented. The following strategies contribute to carrying out this role:

- Plan ahead and provide active group experiences.

- Gather materials and offer them to children.

- Respect children's choices and ideas about using the materials.

- Comment briefly and specifically on what you see children doing.

- Interpret children's actions and communications for other children.

- Let children's actions tell you when group time is at an end.

Plan ahead and provide active group experiences

In a High/Scope active learning infant-toddler program, the caregiver team meets daily for planning (see p. 303). This is when they think ahead about what they will present in the way of materials or experiences at a future group time. Building on the key experiences and reflecting on what they know about the children in their care helps them to think of group-time experiences that the children will enjoy, find challenging, and be able to master. They might decide to build group time around *some materials and simple actions that will be new to the children,* around *some favorite and familiar materials or actions,* or around *opportunities for music and movement.*

It is important that group time be an *active* time for children rather than a school-like "lesson," because infants and toddlers are geared for movement and learning through sensory exploration; they are not likely to submit passively to adult instruction. When group-time experiences are planned *ahead of time,* children do not have to wait as caregivers gather materials, group time can begin and end smoothly, and the daily routine can flow, for example, from outside time to group time to lunch.

✦ *Building group time around new materials and actions*

Planning group times around materials new to the children is one way to introduce and add materials to the play space that children can then explore or play with at choice time. Caregiver Debbie, for example, plans a toddlers'

At group time, these toddlers and their caregiver spread out to explore plastic detergent-bottle caps and baskets.

group time around some new plastic stacking pegs and pegboards she thinks they are ready to handle (p. 276). These later become part of the toy area. In a similar way, a group-time activity can be an initiation for new blocks, large shells, push vehicles, picture books, paintbrushes, finger paints, cartons, musical instruments, or climbing equipment.

Group time can also be a chance for children to explore the properties of materials and try out such actions as splashing or squeezing. (See Sonja's group time and Jenna's group time, both on pp. 274–276.) Other actions to try out at group time might be tearing or crumpling paper, pouring water or sand, mixing sand and water, balancing blocks, pushing golf tees into blocks of Styrofoam, spreading finger paint, smooshing dough or clay, washing baby dolls, climbing up and down the climber, or opening and closing the hinged lids of boxes.

Remember two things while planning a group time around new materials and actions: First, keep the overall idea simple. You should be able to introduce the experience to children in one short sentence ("Here are some new blocks to try") or with a simple action (standing one block on top of another). Second, focus on *doing* rather than *making*. Jenna, for example, plans an opportunity for her toddlers to squeeze dribble salt on paper, and this they do with gusto. She does not expect them to make dribble salt pictures to hang up or take home. (See "Sample Plan for Group Time: Finger Paints" on p. 282 and "Sample Plan for Group Time: Filling and Emptying" on p. 283.)

✦ *Building group time around favorite, familiar materials and actions*

Planning group time around materials or actions children are already used to and particularly enjoy might be done for several reasons: to support children's interests, to allow them to gain a sense of mastery, or to encourage them to extend their knowledge by trying out slight variations on what they already know. Caregiver Joanne, for example, knows her children like to crumble their bread and crackers at mealtime. She plans a group time around crumbling stale bread for the birds to provide children with the opportunity to crumble bread in a slightly different context. In another setting, a caregiver notices that her children often ask her to read them the book *Goodnight Moon* (by Margaret Wise Brown), so she plans to read this favorite story to them at group time in a cozy setting on the pillows in the book area.

Caregivers can plan group times around any of their children's favorite equipment or materials: steps and ramps, tennis balls, rubber or plastic animal or people figures, small photo albums, puzzles, interlocking blocks, quart-size milk cartons and chestnuts, markers and paper, play dough, riding toys. Depending on the particular children involved, favorite actions might include twisting off jar lids, washing furniture with sponges and warm water, tearing paper bags, filling and emptying buckets at the sand table, rolling

Sample Plan for Group Time:
Finger Paints

Originating idea:
New material—Introduce the children to finger painting.

Materials:
White butcher paper to cover the art table, pieces of masking tape to fasten the edges of the paper to the table, red finger paint emptied into a flat cake pan, painting smocks.

Possible key experiences:
Exploring objects—exploring objects with the hands, feet, mouth, eyes, ears, and nose
Sense of self—doing things for themselves
Creative representation—exploring building and art materials

What children may do:
Children may put on their own smocks, help spread butcher paper on the table, and tape down the edges. They may dip their fingers or whole hand in the finger paint or watch others before attempting to do this themselves. Children may spread finger paint on their hands or smear it across the paper. Some children may taste the finger paint (which is nontoxic). They will probably take longer than usual washing their hands and may notice or comment on the "red soap."

Adult support:
Gather in the art area and say, "We need to put on smocks so we can paint." Be ready to help with smocks and long sleeves. Ask the children for help spreading the paper: "Now we'll spread the paper on the table so we can finger-paint on it." Show children how to tape down the edges, and provide them with tape pieces.

Place the cake pan of finger paint in the middle of the table: "This is finger paint. You can put your hands in it and spread the paint on the paper." Watch to see what each child does. If no child approaches the finger paint, try dipping your own fingers in the paint, to give them an idea of what to do. Once children begin exploring the paint in various ways, try out and comment on children's various actions. Listen for children's observations. Be ready to add another layer of butcher paper if children want a clean work surface. As children finish, have them go to the sink and wash their hands. Leave the paper on the table to dry, or roll it up and discard.

Follow-up:
Store a day's supply of red finger paint in a flat, plastic "sandwich" container with a tight lid to keep it from drying out. Add this container of finger paint to the art area for children to use at choice time. During choice time, be ready to help children spread out some paper, or skip the paper and have them use the table top as a finger-painting surface. (When children are finished, provide them with sponges and buckets of warm soapy water for cleaning the paint off the table.)

Sample Plan for Group Time: Filling and Emptying

Originating idea:
New and favorite actions—Children enjoy emptying containers of toys. What happens when they start with empty containers they can fill?

Materials:
Sandbox and sand, small buckets, shovels, scoops, empty food containers, wagon next to sandbox

Possible key experiences:
Exploring objects—exploring objects with the hands, feet, mouth, eyes, ears, and nose
Space—filling and emptying, putting in and taking out

What children may do:
Children may sit or squat in the sand, scoop sand with their hands, try out shovels and scoops, put sand in containers, dump sand out of containers, use containers as scoops, pat sand, empty sand on the grass outside the sandbox, carry buckets of sand, use buckets to fill the wagon with sand.

Adult support:
Let children know where group time will be: "Today, we're going outside to the sandbox for group time." Get into the sandbox with the children. Watch to see which materials they use and how they use them. Listen for children's words and ideas. Describe children's actions and try them out. You might attempt a slight variation on a child's actions if the child seems open to trying something new.

Follow-up:
Watch to see if children carry out similar actions at choice time at the sand table.

---

balls toward each other, rolling dough or clay, filling and shaking tins filled with corks. Again, for very young children, it makes sense to plan group experiences that are simple, can be introduced briefly and simply, and incorporate materials and actions related to what you see children enjoying at other parts of the day. (See "Sample Plan for Group Time: Steps, Ramps, and Boards" on p. 284.)

✦ *Building group time around music and movement experiences*

Singing and moving with children at group time gives them opportunities to explore movement, to build a common repertoire of songs and rhymes, and to experience steady beat.[11] Mike and Shawna, for example, plan a group time in which their toddlers select and play rhythm instruments to fast and slow recorded music. In one infant-toddler program, caregivers planned a group time in which children walked (and enjoyed falling down) on the

---

[11]For more about young children and steady beat, see Phyllis S. Weikart (in press) in the "Related Reading" list on p. 293.

Sample Plan for Group Time:
Steps, Ramps, and Boards

Originating idea:
Favorite materials and actions—The children like climbing up and down steps and ramps and walking along the edge of the sandbox.

Materials:
The rocking boat turned step-side-up, vinyl-covered wedges and cubes, ramps made from the hollow-blocks and boards

Possible key experiences:
Movement—moving the whole body (rolling, crawling, cruising, walking, running, balancing)

Space—observing people and things from various perspectives

What children may do:
Children may concentrate on walking up and down steps, walking or running up and down ramps, or balancing on boards, or they may try each action. They may re-

arrange the boards and ramps. A child may climb up to sit on top of the rocking-boat steps or on top of a vinyl cube and watch the others from there.

Adult support:
Gather children in the movement area for group time, and open with "Let's see how many things we can do on the steps, ramps, and boards." Sit or kneel on the floor. Watch how children balance and pick themselves up if they fall. Be ready to offer comfort and contact as needed. Comment on children's actions. Assist as needed with rearrangements if children decide to move equipment.

Follow-up:
Bring the boards outdoors at outside time for children to walk on and use for making low bridges that they can cross. Place the boards near the steps to the deck.

"bumpety bump" (which was the children's name for a lumpy surface made from two full-sized bed sheets sewn together and stuffed with fist-sized scraps of foam rubber). For a variation, caregivers also covered the bumpety bump with mats before children walked on it. (Caregivers got the idea for this activity from the 1982 book on movement exploration by Molly Sullivan, listed on p. 292.)

Group times can be planned around simple children's songs and rhymes, such as the following:

- **Nursery Rhymes**—*Deedle, Deedle, Dumpling; Hey Diddle Diddle; Hickory, Dickory, Dock; Humpty Dumpty; Jack Be Nimble; One, Two, Buckle My Shoe; Pat-a-Cake, Pat-a-Cake; To Market, to Market; Pease-Porridge Hot; Ride a Cock-horse to Banbury Cross; This Little Pig Went to Market; Two Little Dicky Birds.*

- **Children's Songs**—*Are You Sleeping?; The Muffin Man; Happy Birthday; I'm a Little Teapot; Jingle Bells; London Bridge; Open, Shut Them; Rain, Rain, Go Away; Ring Around the Rosy; Rock-a-bye, Baby; Row, Row, Row Your Boat; The Bear Went Over the Mountain; Twinkle, Twinkle, Little Star; Where Is Thumbkin?*

"Twinkle, twinkle, little star," sing children and caregivers holding their own twinkling stars. Another day, everyone had two stars—one for each hand!

In addition to these traditional songs and rhymes from Mother Goose, include traditional songs and rhymes from the cultures of the children and families in your setting. Ask parents to teach them to you, or if possible, to join you at group time.

Young children often want to sing or chant their favorite songs and rhymes in group time after group time, and even then, they ask for them "Again!" They may ask for a song or rhyme, then listen while others sing or chant it, and join in on only a few favorite words or phrases. Some caregivers make a picture card for each song or rhyme the children know (for example, a drawing of Humpty Dumpty on a wall might be used for *Humpty Dumpty,* and a picture of rain falling on children standing under an umbrella, for *Rain, Rain, Go Away).* Some children then use the cards to indicate their choice of a song or rhyme to sing or chant. Other children refer to their song or rhyme choice by saying a key word like "Dumpty" or "Rain."

Many times a caregiver will sing and chant songs and rhymes unaccompanied by records, tapes, or CDs. Using your own voice (which infants and toddlers will love even if you believe you can't sing) and perhaps accompanying yourself on a keyboard, guitar, or Autoharp allows you to set the pitch within the children's singing range and to adjust the tempo of the song to the children's pace. It also frees children to add their own ideas. On a very windy day, for example, the children in one program decided to sing "wind, wind go away" to the tune of *Rain, Rain, Go Away.* Another day, the children substituted their own names in *The Bear Went Over the Mountain,*

The children in this group have their own ideas about which bells to choose and what to do with them!

singing, for example, "Jason went over the mountain . . ." Later in the year, this version turned into a song to sing at cleanup, while putting toys away: "Jason's putting the blocks on the shelf, Jason's putting the blocks on the shelf . . ."

Some movement experiences you might plan for children at group time include these: walking to music; waving scarves to music; patting or moving various body parts to music; crawling through tunnels of different lengths and widths; rolling on mats or up and down ramp-shaped cushions; playing with rubber playground balls; playing in cartons; tossing balls into large cartons; running around the climber (a tree, or an easy chair) while singing "Run around, run around, run around the climber" to the tune of *Yellow Bird*. (See "Sample Plan for Group Time: Moving to Music With Scarves," p. 288.)

Gather materials and offer them to children

Before the children arrive in the morning, or while they are napping in the afternoon, gather the materials that will be used for group time, and place them close to where you will be using them. Make sure to have some materials for each child to use. These preparations allow the group time to begin immediately so children do not have to wait while you prepare things and so you can let the materials, songs, or actions involved help to draw children to group time. In presenting the materials to children, keep your introduction brief and to the point. "What can you do with these blocks?" "Choose an instrument you want to play." Generally, children themselves will begin to handle and explore the materials as soon as they are close enough to reach them. On the rare occasion when children hesitate or show no interest in the materials you have selected, begin by using the materials yourself. If your actions do not inspire children, set the materials aside for another day, and offer children instead small cars, blocks, animal figures, puzzles, or whatever it is you know they currently enjoy.

Respect children's choices and ideas about using the materials

As active learners, children make a variety of choices at group time. For example, they decide whether or not to participate, how long to stay, what to do with materials, what materials to add, and how to vary actions and words to songs. Caregivers strive to provide interesting materials and experiences children will want to explore and try out at group time. Then they support children's choices and ideas, because they understand children's need to learn in their own way and in a hands-on manner.

Caregivers respect children's group-time choices and ideas by putting themselves at the physical level of the children, watching what they are doing, and listening to what they say. Following children's leads and imitat-

---

Sample Plan for Group Time:
Moving to Music With Scarves

Originating idea:
Music and movement experiences—
The children enjoy moving to music.
What might they do with scarves?

Materials:
CD player; recordings of musical selections, both fast and slow (see p. 363); a scarf for each child

Possible key experiences:
Communication and language—listening and responding; communicating nonverbally

Movement—moving with objects; moving to music

Time—experiencing "fast" and "slow"

What children may do:
Children may select a scarf, stay in one place and move the scarf, move from

place to place holding their scarves, watch one another, and try out one another's movement ideas.

Adult support:
Put the basket of scarves in the middle of the movement area and say "Here are some scarves you might like to use for dancing." As children select scarves, put on the first musical selection and watch to see what children do. Describe and imitate their actions. Watch to see how children move with the second musical selection. End with a slow selection, and ask children to put their scarves back in the basket.

Follow-up:
Add the basket of scarves to the movement area for children to use at choice time.

---

ing children's actions both indicates to children that you see what they are doing and helps you to understand what children are thinking and learning. During Jenna's group time (p. 276), it may be that Conner and Nick feel free to squeeze all the bottles dry because Jenna, their caregiver, has joined them in a companionable manner, takes her cues from them, and dribbles salt just as they do.

Comment briefly and specifically on what you see children doing

Another way to let children know you see and appreciate what they are doing is to describe their actions. "You're stacking one peg on top of another!" caregiver Debbie comments to Sean (p. 276). Such comments open the door to further observations from children without pressuring them to respond. Brief, factual comments also help children recognize that their actions can be described in words. Being on the child's physical level, looking for a momentary pause in the action, and catching the child's eye are ways to address these comments to the child in a way that is personally meaningful. In contrast, nonstop talk from the caregivers, however well-intentioned, may distract children from what they are doing or serve as background noise children filter out as they explore and play; it may even discourage them from talking.

Interpret children's actions and communications for other children

Infants and toddlers combine nonverbal and verbal expressions to create their personal communication styles. Sometimes they understand one another, and sometimes they need "translation." At group time, as several children work in the same general area using the same materials, they have many opportunities for give-and-take communication with peers, but they may need caregivers to help them out from time to time. When Conner (p. 276) says "Bottle?" as he places a bottle of dribble salt

Unhurried by her caregiver at group time, this child takes on a toddler-sized challenge—balancing one cylindrical block on top of another.

in front of Nick, for example, Nick simply looks at the bottle. Aware of Conner's gesture and Nick's apparent confusion, caregiver Jenna offers an interpretation of Conner's words and gesture: "Nick," she says, "it looks like Conner is giving you a bottle to squeeze." This appears to make sense to Nick, because he reaches for the bottle and starts squeezing.

Sometimes caregivers will be confused about what children mean. At one point as he stacks pegs, for example, Timmy knocks one of his stacks over and says "Bo!" Debbie, his caregiver, has no idea what he means, but she knocks her stack over and says "Bo!" Whatever it means, this becomes a turn-taking game Debbie and Timmy play for several rounds. Later, when Timmy says "Mo eg," Debbie responds with, "Timmy, I don't understand. Can you show me what you mean?" Timmy gets up, walks around her to a container of pegs, picks one up with each hand, and takes them back to his peg stacks. "Oh," says Debbie, "I see—you want more pegs." She moves the container within his reach.

Let children's actions tell you when group time is at an end

The length of group time varies from day to day. It may last 3 minutes or 10, depending on the children's involvement. Some days, the children will want to sing one song and no more. Other days, they will want to sing every song they know—and to sing some more than once. At each group time, however, caregivers know when group time is at an end by the signals children send them. For example, you know group time is at an end when all the children are at the sink washing their hands; when all the children have left the movement area to play with the dolls, zoom cars, or sit at the lunch table; or when the children have rolled up all the newspaper covered with dribble salt and stuffed it into the wastebasket.

On the occasions when, for example, children in your group are still finger-painting or splashing in water when the lunch tray is arriving, warn children so they have time to come to a stopping point. "In three more minutes we will have to stop for lunch."

This little boy continues his group-time play while the other children wash up for lunch.

How Caregivers Support Children Throughout Daily Events and Caregiving Routines: A Summary

Arrival and departure
- ❑ Carry out your greetings and good-byes calmly to reassure the child and parent.
- ❑ Acknowledge the child's and the parent's feelings about separation and reunion.
- ❑ Follow the child's signals about entering and leaving the activities of the care setting.
- ❑ Communicate openly with the child about the parent's comings and goings.
- ❑ Exchange information and child observations with the parent.

Feeding and mealtime
- ❑ Hold and pay close attention to the bottle-feeding infant.
- ❑ Support the older infant's interest in feeding him- or herself.
- ❑ Join toddlers at the table during meals.
- ❑ Include older toddlers in mealtime setup and cleanup.

Bodily care routines
- ❑ Fit bodily care around the child's exploration and play.
- ❑ Focus on the child at hand during the care routine.
- ❑ Give the child choices about parts of the routine.
- ❑ Encourage the child to do things for her- or himself.

Nap time
- ❑ Schedule nap time around each child's individual needs.
- ❑ Help children settle down to nap.
- ❑ Provide quiet alternatives for nonsleepers.
- ❑ Provide for children's various styles of waking up.

Choice time
- ❑ Pay close attention to children as they explore and play.

- ❑ Tailor your actions and responses to follow children's leads and ideas.
- ❑ Engage in communication give-and-take with children.
- ❑ Support children's interactions with peers.
- ❑ Use a problem-solving approach to children's social conflicts.
- ❑ Offer older toddlers opportunities to plan and recall.
- ❑ Encourage toddlers to put materials away after choice time.

Outside time
- ❑ Provide loose materials for children's comfort and play.
- ❑ Provide a variety of experiences for nonmobile infants.
- ❑ Use the support strategies appropriate at choice time.
- ❑ Observe nature with children.
- ❑ Bring outside time to a gentle close.

Group time
- ❑ Plan ahead and provide active group experiences.
  - ❑ Introduce new materials and actions.
  - ❑ Revisit favorite materials and actions.
  - ❑ Provide music and movement experiences.
- ❑ Gather materials and offer them to children.
- ❑ Respect children's choices and ideas about using materials.
- ❑ Comment briefly and specifically on what you see children doing.
- ❑ Interpret children's actions and communications for other children.
- ❑ Let children's actions tell you when group time is at an end.

References

Evans, Judith, and Ellen Ilfeld. 1982a. *Activities for Parent-Child Interaction, Supplement to Good Beginnings.* Ypsilanti, MI: High/Scope Educational Research Foundation.

Evans, Judith, and Ellen Ilfeld. 1982b. *Good Beginnings: Parenting in the Early Years.* Ypsilanti, MI: High/Scope Press.

Goldschmied, Elinor, and Sonia Jackson. 1994. *People Under Three: Young Children in Day Care.* New York: Routledge.

High/Scope Child Observation Record (COR) for Infants and Toddlers, field test ed. 1999. Ypsilanti MI: High/Scope Educational Research Foundation.

Kagan, Jerome, Richard B. Kearsley, and Philip R. Zelazo. 1978. *Infancy: Its Place in Human Development.* Cambridge: Harvard University Press.

Mangione, Peter L. 1990. *Child Care Video Magazine, It's Not Just Routine: Feeding, Diapering, and Napping Infants and Toddlers.* Sacramento, CA: California Department of Education.

Schiller, Pam. 1997. "Brain Research: Support and Challenges." *Child Care Information Exchange* (September): 6–10.

Sullivan, Molly. 1982. *Feeling Strong, Feeling Free: Movement Exploration for Young Children.* Washington, DC: National Association for the Education of Young Children.

Wood, David, Linnet McMahon, and Yvonne Cranstoun. 1980. *Working With Under Fives: Volume 5 Oxford Preschool Research Project.* Ypsilanti MI: High/Scope Press.

Related Reading

Bredekamp, Sue. 1997. "Developmentally Appropriate Practice for Infants and Toddlers." In *Developmentally Appropriate Practice in Early Childhood Programs,* rev. ed., eds. Sue Bredekamp and Carol Copple, 55–94. Washington, DC: National Association for the Education of Young Children.

DaRos, Denise A., and Beverly A. Kovach. 1998. "Assisting Toddlers & Caregivers During Conflict Resolutions: Interactions That Promote Socialization." *Childhood Education: Infancy Through Early Adolescence* 75(1): 25–30.

Dombro, Amy Laura, Laura J. Colker, and Diane Trister Dodge. 1997. "Putting Quality Into Action: Routines Day by Day." Chapter 3 in *The Creative Curriculum for Infants and Toddlers.* Washington, DC: Teaching Strategies.

Evans, Betsy. 1996. "Helping Children Resolve Disputes and Conflicts." In *Supporting Young Learners 2,* ed. Nancy Altman Brickman, 27–36. Ypsilanti, MI: High/Scope Press.

Flyer, Jill. 1998. "Putting the Peaceful, Sleeping Baby Notion to Sleep." *Educaring: Resources for Infant Educarers* 19(2): 1–2, 6.

Godfrey, Athleen, ed. 1998. "Babies, Parents, and Sleep." *Zero to Three* 19(2): 1–29.

Gonzalez-Mena, Janet. 1990. *Infant and Toddler Caregiving: A Guide to Routines.* Sacramento, CA: California Department of Education.

Hammond, Ruth Anne. 1998. "A Developmental Approach: When to Toilet Train, A Brief Review of the Literature." *Educaring: Resources for Infant Educarers* 19(2): 3–6.

Throughout the day in a High/Scope program, even the very youngest children make choices.

Honig, Alice, and A. Thompson. 1994. "Helping Toddlers With Peer Group Entry Skills." *Zero to Three* 14(5): 15–19.

Lally, J. Ronald. 1995. "The Impact of Child Care Policies and Practices on Infant/Toddler Identity Formation." In *Young Children* 51(1): 58–67.

Small, Meredith F. 1998. *Our Babies, Ourselves: How Biology and Culture Shape the Way We Parent.* New York: Anchor Books.

Vinczc, Maria. 1979. "Feedings as One of the Main Scenes of the Adult-Child Relationship." In *The RIE Manual for Parents and Professionals,* ed. Magda Gerber, 125–31. Los Angeles: Resources for Infant Educarers.

Weikart, Phyllis S. (in press). *Round the Circle: Key Experiences in Movement for Children,* 2nd ed. Ypsilanti, MI: High/Scope Press.

Wein, Carol Anne, and Susan Kirby-Smith. 1998. "Untiming the Curriculum: A Case Study of Removing Clocks From the Program." *Young Children* 53(6): 8–13.

Related Media

The Ages of Infancy: Caring for Young, Mobile, and Older Infants. 1990. Color videotape, 26 min. Sacramento, CA: California Department of Education.

First Moves: Welcoming a Child to a New Caregiving Setting. 1988. Color videotape, 27 min. Sacramento. CA: California Department of Education.

The High/Scope Approach for Under Threes, U.S. Edition. 1999. Color videotape, 68 min. London, England: High/Scope Institute U.K. (Available from High/Scope Press.)

It's Not Just Routine: Feeding, Diapering, and Napping Infants and Toddlers. 1990. Color videotape, 28 min. Sacramento, CA: California Department of Education.

Rhythmically Moving 1–4. International folk music recordings (CDs, cassettes), Phyllis S. Weikart, creative director. Ypsilanti, MI: High/Scope Press.

Supporting Children in Resolving Conflicts. 1998. Color videotape, 24 min. Ypsilanti MI: High/Scope Press.

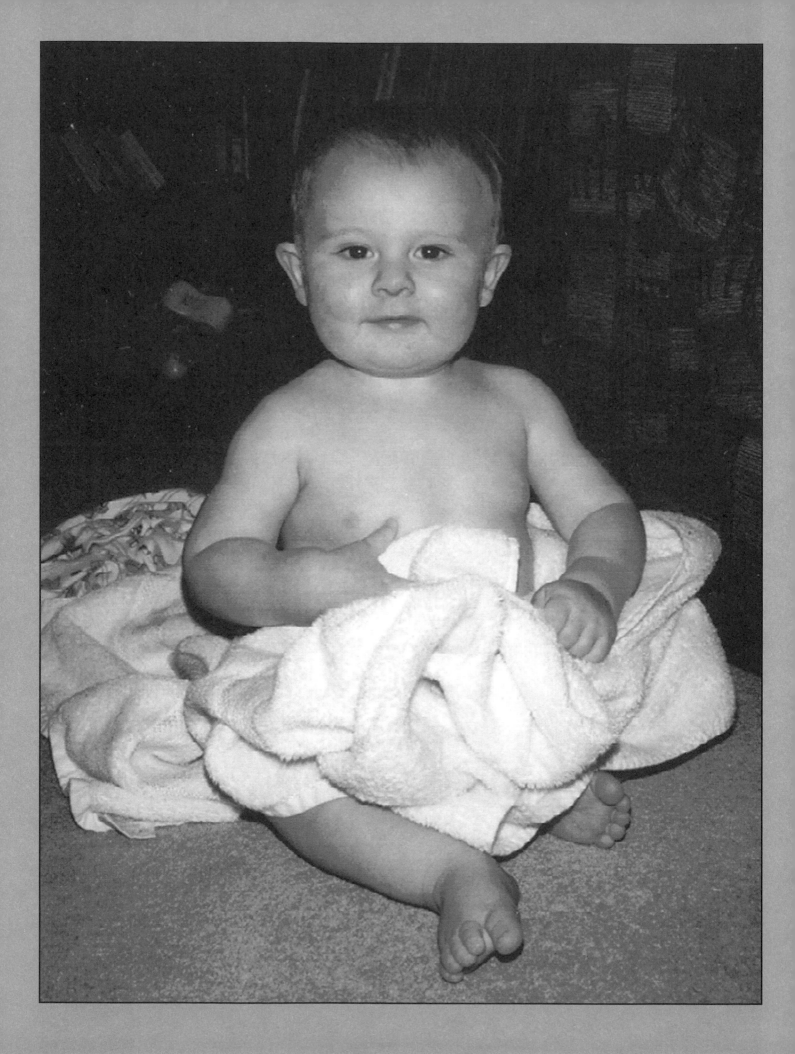

5
The Caregiver Team and Their Partnership With Parents

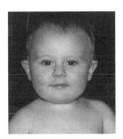

At the same time that parents and [caregivers] are learning about children and each other, each child benefits from the relationships that are developing between the adults.

—*Chiara Bove (1999)*

Active learning, adult support, a safe and inviting environment, child-centered schedules and routines—what draws these elements together and makes them work? *The focused, collaborative efforts of the adults in children's lives!* Throughout each day, members of the caregiver team work together to observe and support the children in their program. The caregiver team also works in partnership with parents, exchanging child observations and striving to provide consistency between children's at-home and away-from-home experiences. Caregivers, parents, administrators, and community members form even wider partnerships to advocate for children and to secure the resources needed for high-quality early learning and care settings. The cooperation of all these adults is needed to create safe, secure active learning environments for very young children.

In the infant-toddler group-care setting, the goal is to build strong, supportive relationships between caregiver and child, between caregiver and parents, and among caregivers themselves; these relationships can then support the vital relationship between parent and child. This chapter focuses on all these relationships in discussing the dynamics of the caregiver team and the caregiver-parent partnership.

The Caregiver Team

Chapter 2 introduced the issue of a group of children remaining with the same primary caregiver for the duration of their stay in an infant-toddler program. This stable arrangement allows children and families to form trusting relationships with the caregiver, eliminates painful and confusing transitions from caregiver to caregiver for children, and promotes a sense of well-being and belonging for everyone involved. To provide their children with consistent and continuous care and to provide mutual support, a pair of primary caregivers (sometimes three primary caregivers) work together in a team.[12] Caregivers may choose to form teams in a variety of ways, depending on what makes the most sense for their particular setting and circumstances. The three options described on the following pages are currently being used by child care teams that the authors have visited, met at conferences, or spoken with around the country. Bear in mind that these options are illustrative examples, not strict guidelines. Your program may have a room for "nonmobile infants," a room for "mobile infants/young toddlers," and a room for "older toddlers," for example, rather than having the three rooms described in Option 1. Also four, rather than three, toddlers may be assigned to each primary caregiver in your program.

---

[12]A caregiver in a family child care home often works alone, but the caregiver might form a team with another family member, another family child care provider, or a hired assistant.

Option 1: Multiroom With Looping
(three 2-person teams, 3 rooms, 3-year looping)

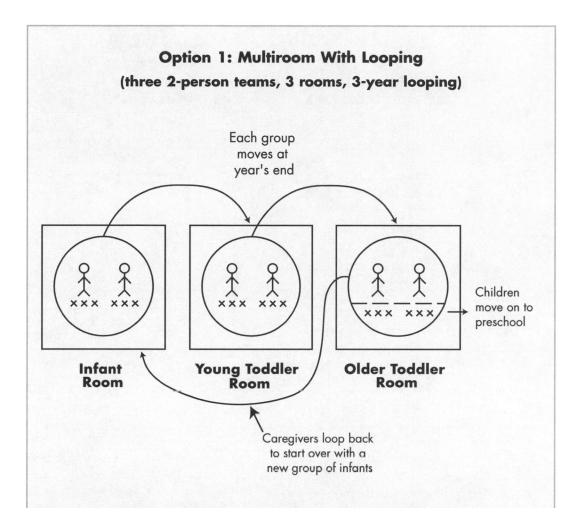

Each group
moves at
year's end

**Infant
Room**

**Young Toddler
Room**

**Older Toddler
Room**

Children
move on to
preschool

Caregivers loop back
to start over with a
new group of infants

This center has an "infant room," a "young toddler room," and an "older toddler room." Each room has a two-caregiver team with six young children of about the same age. Each year, as the children in a given room grow older, they and their caregivers move on to the next room (for example, the former young toddlers move on to the older toddler room with their two primary caregivers). At the same time, children who have been in the older toddler room move on to preschool, and their caregiver team then loops back to the infant room to begin caring for an incoming group of infants.

Option 2: Multiroom Without Looping

(three 2-person teams, 3 rooms, each team stays in the same room for their children's 3-year cycle)

ROOM 1

ROOM 2

ROOM 3

Year 1:   6 infants
Year 2:   Children become young toddlers
Year 3:   Children become older toddlers
Year 4:   Start-over with infants, in same room

etc.

Year 1:   6 young toddlers
Year 2:   Children become older toddlers
Year 3:   Start-over with infants, in same room

etc.

Year 1:   6 older toddlers
Year 2:   Start-over with infants, in same room

etc.

This center has, at any given time, three separate rooms—one for infants, one for young toddlers, and one for older toddlers—but the two-person caregiver team in each room stays in place with their six (possibly up to eight children) from year to year. Thus, as their children grow from infants to young toddlers and then to older toddlers, the caregivers arrange and adapt their room to support children's developing abilities, and the room changes in designation from one year to the next: It is the center's "infant room" one year, its "young toddler room" the next, and its "older toddler room" the next.

Option 3: Shared, Subdivided Space With Looping

(one 3-person team, shared space with separate areas for 3 different ages, 3-year looping)

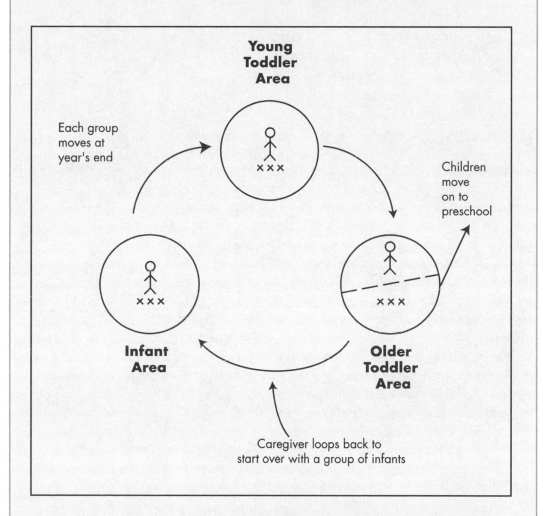

This center has one large space that is subdivided into three areas, each adapted for a different age group. (Additional kitchen and diapering/bathroom facilities are available to be shared by all three age groups. Also, the age-adapted play areas are situated so children may see and even at times interact with those in other age-groups.) A team of three primary caregivers rotates in using the three age-adapted areas. One cares for her three infants in the "infant area"; another cares for her three young toddlers in the "young toddler area"; and another cares for her three older toddlers in the "older toddler area." Each caregiver moves along to the "next-age" area with her children as they reach that age. The caregiver whose children move on to preschool loops back to begin with an incoming group of infants in the area adapted for infants.

The teamwork arrangement of Option 1 permits child-centered settings, with each room tailored to roughly a single age-group; it also promotes a sense of community and collaboration among the three caregiver teams as they move in and out of rooms they have all "lived in" for a year at a time.

A variation on Option 2 is an arrangement in which a small center (perhaps a family child care home) or each room of a larger, multiroom center has a stable, ongoing caregiver team that stays in one place and works with the same, *multiage* group of children from year to year. As a toddler in this program leaves for preschool, a new infant fills the vacancy. When a child of less-than-preschool age leaves the program, he or she is replaced with a child of similar age, when possible, to preserve the multiage mix.

Of the options described here, Option 3 is the most problematic teamwork arrangement, because having nine infants and toddlers in one space may create more commotion than some children can comfortably tolerate. However, the arrangement can work reasonably well when used with a lot of thought and care. For example, if the two toddler groups (younger and older) alternate their choice times and outside times, there will be only six children and two caregivers indoors for a large part of the time. The challenge is in providing the youngest infants with the safe, quiet space they need. The payoff is in seeing the strong, caring relationships younger and older children often form with one another when they are in daily contact.

All three of these options (and the variation of Option 2) can be adapted to an extended-hours program by doubling the number of staff (so each child has two primary caregivers—one in the morning, one in the afternoon) and having half of the staff work the first part of the day and half of them work the second part of the day, with an overlap of an hour or so in the middle of the day. So the pair of caregivers in the Option 1 infant room, for example, might work from 6:30 a.m. until 1:00 p.m., and another pair of caregivers might replace them for the afternoon, working from 11:30 a.m. to 6:00 p.m. During the overlap time, while children nap, both caregiver teams have a chance to meet together as a foursome to share child observations and plan for the following afternoon or morning.

For the infant or toddler who is to spend an extended period (perhaps 3 years) in the same group-care setting, it is important that his or her caregiver team be *a team that remains together for that time,* insofar as it is humanly possible. The practice of keeping teams together for an extended period provides continuity of care for the children involved, continuity for parents, and continuity for the caregivers themselves. Programs that have put team continuity into practice find that stable, consistent caregiver teams—compared with ones that change from day to day, month to month, or year to year—are more conducive to forming the trusting relationships that allow infants and toddlers to thrive and grow in their parents' absence (Smith, Goldhaber, and Cooper-Ellis, 1998). Over a 3-year period, for example, the children, families, and caregivers involved in a particular caregiver team have time to

Continuity of care gives children the stability and courage they need to explore challenges like this one—taking a step from caregiver to Daddy!

know and become invested in one another. Continuity of caregivers gives children the stability and courage they need to explore challenges and form new relationships with peers and other adults.

At the same time, caregivers themselves benefit from taking part in sustained teamwork. They usually learn one another's interests and strengths and develop a rapport that allows them to share the pleasures of their work as well as support one another in meeting the unavoidable physical, emotional, and intellectual challenges involved in child care. Moreover, when one caregiver team shares space, observations, concerns, and insights with other caregiver teams (as the three teams in Option 1 on p. 297 might do, for example), the teams come to rely on one another for support and advice instead of walling themselves off in "the infant room" or "the toddler room." When this *teamwork between teams* occurs, the center acts like a community. Caregivers, for example, are on the lookout for natural and found materials for their own and one another's children. They each open their doors to curious children from other rooms who wish to peek in on and even visit the children next door or down the hall. They may meet together as a larger group of four or six from time to time for daily team planning as time and schedules permit. They all become knowledgeable about the whole range of infant-toddler behavior and can act as a resource for any parent connected with the center.

Of course, there will be unavoidable departures of children or staff in even the best of programs. So establishing working conditions that encourage staff retention and providing program quality to ensure stability of the child population must go hand in hand with planning for team continuity. Both working conditions and program quality depend on staff having ongoing administrative support and opportunities for training and professional development.

A new program hiring new staff can establish caregiver continuity from the outset. An ongoing program, however, may need time to shift from the practice of moving infants and toddlers from room to room with a different caregiver team in each room. The administration and staff will need opportunities for discussion and problem solving, a strong commitment to providing

This new caregiver (left) is used to working exclusively with young toddlers—so she spends time observing older toddlers and their caregivers, in preparation for "moving up" with her children to the older toddler room.

continuity of care for children and families, and a firm belief in each caregiver's ability to observe children and support them through all of their infant-toddler stages. While caregivers who are used to caring only for infants, for example, may initially miss the security of working with one, familiar age group, they generally enjoy their deepening relationships with children and parents as they make the shift to working with their children at older ages as well. Further, by staying with children as they mature, caregivers witness the same continuum of infant-toddler development that parents do. Instead of focusing on just the timetable and milestones within a narrow band of that continuum, they come to see early child development as encompassing a broad range of individual differences.

To provide a program of quality, one that serves children and families as effectively as possible, *daily team planning* is essential. Meeting together for about 30 minutes each day, the members of the caregiver team discuss, interpret, and plan around child observations, using the ingredients of active learning and the key experiences as a guiding framework. This is a time when caregivers reflect on their own practices to solve any practical problems that have arisen. Together, based on their knowledge of child develop-

During team planning, caregivers discuss, interpret, and plan around child observations using the ingredients of active learning and the key experiences as a guide.

ment, they build a common understanding of their children as sensory-motor learners and social beings and devise strategies to support their strengths, interests, and emerging abilities.

Although it may be a tall order for infant-toddler caregiver teams, finding a half hour daily for team planning can be done. It takes determination, creative scheduling, and administrative support. Here are several strategies that teams have found to work:

- Set aside as daily planning time the first 30 minutes after children have settled down for afternoon naps.

- In programs with younger children who nap at various times, plan during the time of day when the fewest children are awake. In some such programs, the center director plays with the non-nappers or hires an aide to do so while the caregiver team plans.

- Try meeting together during a 30-minute segment of morning or afternoon outside time. Replace the primary caregivers with administrative staff, early childhood education students (if your program is associated with a college or university), or an aide hired specifically to cover for teams during daily planning time.

- Plan a daily schedule for caregivers that includes 30 minutes for planning either before children's arrival or after their departure each day.

There may be no *ideal* time for daily team planning in infant-toddler programs, where children rely on the constant presence of their primary caregivers even when other competent adults are standing in for them. Nevertheless, it is important for caregiver teams and administrators to work together to designate and schedule such a time. In the long run, team members are more effective caregivers when they take time together each day to think about what they are observing in children, how to support them, and how to solve problems as they arise.

Caregivers' Strategies for Collaboration

As they work together with children throughout the day, talk with parents, and meet together for their daily planning, the two (or three) caregivers who form a team try to support one another, draw on their respective strengths, and turn their understanding of children and child development into practical ideas to try. The following strategies help them carry out this role:

- **Practice open communication.**
- **Make joint decisions about program issues.**
- **Observe children, discuss child observations, and plan ways to support individual children.**

Practice open communication

Open communication involves speaking in an honest, straightforward manner. Psychologist Virginia Satir (1988) calls this process *leveling*. When you level with others, you strive to communicate what you mean as clearly as possible. Your emotions, physical posture, facial expressions, and tone of voice match what you are saying. When you are upset, for example, you look upset and say so when asked. ("I'm upset," Kim says to her teammate, Yvonne, "because, when there weren't enough shovels to go around at group time, Carlos bit Tanner to get his shovel. He's *never* done that before!") This contrasts with the confusing practice of looking upset, acting upset, but saying otherwise or refusing to talk about what is troubling you. An example would be Kim saying "Nothing's wrong! Everything's okay!" at the same time that she was acting very upset about the biting incident.

Practicing open communication, or leveling, calls for recognizing and avoiding confusing conversational habits. Satir identifies four such behaviors—*placating, blaming, computing,* and *distracting.* The following descriptions of these negative behaviors may help team members assess their own conversational styles.

Placating involves soothing or reducing another person's anger by yielding to that person's ideas or demands. When you placate, you agree with others, no matter what you really think or feel, so they will not get angry with you. Physically, you may assume a posture that suggests humility as you

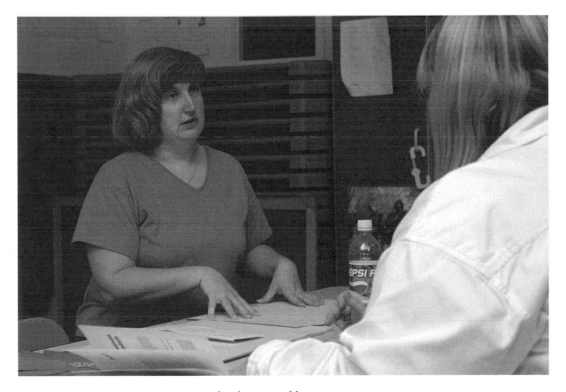

Caregivers strive to communicate as clearly as possible.

apologize or admit responsibility for what has gone wrong, effectively closing the subject and preventing constructive discussion from taking place. For example, if Yvonne were to reply to Kim as a placater, Yvonne might say, "I'm really sorry about the biting, Kim. It's all my fault. If I had set out enough shovels, maybe it wouldn't have happened. Don't be upset, okay? I'll try to do better tomorrow!" This would have cut off open discussion in which the team members might have, together, agreed to insure that group-time materials were always ready and in sufficient supply. They might also have gone on to discuss how to best handle biting situations.

Blaming involves accusing, holding the other person responsible, or criticizing that person. When you blame, you may assume what appears to others to be a fairly aggressive posture. You may cut a person down, talk in a loud voice, ask questions but not wait for answers, or make "you" statements that deflect the conversation from the real issue at hand. For example, if Yvonne were to act as a blamer in responding to Kim, she might say, "You get upset too easily, Kim! You'll get grey hair before your time if you get this upset when one toddler bites another one." Kim herself might have, but did not, act as blamer in making her original statement. She didn't say to Yvonne, for example, "This kind of thing [biting] always happens because *you* don't think ahead about what we will need for group time!"

Computing involves speaking in an unfeeling way, using big words so people will think you know a lot and be afraid to prolong a discussion with you. When you compute in responding to someone who is upset, for example, you may talk at length in a calm and reasonable tone, sitting stiffly, with your hands and face still. If Yvonne were to respond in this manner to Kim, she might say, "Well, Kim, Carlos clearly needs to learn to delay gratification. I'm not surprised at his regressive behavior, since he comes from a dysfunctional situation." Once again, Kim's chances of having an extended discussion with Yvonne could have been thwarted by this mechanical response delivered with a superior air.

Distracting is sidetracking the conversation by bringing up a totally irrelevant issue, to avoid an uncomfortable subject. Physically, you may show your discomfort by nervously moving your arms or legs, repeatedly standing up and sitting down, fiddling with a pen or pencil. If Yvonne were to respond as a distractor to Kim, she might jump up and say, "I just remembered, we're out of diapers for Bobby. I'd better call his mom. She's such a nice person. I really like talking with her. I think she knows my neighbor, the one with the grape arbor."

When team members make a habit of placating, blaming, computing, or distracting, the dialogue of teamwork becomes very difficult. By contrast, although it may seem scary at first, leveling brings great relief. People share their real thoughts and feelings, take turns speaking and listening, and respectfully give their full attention to others as they speak. They speak honestly but also address one another with respect instead of hurling guilt-inducing personal assaults. The urge to "let it all hang out" is tempered by a stronger

Team members share their real thoughts and feelings, take turns speaking and listening, and respectfully give their full attention to one other.

desire for civility. Each person participates in a give-and-take manner in the focused discussion that further unfolds with each contribution. As levelers, team members find themselves relying on one another's strengths and differences to co-create the strategies they need to support their particular children in their particular setting. At the same time, they practice among themselves the same honest, straightforward exchanges they have with the children in their care. Following is an excerpt from Kim and Yvonne's conversation about biting, in which both speak as levelers:

Kim: *I'm upset because, when there weren't enough shovels to go around at group time, Carlos bit Tanner to get his shovel. He's* never *done that before!*

Yvonne: *Biting is upsetting to see, especially when you weren't expecting it. We could probably have avoided that incident by better planning on our part—making sure that at the start there's enough for everyone at group time.*

Kim: *I know that toddlers bite (sometimes even when there are enough shovels), and Carlos is very active. I'm glad that he knows what he wants, but it's not okay for him to hurt another child. There have to be some limits.*

Yvonne: *Right. I guess, to a toddler like Carlos, who's just beginning to talk, biting seems to be a good way to get a point across quickly. But even if biting's just an attempt to say something in a hurry, we don't want children biting other children. Kim, since you're obviously so upset now, how did you stay so calm at the time? How did you deal with the situation?*

Kim: *Well, I could see that the bite didn't break the skin. I tried to be calm and matter-of-fact so the children wouldn't get any more upset than they already were. I stroked Tanner's bitten arm, telling Carlos "Be gentle with Tanner. He doesn't like to be bitten." Then I stroked Carlos's arm as well and said to him, "Be gentle." Then I said, "Carlos, it looks like you want Tanner's shovel, but he doesn't want to give it up."*

Yvonne: *Oh, I wondered what you said, because I saw Tanner take another shovel off the shelf and give it to Carlos. That seemed to end the whole episode.*

Kim: *It did. Carlos wanted Tanner's shovel, but he was satisfied with the one from the shelf. I do think I have to watch Carlos in a new way, though, so biting doesn't become a habit.*

Yvonne: *Well, I guess that by helping Carlos identify the problem—he wanted Tanner's shovel—you gave both children the opportunity to come up with a satisfactory alternative to biting.*

Even as levelers, team members like Kim and Yvonne do not always agree. They learn, however, to examine their differences and do joint problem-solving. For example, when two levelers discover differences, they try to remain calm and patient with each other and acknowledge the strong feelings involved. They are ready, as early childhood educator Katie Gerecke (1998) has pointed out, to listen carefully to each other's ideas and concerns, state their own beliefs clearly, look for areas of agreement, brainstorm for solutions, and choose one to try. After trying their ideas, they reflect on how well they worked. Here is an excerpt from a conversation between Kim and Yvonne in which they attempt to talk openly about their different opinions on what position they should place nonmobile infants in at choice time.

Kim: *Today I put Mallory in the infant seat at choice time to protect her from Jamal and Jai. They're really getting good at crawling, and Jamal almost crawled right over her head when she was lying on the floor yesterday!*

Yvonne: *Hey, I thought we weren't going to restrict babies to infant seats for choice time! I think* not *putting Jamal and Jai in those things at choice time was what led to their crawling.*

Kim: *Well, look at us! We're getting a little worked up here! I guess we both have pretty strong feelings about where infants should be!*

Yvonne: (Laughs) *Yeah, I guess we do! Okay, let's talk about this. You want Mallory to be safe, right?*

Kim: *Yes, and I think that now that Jai and Jamal are crawling, she's safer when sitting in the infant seat than when lying on the floor.*

Yvonne: *I want her to be safe, too, but I also want her to have a chance to get ready for crawling. Right now, she needs to kick her legs, wave her arms, turn her head, and work her way up to rolling over. She's free to do all these things on the floor, but not in an infant seat.*

Kim: *Well, I want her to be safe, but I don't want to restrict the way she moves, either. Maybe I could put Mallory back on the floor and put the big pillows around her—not too close, but as sort of a speed bump for our two creeper-crawlers.*

Yvonne: *That might work. She could still move freely, but the pillows would create a safety barrier around her until she's ready to crawl.*

Kim: *Let's try that tomorrow.*

(Several days later.)

Kim: *Well, the pillows seem to be working for Mallory.*

Yvonne: *Yes, Jamal and Jai do try to climb over them, but the pillows slow them down so you or I can move over to Mallory soon enough to make sure they don't crawl on top of her!* (See "Steps in Resolving Conflicts With Adults," p. 330.)

Make joint decisions about program issues

It is important for caregivers to discuss and reach agreement on the issues that underlie working well together. Team members need to sort out and deal with their individual concerns about space and materials, schedules and routines, roles and responsibilities, so their interactions with children and families can reflect their ease with one another rather than their unresolved tensions. By wrestling with these issues, the caregiver team lays the groundwork for a welcoming early childhood environment. The following are examples of the kinds of questions that infant-toddler caregiver teams need to address and work out together.

✦ *Space and materials*

- How will we arrange (or rearrange) our indoor and outdoor space to promote active learning?

- How might the arrangement of this space work better for nonmobile infants? For mobile infants? For young toddlers? For older toddlers?

- What might we do to make this space more comfortable for children and adults?

Team members make joint decisions about space and materials, schedules and routines, and roles and responsibilities.

- What materials might we add, eliminate, or supplement to support children's interests and sensory-motor development?

- Are there any physical changes we can make to the indoor and outdoor space to enhance children's opportunities for movement? For sensory exploration? For social interaction?

- Whose help and support do we need to make these changes?

◆ *Schedules and routines*

- How will we organize our overall daily schedule? How can we make sure it is predictable (so everyone knows what happens next) yet flexible enough to accommodate individual children and their care routines?

- To what extent are we incorporating all the ingredients of active learning and adult support into each part of the day?

- What does (or might) make it possible for us to give our full attention to each child during feedings, mealtimes, and bodily care routines?

- What choices do our children have at mealtime and nap time?

- What roles do we assume at choice time and outside time?

- What are our children doing at group time?

- What can we do to make arrivals and departures smoother for children and parents?

✦ *Roles and responsibilities*

- How will we divide up our daily tasks? (Who loads, runs, unloads the dishwasher or the washer and dryer? Restocks snack foods and utensils? Restocks the diaper-changing area? Washes toys? Changes bedding? Takes out and puts away outdoor play materials? Cleans paintbrushes? Restocks art materials? Fills and empties the sand and water table(s)? Adds or replaces materials? Feeds the fish, the animals? Waters the plants?)

- How do we keep track of what needs to be done each day and by whom?

- What daily records do we keep, for what purpose?

- What are our respective roles during team planning?

- How do we record our observations and plans?

- How do we support one another throughout the day as we work together with our children?

- How do we communicate with one another while maintaining our focus on the children?

As caregivers work together over time, they construct their own responses to these and similar questions. While each team comes up with its own strategies to try, every team relies on open communication, patience with themselves, and a belief in their ability to solve problems and seek out support from administrators and others as needed.

Observe children, discuss child observations, and plan ways to support individual children

At the heart of the daily teamwork process lie three questions:

- What did we see children doing today?

- What do their actions tell us about them?

- How can we provide materials and interact with children to support their play and learning tomorrow?

These questions prompt the caregiver team to examine children's actions, interpret them in terms of child development, and plan follow-up support strategies. Overall, the team reflects on the nature and implications of each child's actions and communications.

✦ *Observe children throughout the day*

As infants and toddlers continually grow and develop through their day-to-day active learning, their caregivers attempt to see who they are and what they are doing, so they can be present and ready with individual support. This is why caregivers are careful observers as they interact with children during their mealtimes, their bodily care routines, their naptime routines, and during their exploration and play with materials and peers at choice time, outside time, and group time. Caregivers take note of a wide range of behaviors: how children move, how they express themselves, what materials interest them, what causes them frustration, how they attempt to solve problems, and which other children they enjoy being with.

Because so much happens in a child care setting on any given day, infant-toddler caregivers have devised a number of ways of reminding themselves of all the interesting things they have seen and heard. They bring these reminders to team planning for discussion. Some ideas for remembering these observations follow. The ideas may work for your team, or they may suggest to you other self-reminder strategies to try:

- Carry in your pocket a pen or pencil along with index cards or a pad of sticky notes. When you observe something concerning a child, jot down the child's name and key words, drawings, or symbols that will help you at team planning to reconstruct what you saw. (Jamal, ramp, pillows, babble - - - > Mallory)

- Place spiral notepads or clipboards supplied with paper and a pencil in strategic places around the room(s). When making an observation, jot the child's name and key words on the notepad or clipboard nearest you.

- Keep an instant camera and film on a shelf above the children's reach. Take photos of actions you want to remember, and bring them to team planning. (Ask local camera shops and discount stores for donations of "expired" film.)

- As you log routine entries about a child's feedings, diaper changes, and naps, jot down key words to remind you of any unique or striking actions you saw and want to share. If you don't want to write directly on the child's log sheet, keep nearby a pad of sticky notes to write on, and attach these to the log sheet.

- At a convenient level where caregivers can write on it, tape a blank piece of paper to the wall for jotting down notes on each child, or keep a tape recorder handy. When you see actions you want to remember for a particular child, jot key words on that child's paper, or record a brief statement on tape.

As you observe children, watch and listen carefully, with an open mind. You want to see and hear as much as you possibly can without making snap judgments or jumping too quickly to conclusions. To help you remember what you have seen and heard, make brief notes to yourself. Because your time with the children is so action-packed, it is often difficult to write much more than key words. These brief, personal notes, however, will help you reconstruct your observations later in the day, when you have a chance to record them in more detail and decide with your teammate what they mean and what to do about them. However, whenever you are able to write in more detail, by all means, do so! Again, stick with the facts, and avoid making judgments. For example, you might note that "Liam banged his spoon on the table" rather than that "Liam deliberately annoyed everyone at the table by banging his spoon."

✦ *Discuss, interpret, and record child observations, using the key experiences as a guide*

Each caregiver arrives at team planning with a head full of child observations and some quickly jotted notes or photos to refresh her memory. As team members review the day, they share their observations, and by using the key experiences as objective referents, they figure out what the observations might mean. They then record the observations, for example, by writing short anecdotes under the relevant key experience categories on a form. The notes staff record on each child's form serve to chart growth and development and can be shared with parents and other caregivers as needed. Following is a portion of Kim and Yvonne's team-planning meeting that illustrates this process:

Having just changed the diaper of the child she is holding, this caregiver takes a minute to jot a note about his play. "I'm writing about how you pushed the truck," she tells him.

Discuss

Kim: (Looking at the note she made to herself that reads "Jamal, ramp, pillows, babble - - - > Mallory") *I was struck by something that happened between Jamal and Mallory today. I put Mallory on a blanket on the floor at choice time and put the big pillows around her so she'd have lots of room to move. Jamal was crawling up and down the carpeted ramp, as he has been doing for the past couple of days. At one point, he seemed to pause and catch sight of Mallory inside her pillow barricade. He crawled down the ramp and headed straight for her. It looked like he really made a choice to go see her!*

Yvonne: *Well, you know, they did spend a lot of time on the floor next to each other before Jamal learned to crawl.*

Kim: *Yes, they did, and I'm wondering if maybe he misses her. Anyway, he crawled up to one of the pillows, and then he crawled onto and over it. I was close to both of them, but this time I didn't try to stop him, because it seemed that he really wanted to make some kind of connection with Mallory.*

Yvonne: *You were probably ready to prevent him from hurting her!*

Kim: *Yes, I was, but what was really interesting was that once she saw him struggling to get over the pillow, Mallory started to wiggle all over and smile and coo as though she was really happy to see him! When Jamal did get over the pillow into Mallory's little space, he just sat next to her and waved his arms and babbled back to her!*

Yvonne: *So they had what looked like a conversation?*

During team planning, these caregivers discuss and record their observations of children.

Kim: *Yeah! Sort of like two long-lost pals! They both wiggled and vocalized. I thought Jamal might try to pat her or something, but he didn't. And then after a bit, Mallory turned away, and eventually Jamal crawled back over the pillow and back to the ramp.*

Interpret

Yvonne: *So what do you think was going on here?*

Kim: *Well, let's see.* (To help them interpret Jamal's actions objectively in terms of child development, she turns to a list of the infant-toddler key experiences and studies them. Yvonne moves closer so she too can see the list.) *First, I'm looking at the category of "social relations." The key experiences* building relationships with peers, *and* expressing emotions *might help us interpret Jamal's actions. Jamal wanted to get close to Mallory. He was pleased to see her. When he "talked" to her, he used his whole body.*

Yvonne: *Yes, and even though Mallory is so young, she also showed pleasure at seeing Jamal by the way she wiggled, smiled, and cooed at him! So there seems to be some kind of social relationship between the two, maybe one that started before either of them could crawl.*

Kim: (Turning back to the key experience list) *I guess, looking under the "communication and language" category, we could interpret their actions as* communicating nonverbally, *because they did seem to be having a little conversation. They looked at each other and wiggled and babbled. This went on till Mallory turned away.*

Yvonne: *Yes, and under the category "sense of self," they both* expressed initiative. *Jamal decided to climb down the ramp and over the pillow to get to Mallory, and Mallory turned away when she decided she had had enough social exchange!*

Kim: *The other thing that strikes me as I look at the "space" key experiences is that Jamal really was* observing people and things from various perspectives. *He actually saw Mallory from the top of the ramp, and then he remembered where she was even when she was hidden behind the pillow! That seems like quite an accomplishment!*

Yvonne: *Yes, and he had to climb over the pillow to see her again! I'm beginning to see that he was actually* problem solving, *too—going back to the "sense of self" category. So his mind was as busy as his body!*

Record

Kim: *Okay, so I'm going to record this on Jamal's observation form under what?* (Pause.) *I think under "social relations," since that's what first struck me,* (pause) *and then I'll also make a note under "space."* (Kim writes the following in the "social relations" column of Jamal's form: "12/15 At CT [choice time], J. [Jamal] crawled up the ramp, looked down from the ramp at Mallory surrounded by pillows on the floor, crawled down the ramp and over a pillow, and sat on the floor next to her. He looked at her, waved his arms, and babbled at her, 'Oooweee, bebebe . . .' Mallory smiled, wiggled, and cooed back to him." In the "space" column of Jamal's form, Kim writes: "12/15 [See 12/15 anecdote under 'social relations' related to *observing people and things from various perspectives*]".)

Before we continue with Kim and Yvonne's plans for the next day, a word about recording child observations. The most useful anecdotes paint a picture that is clear to people who did not witness the original event. Effective anecdotes include the following characteristics:

- *Context:* Include the date (12/15; also be sure to indicate the *year* at the top of the sheet on which you record anecdotes), each child's name (Jamal, Mallory), the time of day (choice time), and where the action occurred (the ramp, on the floor next to Mallory).

- *Actions and sounds or words:* Describe what the child did and said (for example, "crawled up the ramp," "looked down from the ramp at Mallory," "Oooweee, bebebe . . . ").

- *Facts:* Include objective details rather than general or subjective statements (for example, "He looked at her, waved his arms, and babbled at her, 'Oooweee, bebebe . . .' Mallory smiled, wiggled, and cooed back to him," rather than "They were glad to see each other").

To keep track of each child's development, Kim and Yvonne use a form to record the anecdotes from their child observations, keeping one such form for each child. On the form, they organize the anecdotes according to the nine key experience categories—**sense of self, social relations, creative representation, movement, music, communication and language, exploring objects, early quantity and number, space,** and **time.** For a sample of this system of recording and organizing child observations, see "Child Observations" (pp. 318–319), which illustrates how Kim and Yvonne have recorded their observations of Jamal.

✦ *Plan ways to support individual children*

After discussing child observations and using the key experiences as a guide for interpreting and recording them, members of the caregiver team ask themselves, "So, what do we do tomorrow based on what we have learned about our children today?" To illustrate this step of the teamwork process, let's return to the conversation between Yvonne and Kim.

Yvonne: *So, what are these two babies telling us? How can we support them tomorrow?*

Kim: *Hmm . . .* (Both team members pause to think.)

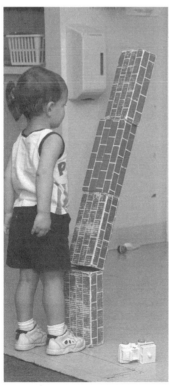

*Kent's caregivers wrote this anecdote during their team planning: "7/7 At choice time in the block area, Kent stacked up three cardboard brick blocks end-to-end. When he added a fourth block, the stack toppled, so he began all over again!" They recorded this anecdote on Kent's observation form under **creative representation**, with the key experience* exploring building and art materials *in mind.*

Child Observations

Child: Jamal   Year: 20___   Observers: Kim and Yvonne   J = Jamal, CT = choice time, OT = outside time, A = arrival

Sense of Self	Social Relations	Creative Representation	Movement and Music
8/22 J. reached for and grasped a dry diaper during diapering.	8/15 At A, Jamal cried when his mom gave him to Kim. Kim gave him back to his mom, and he stopped crying. She talked to him, held him for about 10 minutes, then said, "I'm going to give you to Kim now." Kim held him the same way his mom held him. He looked sad but did not cry.	8/25 Waking up from his nap, J. lay on his back and watched his hands as he moved them back and forth above his head.	8/19 Lying on his back at CT, J. kicked his legs vigorously.
9/6 J. watched himself in the mirror during CT. He smiled at his reflection when Kim said, "There's Jamal!"	8/20 Jamal snuggled in Kim's arms and gazed at her intently while he drank his bottle.	9/11 At CT, J. selected a crumpled piece of blue kraft paper to hold and taste. When it made noise, he made a blowing noise.	8/23 When Kim sang London Bridge with Latisha, J. turned his head toward their singing.
10/1 Waking from nap, J. cried. When Kim stroked his arms and legs and asked him what was troubling him, J. grabbed his foot and put his toes in his mouth. When Kim said, "You've got your toesies in your mouth," he looked up at her with a slight smile.	9/9 At CT, J. watched Mallory, who was lying on the next blanket.	11/4 At CT, J. babbled "Bebebebe . . . " at a bear in a board book, then cheered on that page.	10/12 At CT on the floor, J. rolled over from his back to his front!
12/10 J. picked up banana pieces and fed himself. After smooshing some pieces, he licked banana off his fingers.	12/15 At CT, J. crawled up the ramp, looked down from the ramp at Mallory surrounded by pillows on the floor, crawled down the ramp and over a pillow, and sat on the floor next to her. He looked at her, waved his arms, and babbled at her, "Ooowee, bebebe . . . " Mallory smiled, wiggled, and cooed back to him.		11/2 Lying on his back at CT, J. held a short-handled spoon with both hands, let go with one hand, waved it around, then reached over and held it in his other hand.
			11/10 At CT, J. got himself into a sitting position!

Child Observations (continued)

Exploration and Early Logic

Communication and Language	Exploring Objects	Early Quantity and Number	Space	Time
8/17 Hearing his dad's voice at the end of the day, J. cooed and wiggled all over.	8/18 On the floor at CT, Jamal reached for and grasped a rubber duck.	11/1 During diapering, J. laughed when Kim hid her face behind the clean diaper and then appeared again and said, "Peek-a-boo, I see you!"	11/30 When J. heard and saw his dad at the end of the day, he crawled toward him as fast as he could go.	10/8 At CT, J. grasped a rubber duck and banged it against the floor, causing it to squeak. He looked at the duck in surprise, then banged it to make it squeak again. He repeated this action several times, making high-pitched squeaking noises as he did so.
9/1 At OT, J. stilled each time he heard the toddlers next door shake the jingle bells.	9/7 During diapering, J. reached for and grasped Kim's braid. He let go and grasped her other braid.		12/12 J. crawled onto the low wooden box, sat on it, and looked around.	
9/14 During diapering, J. made a lip-smacking noise. Kim repeated it, then J. repeated it, and so on, for several rounds.	10/3 At CT, J. held a large shell, gazed at it, mouthed it, and made a funny face.		12/14 J. crawled into a large carton and began to cry. When Yvonne lay next to the open carton and said, "It looks like you want to turn around, Jamal," he turned himself around and sat looking out.	
10/20 Waking from nap, J. looked at and babbled to his stuffed bear, "Beboo, beboo . . ."	12/23 Sitting next to a basket of household objects, J. selected a wooden spoon, then a tea strainer to hold and mouth.		12/15 (See 12/15 anecdote under "social relations" related to observing people and things from various perspectives.)	

Yvonne: *Well, I'm thinking about the "space" key experiences. Maybe we could provide both of them with more chances to see things from different vantage points. What if we put Mallory on the mattress instead of surrounding her with pillows? Then she'd still be free to move, but she'd be able to see other children better, and Jamal could see her better, since no pillows would be blocking his view. She'd still be protected, because the mattress would act as a speed bump to slow down anyone crawling toward her. If Jamal crawls up there with her, he'd be up off the floor too, seeing things from a little different perspective.*

Kim: *That might work. We'd still have to be close by, watching. And we could put the mattress in the corner so Jamal could approach it from only two, not all four, sides. This idea might lead to even more interaction between them.*

Yvonne: *Yes, and for Jamal, I'm trying to think of other things he might climb or crawl onto. I could put out a couple of large hollow wooden blocks tomorrow and see if he climbs onto them.*

Kim: *How about using the small packing cartons too? If we stuffed them with newspaper for extra support and sealed them up, they'd be sturdy enough to climb on or sit on.*

Yvonne: *Great! And here's another idea—we could bring out the rocking boat and turn it step-side-up. If Jamal's ready for steps, he'll try them; if he's not, he won't—but Jai might. Jai's mom said he's been trying out steps at home.*

Kim: *It just occurred to me that the changing table might provide Jamal or Jai with another perspective! Maybe for Jamal, especially, we could take some time during diapering for him to sit on the changing table and just look around at the rest of room. We could try describing what he seems to be looking at. It might work, it might not. We could try it and see.*

Yvonne: *Okay! Now, what about "social relations"? What can we do to further the friendship that seems to be forming between Mallory and Jamal?*

Kim: *Well, we could try putting Mallory down on the floor near Jamal or move the mattress she's on so it's closer to where Jamal is playing. I mean, if Jamal is climbing on ramps and boxes, we could put Mallory closer to him than she was today, but of course not so close that she's in danger.*

Yvonne: *And the other way around—we could move Jamal closer to her by putting his toy basket on the floor a bit closer—even quite close—to Mallory, since they're used to being on neighboring blankets.*

Kim: *Now that Jamal's crawling, Mallory can't always be near him, or vice versa. So sometimes we could try putting Bobby and Mallory closer together on the floor or mattress—since Bobby isn't crawling yet. This wouldn't support Jamal and Mallory's friendship, but it might mean Bobby and Mallory could keep each other company the way Mallory and Jamal did before he learned to crawl.*

Yvonne: *That might work. But I think we need to continue respecting babies' preferences when they seem to be seeking each other out* and *when they withdraw. I just think we need to be sensitive to both situations.*

Kim: *I agree!*

Yvonne: *Now, let's figure out which of these ideas we can work into tomorrow's plan.*

The chart on p. 322 is a summary of Kim and Yvonne's discussion of their observations of Jamal and Mallory. After discussing the possible support strategies in this chart, Kim and Yvonne decide how they can include some (but not all) of them in their plan for the next day. To see how they record their ideas, see "Sample Evolving Daily Plan: Kim and Yvonne" on p. 323. As they go on to discuss observations of other children, they will generate other ideas and strategies to record on this daily planning sheet.

During the daily process of team planning, it is important to (1) record your anecdotes from child observations and (2) record your plans for the next day. Kim and Yvonne, for example, take turns at this: One day, Kim

During team planning, one team member records child observations while the other records the ideas they will try the next day.

Summary of Kim and Yvonne's Discussion

Observation	Related Key Experiences	Possible Support Strategies
12/15 At CT [choice time], Jamal crawled up the ramp, looked down from the ramp at Mallory surrounded by pillows on the floor, crawled down the ramp and over a pillow, and sat on the floor next to her. He looked at her, waved his arms, and babbled at her, "Oooweee, be-bebe . . ." Mallory smiled, wiggled, and cooed back to him.	**Social Relations** • Building relationships with peers • Expressing emotions **Sense of Self** • Expressing initiative • Solving problems encountered in exploration and play **Communication & Language** • Communicating nonverbally **Space** • Observing people and things from various perspectives	**Social Relations** • Put Mallory closer to Jamal. • Put Jamal's toy basket close to Mallory. • Put Bobby close to Mallory. • Respect children's preferences for approaching and withdrawing. **Space** • Put Mallory on the mattress, in a corner. • Add things to climb on: large hollow blocks, packing cartons, step-side-up rocking boat. • Give Jamal time to sit on the changing table and look around.

records the observations on the children's individual forms while Yvonne records ideas for the next day on the planning sheet; the next day, they switch tasks. They keep all the children's observation forms together (but separated by divisions) in a looseleaf notebook. At various times, Kim and Yvonne personally add to the notebook their anecdotes from any observations they have not had time to discuss on a given day. They both refer to this growing collection of anecdotes when they are talking to parents, preparing parent reports, and assessing children's growth and development using the High/Scope Child Observation Record (COR) for Infants and Toddlers (1999).

Sample Evolving Daily Plan: Kim and Yvonne

Date: *Tues. 12/15*	**a.m.**	**p.m.**
Arrival		
Choice Time *Put Mallory on mattress in corner.*		*Put out large hollow blocks and turn rocking boat step-side-up for Jamal.*
Group Time		
Outside Time *Try putting Bobby and Mallory on blankets near each other.*		
Departure		
Bodily Care *After diaper change, see if Jamal wants to sit on the changing table and look around.*		
Meals		
Naps		
To Remember *Gather, stuff, and seal packing boxes to climb on (for next week).*		

The Caregiver-Parent Partnership

Caregivers like Yvonne and Kim form partnerships with the parents of their infants and toddlers. These partnerships are characterized by mutual trust and respect and include an ongoing conversational give-and-take about the growth and development of the children in whom all of them have a common, abiding interest. Because infants and toddlers cannot yet speak clearly for themselves—*Hey, let me sleep! I had a rough night last night. My new teeth were driving me crazy!*—caregivers and parents have no alternative but to share what they know about the nonverbal but communicative children in their care. By paying close attention to each other and participating in joint activities, caregivers and parents use a teamwork approach to creating a supportive environment for their children. According to infant and toddler specialist Abbey Griffen (1998),

> Since the parents are the child's primary caregivers, the time required to build trust between caregiver and parent benefits the baby in the long run. Relationships are central to quality care. Relationships between baby and caregiver take time, understanding gained from the parents and family members, and careful observations. The caregiver, although knowledgeable and skilled, cannot

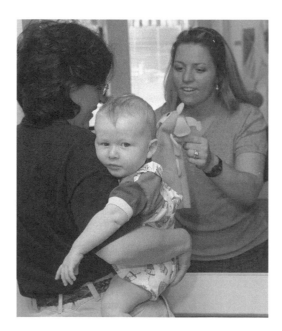 

Caregivers and parents work in partnership to create a supportive environment for their children. During arrival, for example, this mom explains to her child's caregiver how important the little puppet is to her child today. And, on the caregiver's hand, the little puppet does seem to make saying goodbye to Mom a little easier.

presume to know more than the parent before doing the work of relationship building. That work requires gathering information, testing strategies, and observation over time. Finally, each baby deserves a secure, predictable emotional environment; for that reason, professional infant/toddler caregivers know that building a trusting relationship with the parent is essential. (pp. 26–27)

While caregiver-parent partnerships take time and effort to establish and sustain, everyone involved benefits. Together, parents and caregivers collect, exchange, and interpret specific information about the child's ever-changing actions, feelings, preferences, interests, and abilities. They learn from each other what does and does not work with the particular child at the center of their relationship. New parents gain confidence in their parenting skills. Experienced parents receive support as they adapt to new stages of parenthood or deal with relatives or friends critical of their child care arrangements. Caregivers grow in their ability to attune themselves to each child. Both parents and caregivers are reassured by their mutual efforts to smooth the transition between home and center, and parents and caregivers with differing beliefs about childrearing, care, and early learning often expand their perception of the possible. The child, in turn, sensing the comfortable bond between parent and caregiver, reflects their ease with each other in his or her behavior— a happy mom makes Baby happy; a happy baby makes Mom happy. Further, the parent-caregiver "team" serves as a strong advocate for the child in other settings, as needed.

Guidelines for Effective Caregiver-Parent Partnerships

For caregivers, following these basic guidelines can contribute to the success of the caregiver-parent partnership:

- Recognize role separation.
- Practice open communication.
- Focus on parents' strengths.
- Use a problem-solving approach to conflict.

Recognizing role separation

Caregivers can best support active learning when they recognize the difference between supporting parents and competing with them. The overriding goal is to provide a warm, secure, interesting environment for the children parents entrust to them. Caregivers make a conscious effort not to compete

Parents, in general, love their children passionately. Their emotions play a large part in guiding their interactions with their offspring.

with parents for children's love and attention, and they do not try to glorify their own child care abilities. Rather, they respect the primacy of the parent-child bond and see themselves as mature, knowledgeable adults children can trust and rely on in the absence of their parents.

Understanding their separate roles allows caregivers and parents to work together without stepping on each other's toes. While the child is at the heart of the caregiver-parent relationship, the parent's and the caregiver's respective roles relative to the child are different and complementary. Parents, in general, love their children passionately. Their emotions play a large part in guiding their interactions with their offspring. Caregivers, as professionals, take great interest in the well-being of the individual children in their care. They tend to think very carefully about how they interact with them. In a sense, one might say that parents feel first and think later, whereas caregivers think first and then feel. "Parents operate (and should operate) from the gut level, reacting emotionally rather than responding reasonably," early childhood educators Janet Gonzalez-Mena and Dianne Widmeyer Eyer have said (1993). "Of course, parents should also use their heads, should be objective now and then. . . . Caregivers should also be human . . . but they should mostly be fairly objective and thoughtful in goals and reactions. . . . The point is balance. The balance swings more to feelings and spontaneity in the parenting role and more to thoughtfulness, objectivity, and planning in the caregiver role" (pp. 221–222). Fortunately, children need both passionate adults and thoughtful adults, or as psychologist Urie Bronfenbrenner (1985) distinguished them, *irrational* and *rational* adults:

> You [as a child] need both kinds of involvement: rational and irrational. First, you need somebody who thinks you're the most wonderful creature in the world . . . who's that crazy about you. . . . You also need somebody who is *not* irrational about you; who values you as a child but considers you no more wonderful than another child. Such a person works for your development in a fair, rational manner. If you don't have somebody like that in your life, it is very difficult to become a full human being. Another problem is that the same person can't play both roles, because a person really can't be crazy and fair at the same time. (pp. 47–48)

Parents and caregivers, then, are not in competition. Rather, they play quite different roles in relation to the child, roles the child relies on them to carry out in their own particular ways in a consistent and dependable manner. Moreover, it is important for caregivers and parents alike to be aware of one of the findings of an ongoing large-scale research study of early child care (beginning in infancy) involving 1,300 children in nine states. This study is being conducted by the National Institute of Child Health and Human Development (NICHD) and, as reported by education writer Linda Jacobson (1999, p. 5), it has concluded that *"a mother's influence on her child is not affected by the amount of time the child spends in care."*[13] While children are forming new relationships with their caregivers and peers, their primary relationship with their parents remains firmly intact.

---

[13]For detailed reports of this study, see NICHD (1997) and Owen (1999) in the References on p. 353.

In this program, parents (left and right) often play with their children before leaving them for the day. As this mom talks with her child's caregiver (center), it is clear that the child is at the center of the parent-caregiver relationship.

Practicing open communication

Another key to a successful caregiver-parent partnership is open communication—the same approach members of the caregiver team use with one another (see pp. 305–309). During caregiver-parent interchanges, the caregiver always makes an effort to level, so her emotions, physical posture, facial expression, and tone of voice match what she is saying to the parent. She clearly states her thoughts and feelings in a kind and thoughtful manner. The caregiver and parent engage in two-way conversation, meaning they take turns listening and speaking and respectfully give each other their full attention. Open communication provides a set of ground rules that guides conversations about the range of care and early learning issues caregivers and parents together face.

As open communicators, caregivers refrain from "computing" with parents, that is, displaying their child development expertise at the expense of parents' self-confidence. Regardless of how much they know about infants and toddlers, caregivers have a sense of humility about their role. They understand that supporting parents in their complex and long-term role is more effective than "teaching" or "correcting" them. They realize that parents know more than anyone else does about their own child. Most important, they know that their daily interactions with a particular child end after 2 or 3 years, whereas the parent-child bond is lifelong.

Focusing on parents' strengths

While open communication with parents may take considerable thought and effort, it is greatly aided by a caregiver's willingness to focus on parents' strengths rather than on any perceived faults or social barriers. Again, it is important to remember that the child is at the center of the parent-caregiver relationship and to make the assumption that both parents and caregivers have the same goal—to provide the best possible care and education for the child. On a personal level, caregivers interacting with the adults seeking child care today may find themselves presented with a wide range of adults: parents in professional occupations, parents with marginal employment, teen parents, single parents, parents with disabilities, retired grandparents, foster parents, nannies. Children may come from families representing a variety of faiths, cultures, home languages, and political beliefs. Each adult—parent and caregiver—brings who they are and what they know to the unfolding saga of a child's care and education. Therefore, it makes sense to let go of any negative impressions or stereotypes you may have. Acknowledge them to yourself in your own mind. *(Uh, oh. I'm feeling angry at this 15-year-old for having a baby!)* Then allow yourself to *meet parents as they are* rather than to shut them out because they do not fit your image of what parents ought to be. *(All right, this mom is here with her baby in my program. Her child deserves the best from both of us, and together, we can provide it!)* Instead of setting up barriers between yourself and the diverse families you may encounter, it is more productive and useful to the child for you to seek out and build a partnership based on parents' strengths and dreams. *(This mom is young, energetic, very involved with her child, and committed to finishing school. Maybe her determination will open doors.)*

Using a problem-solving approach to conflict

Finally, given the diversity of family experiences and childrearing practices within our communities, it is important to realize that parents and caregivers are bound to disagree from time to time. When they do, caregivers can turn to a problem-solving approach to conflict. The steps they use with adults are related to the problem-solving steps they use with children. (See "Steps in Resolving Conflicts With Adults," p. 330.) Here is a brief example of how this process unfolds:

> *At the end of the day, Lacie, Marlee's mom, arrives to find her baby Marlee sitting on the floor next to a basket of rattles and household items. She is holding and mouthing the cardboard tube from a roll of paper towels. Lacie takes the tube away from Marlee and offers her a rattle. Refusing the substi-*

Steps in Resolving Conflicts With Adults

1. Approach calmly.

Calm yourself, mentally acknowledging your own feelings.

Prepare yourself to listen.

Use a calm voice and gentle body language.

2. Acknowledge adults' feelings.

"You look really upset." "I can see you have very strong feelings about . . ."

3. Exchange information.

Take turns describing the details of the problem situation and your specific needs.

Use "I" statements rather than "you" statements.

Listen attentively as the other person speaks. Remember, this is a dialogue, not a debate.

4. Look at the problem from the child's viewpoint.

"What is the child showing or telling us through actions or words about . . . ?"

"How do our adult needs relate to the child's needs?"

5. Restate the problem.

"So the problem is . . ."

6. Generate ideas for solutions, and choose one together.

"What can we do to solve this problem?"

Together, brainstorm to come up with ideas for solutions.

Select an idea and co-design a strategy to try.

7. Be prepared to follow up the problem.

Take turns describing how the strategy is working.

If necessary, make adjustments together or return to Step 6.

---

tute, Marlee begins to cry. Lacie picks her up, approaches Kerra, Marlee's caregiver, and says, *"Why are you giving my baby trash to play with?"*

As Kerra calmly rises from the floor where she has been sitting with the children, she realizes that Lacie's question makes her feel both dismayed and defensive. But, setting these feelings aside, she also realizes the question is a sign of Lacie's strong, single-minded devotion to Marlee. She gives Lacie her full attention. **(This was Step 1: Approach calmly.)**

"I can see you're upset, Lacie," Kerra says, touching Lacie lightly on the arm. *"Of course I am!"* Lacie replies heatedly. As Marlee begins to cry harder, Lacie pats her to soothe her and then asks in a calmer voice, *"Why do you let my baby play with throw-aways?"* Marlee's crying subsides as her mom becomes calmer. **(This was Step 2: Acknowledge adults' feelings.)**

"Can you tell me what bothers you about the paper-towel tube?" Kerra asks. Thinking for a moment as she rocks and pats Marlee, Lacie explains, *"Well, it's not a real toy, it's not colorful, it's used—and you can't wash it. Besides, my mom would kill me if she saw her granddaughter playing with junk!"* With this last remark, she laughs a little. *"Yeah,"* responds Kerra, *"my mom had the same reaction when she saw my kids playing with wooden spoons and empty cereal boxes! I told her that I gave them household things to play with because they're easy for babies to grasp and handle, and they give them the opportunity for some exploration. Plastic rattles are smooth, but wooden spoons feel a bit rougher, and cardboard boxes and tubes crinkle and crumple and give when a baby squeezes them. Children can learn a lot through their senses when they play with different kinds of materials."* **(This was Step 3: Exchange information.)**

*"And, what did your mom say to that?" Lacie asks. "Well,"
continues Kerra, "she said she still preferred 'real toys' for her
grandchildren, but she also began to watch the children more
and see just how much they gravitated toward everyday things
like wrapping paper, shoelaces, measuring spoons. She'd rather
they play with the rattles and real toys she gave them—and they
do sometimes—but, seeing how much they liked the pots and
pans and butter tubs, she stopped trying to take them away."
"Yeah," says Lacie, "well I guess Marlee does like the cardboard
tube, maybe because it's so light and 'squeezey.' I remember
now that I used to like to use a tube like that as a horn, and it
would drive my mom crazy to hear me blowing through it!"
Laughing, Kerra replies, "I still like to do that!"* **(This was Step 4:
Look at the problem from the child's viewpoint.)**

*"Okay, let's see," Kerra says. "The problem seems to be . . .
what? (She pauses to think.) You're concerned about Marlee
playing with towel tubes because they're not real or colorful
toys, they can't be washed, and they look junky. I am concerned about providing children with materials that offer them
a variety of qualities to explore. And Marlee seems to like the
towel tube because it is light and squeezey." "And she cried
when I took it away," adds Lacie. "Well, she does choose things
that interest her," comments Kerra.* **(This was Step 5: Restate the
problem.)**

*"So," continues Kerra, "what can we do about this prob-
lem?" Both women think for a bit. "Let's just list a bunch of
possibilities and then decide together what might work," says
Kerra. (She knows from experience that making such a list can
help to free each person from clinging to one particular idea.)
"Okay," says Lacie. Kerra finds a nearby clipboard she uses for
jotting down child observations, and together they brainstorm
and list the following ideas:*

- *Don't offer any towel tubes to children.*

- *Offer towel tubes, but replace them after a child has handled them.*

- *Continue to offer towel tubes along with other, conventional toys and household items.*

- *Replace towel tubes with other tube-like things that are light and squeezable, perhaps plastic tubing.*

- *Offer colored cardboard tubes that are a bit sturdier and look nicer (like the ones from a local recycling agency). Check to make sure dyes are nontoxic.*

Both Lacie and Kerra are interested in the last idea. They decide to focus on it, and as they discuss it further, they come up with this strategy to try: For younger children like Marlee, who still put everything in their mouth, replace the towel tubes with sturdier, more colorful cardboard tubes. These are just as easy to grasp but do not deteriorate as readily as the towel tubes when wet. Provide older children with both the towel tubes and the colorful cardboard tubes. Replace all tubes daily. (This was Step 6: Generate ideas for solutions, and choose one together.)

Later that month, as they talk about how the new cardboard tubes are working, Lacie asks about the possibility of bringing up the topic of using household materials as playthings at a meeting for parents and grandparents so her mom could hear from Kerra about why Marlee and other children like to play with everyday household things as well as regular baby toys. "I've talked with my mom, but it would help if she heard it from you!" says Lacie. "Yes, I'd like to do that," says Kerra. She talks with her team member about the idea, and they decide to include this topic in their next parent (and grandparent) meeting. (This was Step 7: Be prepared to follow up the problem.)

As you engage in problem solving with parents (and other adults in your program), it is important to be aware of likely outcomes. Gonzalez-Mena (1992, p. 4) described four typical outcomes to anticipate:

- *"Resolution through understanding and negotiation. Both parties see the other's perspective; both parties compromise."* This is what happened between Lacie and Kerra: They eliminated towel tubes for young infants and replaced them with sturdier, more colorful cardboard tubes; they also provided the sturdier tubes, along with towel tubes, for the older children.

- *"Resolution through caregiver education. The caregiver sees the parent's perspective; the caregiver changes."* This kind of resolution would have occurred had Kerra and Lacie agreed to simply remove the towel tubes, the first idea on their list.

- *"Resolution through parent education. The parent sees the caregiver's perspective; the parent changes."* A resolution of this sort would have occurred had Kerra and Lacie agreed to carry out the third idea on their list—continuing to offer towel tubes along with other, conventional toys and household items.

- *"No resolution. . . . [at best, this can mean that] each has a view of the other's perspective; each is sensitive and respectful but unable, because of differing values and beliefs, to change his or her stance."* For example, Kerra might have continued to offer towel tubes to all children while making an effort not to offer them in Marlee's collection of playthings. Lacie, though still disliking the idea of seeing children playing with "junk," might have ceased complaining, because her own child was usually not playing with towel tubes.

Together, parents and caregivers in this program came up with a solution to children's intense desire to play with their parents' car and house keys—a generous supply of safe key sets for children, and free advertising for the local bank!

While another outcome is also possible—no resolution and no mutual respect for each other's views—this situation creates a tension between parent and caregiver that is bound to affect the child. Had this happened between Kerra and Lacie, Kerra might well have resorted to "resolution through caregiver education" and removed all the paper-towel tubes. For the sake of her ongoing relationship with Lacie, she might have bowed to Lacie's wishes, reasoning that the children will not be seriously harmed by the removal of this one type of plaything when they have such a wide range of other interesting materials to explore and play with. She might also have reasoned that in the long run, Lacie, once she begins to trust that Kerra hears her, will in turn be more willing to trust and hear Kerra. As Abbey Griffen (1998) observed,

> Negotiating conflicts can be very useful in building relationships. The process brings out issues that might undermine the relationship-building process if the parent were silent or, conversely, if the caregiver acquiesced to demands she could not manage well within the group care setting. However, effective negotiation requires a readiness to exchange the habit of being "nice" for the challenge of honest dialog. Knowledge, skill and experience are needed. First and most important, some degree of consistency between home and child care program and trust between parent and care-

giver help each to better meet the needs of the individual baby. Honest dialog helps parents feel respected and listened to. Second, caregivers who are accepting of individual differences among their families help parents cope with the intense emotions experienced when leaving their vulnerable baby in the arms of someone else for long hours during their work week. Finally, caregivers have strong feelings about their caregiving practices and about the individual baby. They need to establish themselves as worthy of respect both by listening and by being clear about their policies. (p. 29)

Whatever the outcome of any occasional disagreement, the caregiver-parent partnership will remain intact if caregivers make a consistent effort to acknowledge the caregiver/parent role difference, communicate openly, focus on parents' strengths, and take a problem-solving approach to conflict. Following these guidelines helps both caregivers and parents to keep an eye on their common goal—to provide a consistently supportive environment for children at home and at the center.

Caregivers' Strategies for Engaging Parents as Partners

Caregivers establish partnerships with parents because they value and respect parents as the major contributors to children's health and well-being. They recognize that their own effectiveness as caregivers and early educators and the ongoing vitality of the center both hinge on whether there is successful teamwork between parent and caregiver. The following strategies help caregivers engage parents as partners and center participants:

- Create a welcoming environment for families.
- Establish a family-centered enrollment process.
- Exchange child observations, but leave the "firsts" to parents.
- Encourage parents to participate in the center.

Create a welcoming environment for families

One way you can prepare the physical setting for caregiver-parent collaboration is to set up a family-oriented space or room somewhere between the center's entrance and the children's rooms. It can be furnished comfortably (with chairs, tables, shelves, coat hooks, a telephone, a sink, a microwave,

This mom enjoys the beginning of her child's day at the center. Today, she spends time with her daughter in the family space just outside the infant room, in the infant eating area, and at the "hello-goodbye" gate.

and access to a bathroom, for example). This transitional area resembles a town square or cafe where parents can easily meet and mingle; sit down with their children, other parents, caregivers, and staff members; eat a sandwich; nurse an infant; make a list or a phone call; or simply collect themselves before leaving. Having a space like this (in addition to or in place of the reception area described in Chapter 3, p. 109) encourages parents to take their time as they enter and leave and to look forward to the center as an enjoyable place for their children *and* themselves.

Caregivers, and the rest of your center staff, can make mental preparations for parents, as well. Before they meet a single family member, they might review their own professional commitment to the guidelines for building effective partnerships with parents (p. 325). Then, from the first contact with parents, genuinely welcome them to your center. Consistently approach parents and family members in a friendly, respectful, nonjudgmental manner, and take the time to introduce parents to one another. When parents are upset, make every effort to remain calm, empathic, and thoughtful. In short, this means seeing parents not as competitors or irritants, but as co-players in the drama of childrearing. Thus, with a welcoming attitude and readiness to listen and converse, you will be able to draw parents into the communal heart of the center.

Establish a family-centered enrollment process

Parents typically experience strong emotion over leaving their baby or toddler in an away-from-home care setting. They see this as shattering the 'round-the-clock intimacy they have established at home with their child. Experienced caregivers anticipate parents' feelings and consider them to be a routine part of the enrollment process. It is important to realize, however, that to the parent who is feeling sad, guilty, fearful, or anxious, these emotions are anything *but* routine—they may, in fact, be overwhelming! At the same time, the young child may also feel anxious and upset. With no sense of time, an infant or toddler has no way of knowing, initially, that his or her parent will actually return, and so the child may feel abandoned. Griffen (1998) drew attention to the vulnerability of parents and children at this time:

> Infants enter child care as early as 6 weeks after birth. Many more enter at 3 months, which corresponds to the 12 weeks of job-protected leave guaranteed by the Family Medical Leave Act as well as many state regulations and child care program policies. Thus, parents and caregivers meet at a fragile time—a time when parents' emotions are high. They are just getting to know their new baby. They are often sleep deprived. Protective feelings and grief

Parents and children have strong feelings about the daily transition from home to center. This toddler is happy when her mom stays to play with her at the center, distressed when her mom leaves, and finally, comforted by her "blankie" and her friend.

at separation are primal feelings that parents express in different
ways. As T. Berry Brazelton observed in *Working and Caring*
(1985), some parents placing young infants in child care openly
express their feelings, some seem almost aloof as they gird themselves for the inevitable, and some are demanding and overbear-
ing in an effort to maintain control. The leaving magnifies their
fears. (p. 24)

A family-centered enrollment process acknowledges parents' and children's sorrows and fears and their manner of coping with them. While these
feelings cannot be eliminated, caregivers can provide families with the time
and support they need to regain their emotional balance and to incorporate
the life of the center into their daily routine. To avoid unnecessarily abrupt
and painful transitions from home to center, following these steps can guide
the enrollment process in a sustained and gradual way: (1) recall your own
transitions; (2) organize enrollment materials; (3) host visits to the center;
(4) make a home visit, if possible; and (5) support and learn from the
parent-child pair through a series of settling-in visits to the center.

✦ *Recall your own transitions*

The enrollment process begins before you ever see a parent, with your own
recollections of the separations and transitions you have experienced. Take
time to remember how you felt, for example, at some time when you were
aware of being all by yourself, without a parent, sibling, or family member.
Perhaps it was your first time being cared for by a new babysitter or your
first day in child care, preschool, kindergarten, or first grade; it may have
been your first time at home by yourself after school or in the evening; it
may have been your first overnight stay away from home. If you are a parent, recall how you felt when you left your own child (or children) in someone else's care, when you left your child at school for the first time, or when
your child moved out of the house to live somewhere else.

Share with your team member some stories about these personal experiences and the feelings you had at the time. Talk together about the support
you received or wish you had received during these times. When you have
done this, remember that the parents and children you will be welcoming
into your center will come to you with similar stories and feelings. Use your
own memories to remind yourself to acknowledge their feelings and provide
the calm support and reassurance that you, from your own experience, know
might help them through this transition. Your goal, after all, is to create
pleasant memories for the children who are making their transition from
home to your center.

✦ *Organize enrollment materials*

One way to reassure anxious parents is to provide them with clear information about your program. To facilitate the enrollment process, put together a packet, file, or booklet containing all the information and permission forms, policies, and descriptive statements pertinent to your program (the forms should include any that your state legally requires parents to sign). Providing such materials to parents in this way reassures them that you are responsible and organized and lets them know from the outset what policies and educational ideas guide your center's approach to children's care and early learning. In general, parent enrollment materials might include your own parent-friendly versions of the following:

- *Information and permission forms* requesting family data (parent/ guardian names, addresses, phone numbers; child's name and birth date); a record of child's immunizations, allergies, illnesses, medications, insurance, emergency phone numbers/contacts; signed release forms (for outings, on-site photographs, administering medications); current information about the child's eating and sleeping and toileting habits, favorite play and comfort items, daily routine

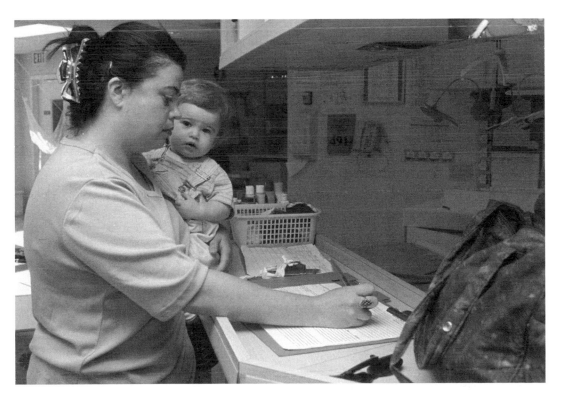

This parent knows that part of her daily routine at the center is to sign in, to indicate her anticipated return time, and after talking with her child's caregiver, to make note of any special requests or concerns for her child that day.

- *A list of center policies* regarding tuition, fees, and payment schedules; center hours, attendance, arrival and departure times, sign-in and sign-out, and policies for children who are ill; staffing, primary caregivers, caregiver teams, continuity of care, group size, staff-child ratios, and staff schedules

- *A list of parent/center responsibilities* regarding provision of diapers, nursing, bottles and formula, food, medications, clean clothes, bedding

- *A center calendar* including, for example, holidays, staff-training days, staff vacations, parent meetings, family potlucks and outings

- *A program overview* including, for example, statements about active learning, supportive adult-child interactions, space and materials for active learners, the overall daily schedule, and individualized caregiving routines, as well as statements describing, for example, the center's approach to inclusion of comfort items and other reminders of home for children, daily outdoor play, learning to use the toilet, using a problem-solving approach to conflict (among toddlers, among adults)

- *A list of the enrollment-process steps* including initial center visit, review of enrollment materials, decision to enroll, possible home visit, and parent-child settling-in visits

Based on these materials, you may draw up an agreement or contract for parents to sign. You may also translate materials into languages other than English, depending on the ethnic background of the families in the community you serve. However you decide to organize and present them, the purpose of these materials is not to overwhelm parents with paperwork, but to let them know up front that the care and learning community they and their child are joining takes its responsibilities to children and families very seriously and that the health, well-being, and active engagement of their child is your first priority.

✦ *Host visits to the center*

On their first visit, parents come to see what your program looks and feels like and to talk with you about their child. It is important to give parents a tour of the setting so they can see and talk with you about where children eat, sleep, and have their diapers changed; where mothers can nurse their infants; where children play with materials, climb, and explore both indoors and outdoors; how caregivers organize and store diapers, bottles, and medicines; how caregiver teams interact with children; and how caregivers keep track of children's individual schedules and regularly record their observations of each child.

Before enrollment, visiting the center together helps children and parents to get a sense of how it might feel to spend some or all of the day there.

It is also important to set aside time during this visit to talk with parents about their own concerns, desires, and goals for their child. Find out what they are looking for in a center and how your center can support and work toward these goals. You will also want to review the materials in the parent packet, answer any immediate questions about them, and encourage parents to read them at home and to call with any further questions they might have.

Once it becomes clear that parents have decided to enroll their child in your program (whether on this visit or on a follow-up enrollment visit), take time to talk with parents about the transition process itself. Encourage them to talk about their own early transitions, and share your own transition experiences and feelings. The idea is not to alarm parents or to scare them away, but to gently guide them through the process of leaving their child with you. Explain that the reason you are asking them to make a series of settling-in visits with their child is to deal as effectively as possible with the feelings they may encounter. Although these visits may take some planning on everyone's part, they go a long way toward easing both parent and child into center participation.

Children benefit when they are included in the visit-planning process. Ask parents to talk with their children ahead of time about visiting the center together, just as they would talk about an upcoming visit from Grandma or a trip to the store. An enthusiastic, straightforward statement, such as "Tomorrow we're going to the Tall Trees Center to play with some other children," lets the child know that a new adventure is imminent. Even though the child may not be able to understand the parent's words, he or she can pick up on a parent's positive attitude and confidence. Suggest that on the day before the visit, parents may wish to walk or drive by the center with their child and say something like "Here's Tall Trees Center where you'll be playing with the other children." This gives the child a glimpse of the center before the actual visit and allows parent and child to gradually approach the idea of going to the center. (This is similar to an adult, on the day before a job interview, going to the interview site to find out where it is and how long it takes to get there.) When parents do make the first visit to the center with their child, ask them to bring a diaper bag packed with diapers, a change of clothes, some food the child normally eats, and the child's favorite comfort items. Let them know that these familiar items serve to comfort and reassure the child in the new setting, and that they also help you, the caregiver, learn what the child likes and is accustomed to.

Introduce prospective parents to others whose children are enrolled at the center. This gives prospective parents the opportunity to ask questions they might be hesitant to ask you and to find out about the program from another parent's perspective. Some "veteran" parents may even be willing to be "buddies" to new parents to support them through the settling-in process.

✦ *Make a home visit, if possible*

While not always easy or even possible to schedule around conflicting work and family demands, a getting-acquainted visit to the child's home at this time helps to ease the transition from home to center for everyone involved. Parents and children feel more at ease on their own turf, and caregivers see for themselves what the child is used to, what feels like home to the child. Also, the child sees the parent and caregiver together in a familiar setting.

Try to schedule home visits at a time when the child is awake. While these visits do not have to be lengthy, they need to long enough to begin to discover what the child likes to do—where he or she likes to explore, play, eat, sleep, and so forth. For example, caregiver Kim, on a visit to infant Bobby's family home, is told by Bobby's mom that "Bobby never stays covered when he sleeps, so I always make sure he sleeps in something warm." Mom shows Kim one of Bobby's blanket sleepers and agrees to send one along with Bobby for naps at the center.

As early childhood specialist Barbara Tizard and her colleagues (1983) observed about their experiences with home visits,

Home visits allow parents, caregivers, and children to get to know one another in a setting where the child is thoroughly at ease.

This informal contact at home made it very easy to relate to both children and parents when we later met them at [the center]. We do not think that home visits should be regarded as a way of finding out about a family's 'problems'—[caregivers] are not social workers. The visits should rather be seen as an opportunity for gaining and giving useful positive information, and laying the basis of a friendly relationship between caregiver, parent, and child. (p. 130)

✦ *Support and learn from the parent-child pair through settling-in visits to the center*

If, over a period of several weeks, the parent and child make a series of visits to the center together, parents can use these visits to continue the process of teaching caregivers about their child. The caregiver can watch the parent to learn how the child is accustomed to being held, fed, changed, and put to sleep. Caregiver Kim, for example, sees that Bobby's mom gently strokes his back or arm as she holds him, so when Kim receives the baby from his mom, she repeats this familiar, soothing gesture. The caregiver watches the

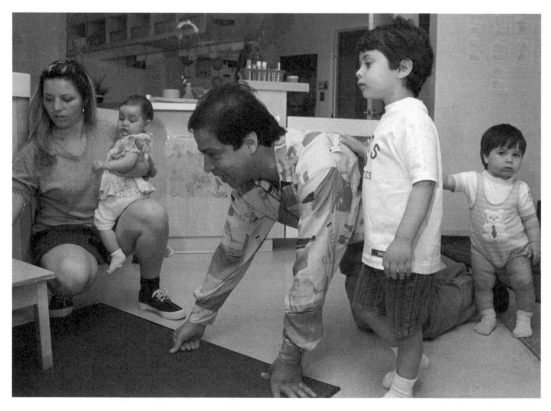

On this settling-in visit, Dad and Big Brother play a major role!

child and also gathers information from the parent to learn about the child's temperament and his likes and dislikes: "Bobby's pretty easygoing most of the time," his mom tells Kim, "but he likes to be bathed by hand, not with a washcloth! That's one thing he's particular about."

The caregiver, in turn, shares her child observations with the parent: "Look," says Kim to Bobby's mom, "Bobby rolls over with no trouble at all. He looks very comfortable on his blanket on the floor." Bobby, in the meantime, sees his mom and Kim together, senses their ease with each other, and is free to turn his attention to the materials and children who have caught his eye.

On a very practical note, these visits are also an ideal time to take photographs of the parent and child together. The child can look at these later on, when the parent is away, and the photos can be put on the bulletin board with photos of other center families.

The first time the parent does leave the child with the caregiver, the parent may simply go down the hallway to chat with another parent in the "town square." Though the child and the parent may both feel some anxiety, by this time they both feel fairly comfortable with the caregiver, the setting, and the routine. This familiarity gives them a confidence and reassurance that helps counter their sadness at parting. Following this series of parent-child visits, when parents finally do leave the child at the center, they will still feel a wrench but perhaps one that is more manageable than if they had dropped off their child and left on the very first visit.

The number of settling-in visits varies from family to family. Some families may adjust to center life in less than 2 weeks. Others may take somewhat longer before they feel ready to leave their child in your care. Still others may skip the visits altogether because of circumstances beyond their control. One thing we know for certain, however, is that these visits ease the transition from home to center for children, parents, and caregivers. They also build the trusting relationships on which the child's ongoing well-being and learning depend. Again, Griffen (1998) has underlined the importance of these settling-in visits:

> The time before the baby enters child care and the first weeks and months of care are a time when it is critical for parents and caregivers to form a trusting relationship that allows concerns, fears and desires to be shared. It is vital that the caregiver learn about the individual baby from the family. In their initial meetings and daily communications with parents, caregivers gather information about the baby's health history, current sleep pattern, temperament, and preferences for holding, soothing in preparation for sleep, and transition into wakefulness. The time they take to understand

the culture and childrearing beliefs of the family and clarify the philosophy, policies, and daily routines of the home or center lays the foundation for identifying and negotiating differences before they become conflicts. When they lay the foundations for open communication from the beginning, parents and caregivers become each other's best source of support; when they fail to build such a foundation, tensions between them are bound to arise. (p. 24)

Exchange child observations, but leave the "firsts" to parents

Once children are enrolled, caregivers continue to build their relationships with parents by exchanging daily child observations. As we have noted, caregivers attentively watch and listen to children throughout the day, and during their daily planning, they discuss and interpret these observations and use them to plan for the next day. (See again the observations caregivers recorded for Jamal, pp. 318–319). Consequently, caregivers have a wealth of stories and child observations to share with parents. ("Today, at choice time, Bobby held on to the red wool ball. He waved it around and even held it with his feet!") Hearing these stories helps parents picture and participate vicariously in the child's life at the center.

At the same time, parents alone know what their children do and feel from the time they leave the center until they return the next day, the next Monday, or after a vacation, so caregivers need to have parents fill in their knowledge gaps. ("Bobby is sitting up now, all by himself!" Bobby's mom tells Kim one morning. "We didn't believe it. One minute he was lying on his back as usual, and the next time I looked, he had gotten himself into a sitting position!") Parents and caregivers rely on each other to stay attuned to the child and to provide care that is as consistent as possible between home and center. (Another morning, Bobby's mom tells Kim, "Bobby just started eating bananas this weekend. He really likes them, so I'm leaving some bananas for him today.") Parents also take great comfort in learning about their children's relationships with other children—for example, how Jovan offered a piece of his clay to Yomena, or how Kayla started up a game of peek-a-boo with Jared by hiding behind and peeking around the wall of the climber.

Note that in the previous paragraph, Bobby's mom reports a "first" to Bobby's caregiver: *Bobby's first time sitting up by himself*. Reporting major milestones like this should belong to parents. Therefore, make a point of *not* sharing the ones you, the caregiver, observe at the center—a child's first independent step or first word, for example. By keeping these observations to yourself, you grant these momentous occasions to parents and family members. If a child takes a first step at the center, he or she will take another step at home the same day or the next. Unless a parent specifically asks you

At the beginning of the day, Mom helps Regina off with her coat. Then she shares a story with Regina's caregivers about what Regina did at home the night before. Later, at the end of the day, her caregivers share this anecdote with Regina's mom: "At choice time, Regina looked closely at the I Spy book with (caregiver) Melody. Then, when she saw it laying on the floor, she pushed it toward Julia and said 'Py boo!' (for Spy book)."

whether you've observed some specific development, wait until you hear about its occurrence from parents, then share your subsequent observations: "Hey," Kim greets Jamal's mom at the end of the day, "Jamal took some steps all by himself today, just as you saw him do last night at home!"

Try to relate some child observations in each of your interactions with a child's parents. Share child observations when the parent brings the child to the center. ("Yesterday, Queen crawled up and down the rocking-boat steps, so I'm going to watch to see if she returns to them today.") And do the same when the child is picked up at the end of the day. ("Nikki spent a long time this morning looking at herself in the mirror.") Call parents at work to relate a story about their child. ("Remember when you told me this morning that Bobby was babbling at the cat?" Kim says to Bobby's mom over the phone. "Well, listen—he's babbling to Mallory!" She holds the phone near Bobby so his mom can hear his conversation with Mallory.)

As you record child observations at team planning or during the day, write an anecdote on a file card and put it in the child's tub or cubby for the parent to read and take along at the end of the day. Some centers have journals that travel to home and back with the child each day. Both caregivers and parents record their brief observations in this journal on a regular basis. For example, Jamal's mom writes, "Jamal stayed up late last night playing with his cousin. He may be cranky today." Yvonne writes back, "Jamal fell asleep at lunchtime today and took an extra long nap. At outside time he crawled in and out of a large carton, full of energy once again!" Journals can also include photographs of children as well as children's own marks and scribbles. For example, one day, older toddler Megan, who was used to hearing her mom say "I'm putting this in your journal for Ellie" and then seeing her mom and her caregiver trade the journal back and forth, brought over to her mom a strand of yarn she was playing with. She laid it on the journal page her mom was writing on and said "Li Li"—her name for Ellie, her caregiver. Her mom taped the yarn to the page and wrote, "Megan was playing with this and wanted me to put it in the journal for you."

Share child observations during parent conferences and home visits, when you might want to give parents a selection of the anecdotes you have collected. These anecdotes will provide a basis for discussing the child's physical, social, emotional, language, and cognitive development; they will also be a way of sharing an appreciation of the child's interests and strengths.

Encourage parents to participate in the center

Once parents have spent some time in the center getting their child settled in, they themselves will most likely feel at home in the setting and comfortable with their decision to enroll their child. Parents' participation in the center need not end there. The benefits of developing ongoing parent involvement in your program are many: Parents and caregivers can strengthen the trust and respect they have for each other and grow together in their ability to provide consistent care and education for children. Parents and caregivers can learn to understand child development issues from each other's viewpoints and to appreciate the time and energy it takes to fulfill each other's roles. Parents are able to see and appreciate their children's abilities to interact with peers. Children can feel reassured because they see their parents as being deeply connected to both home and center. "Experienced" parents can

When parents participate in the program, children come to see their parents as being deeply connected to both home and center.

support "new" parents by giving them a parent's perspective on your program. Parents are able to form a network to support one another as they go through the various surprises and stages of parenthood; being part of such a network can help parents to work through some of the issues that inevitably arise in child care programs ("That child is biting my child!" "I don't want my child to play with her food like So-and-So does!"). Parents with real ties to the center are often willing to offer their time, energy, and resources to assist the center by, for example, donating supplies or helping to make physical improvements. They are also more willing to advocate for the center and for early childhood issues in the larger community.

Experience has shown that, as well as producing all these benefits, parent participation in the life of the center can also raise certain issues. Children may behave differently when their parents are present; for example, they may become more clingy, stubborn, or energetic. Children may not wish to share their parents with other children. Parents present in your setting may discipline or interact with children in a manner inconsistent with your program's philosophy of promoting children's sensory-motor learning, providing adult support of child choices, and using a problem-solving approach to conflict. Parents may require attention that pulls a caregiver away from the children in her care. Caregivers may face parent questions they cannot answer or requests they cannot meet. Although these or similar issues will arise from time to time, they are not reason enough to avoid parent participation. Rather, it is important to acknowledge any potential thorny issues, to talk as a team about ways others have worked through them, and to remain calm when any such issue does arise, because after all, it's another opportunity for adults to do some collaborative problem solving!

With the benefits and issues of parent participation in mind, here are a number of options for participation that an infant-toddler center may wish to offer parents:

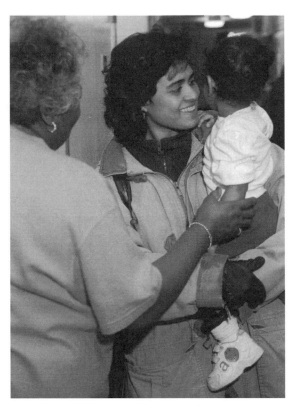

Caregivers work in partnership with parents, exchanging child observations and striving to provide consistency between children's at-home and away-from-home experiences.

- *Join your child at the center*—this might include spending 20–30 minutes with your child at the beginning or end of the day—changing a diaper, nursing, feeding a bottle, playing with toys, or reading a storybook; spending time at noon eating lunch with your child; playing outside with your child at outdoor time; joining group time or offering a group-time experience, such as singing, playing a musical instrument, exploring clay, telling a story, cooking with older toddlers; accompanying your child on an outing or special event; if you are a student, joining your child at the center between your own classes.

- *Attend parent-caregiver meetings*—this might include workshops and discussions led by parents, caregivers, or guest speakers and designed around topics raised by parents or around child development issues;[14] family and center potlucks, picnics, and outings to local events or celebrations; parent-caregiver conferences; home visits.

---

[14]For some suggestions on conducting workshops for parents of older toddlers, see Graves (2000) in the Related Reading list on p. 354.

- *Participate in center-related service projects*—this might include fund-raising events; gardening, grounds improvement, or materials procurement (collecting natural/household items for play or making curtains, blankets, pillows, bibs, smocks, play dough, blocks); updating children's photo albums; repairing toys/ equipment; providing technical assistance with computers, accounting, the parent library, the toy-lending library; serving on the center advisory board, the preschool or kindergarten liaison committee, the community relationships committee, the welcoming committee.

- *Read or write*—this might include reading or contributing to your child's home-center journal; center newsletter articles, notices, and reminders; parent bulletin boards about family and center events, parenting and child development topics, recreational opportunities, upcoming community events; books and articles in the parent library.

This mom takes a moment to jot a note in her child's home-center journal before leaving for work.

However you encourage parents to participate in your center, the relationships that result from these shared experiences strengthen the vital three-way bond between child, parent, and caregiver.

Overall, thoughtful caregiver teams and caregiver-parent partnerships create a strong framework of support for infants and toddlers in child care settings. Working closely together, these key adults observe, interact with, and plan for children in ways that interweave the elements of successful High/Scope infant-toddler programs—active learning and key experiences, supportive adult-child interactions, safe and inviting environments for sensory-motor exploration and play, and child-centered daily schedules and caregiving routines. In such programs, our very youngest children have the opportunity to thrive—they can depend on their caregivers and families for the tender care and early learning that will help sustain them through the rest of their lives.

Caregiver Teamwork and Parent Partnership: A Summary

The caregiver team

- ❑ Remains together from one year to the next
- ❑ Meets for daily team planning
- ❑ Practices open communication
- ❑ Makes joint decisions about
  - ❑ Space and materials
  - ❑ Schedules and routines
  - ❑ Roles and responsibilities
- ❑ Observes children throughout the day
- ❑ Discusses, interprets, and records child observations, using the key experiences as a guide
- ❑ Plans ways to support individual children

The caregiver-parent partnership

- ❑ Caregivers follow certain guidelines in working with parents:
  - ❑ Recognize role separation.
  - ❑ Practice open communication.
  - ❑ Focus on parents' strengths.
  - ❑ Use a problem-solving approach to conflict.
- ❑ Caregivers create a welcoming environment for families.
  - ❑ Establish room or space for families.
  - ❑ Approach families in a friendly, respectful manner.
- ❑ Caregivers establish a family-centered enrollment process.
  - ❑ They recall their own transitions.
  - ❑ They organize enrollment materials, including information and permission forms, center policies, parent/center responsibilities, center calendar, program overview, list of enrollment-process steps.
  - ❑ They host visits to the center.
  - ❑ They make a home visit, if possible.
  - ❑ They support and learn from the parent-child pair through settling-in visits.
- ❑ Caregivers exchange observations with parents, but leave "firsts" to families.
- ❑ Caregivers encourage parents to participate in the center.
  - ❑ Parents join their child at the center.
  - ❑ Parents attend parent-caregiver meetings.
  - ❑ Parents participate in center-related projects.
  - ❑ Parents read or write center-related materials.

References

Bove, Chiara. 1999. "Welcoming the Child Into Child Care." *Young Children* 54(2, March): 32–34.

Brazelton, T. Berry. 1985. *Working and Caring*. Reading, MA: Addison-Wesley/Lawrence.

Bronfenbrenner, Urie. 1985. "The Parent/Child Relationship and Our Changing Society." In *Parents, Children, and Change*, ed. Eugene L. Arnold, pp. 45–57. Lexington, MA: Lexington Books.

Gerecke, Katie. 1998. "Classroom Adaptations for Children With Special Needs." *High/Scope Extensions* (October): 1–5

Gonzalez-Mena, Janet. 1992. "Taking a Culturally Sensitive Approach in Infant-Toddler Programs." *Young Children* 47(2, January): 4–9.

Gonzalez-Mena, Janet, and Dianne Widmeyer Eyer. 1993. *Infants, Toddlers, and Caregivers*. Mountain View, CA: Mayfield.

Greenman, Jim. 1988. *Caring Spaces, Learning Places: Children's Environments That Work*. Redmond, WA: Exchange Press.

Griffen, Abbey. 1998. "Infant/Toddler Sleep in the Child Care Context: Patterns, Problems, and Relationships." *Zero to Three* (October/November): 24–29.

High/Scope Child Observation Record (COR) for Infants and Toddlers, field test ed. 1999. Ypsilanti, MI: High/Scope Educational Research Foundation.

Jacobson, Linda. 1999. "Most Child Care 'Adequate,' Latest Findings in Study Say." *Education Week* 18, no. 21 (February 3): 5.

National Institute of Child Health and Human Development (NICHD) Early Child Care Research Network. 1997. "The Effects of Infant Child Care on Infant Mother Attachment Security: Results of the NICHD Study of Early Child Care." *Child Development* 68 (5, October): 860–79.

Owen, Margaret T., for the NICHD Early Child Care Research Network. 1999. *Cognitive, Linguistic, and Social Consequences of Early Experience: Child Care and the Mother-Child Relationship*. Paper presented at the American Association for the Advancement of Science Conference, Anaheim, CA, January 24.

Satir, Virginia. 1988. *The New People Making*. Mountain View, CA: Science and Behavior Books.

Smith, Dee, Jeanne Goldhaber, and Catherine Cooper-Ellis. 1998. *Multiple Perspectives on the Benefits of Teacher Continuity and Infant and Toddler Centers*. Presentation at the National Association for the Education of Young Children conference, Toronto, November.

Tizard, Barbara, Jo Mortimore, and Bebb Burchell. 1983. *Involving Parents in Nursery and Infant School*. Ypsilanti, MI: High/Scope Press.

Related Reading

Accreditation Criteria and Procedures of the National Association for the Education of Young Children, 30–31. Washington, DC: NAEYC.

Bergman, Roberta, and Sue Gainer. 1998. "Making Multi-Age Groups Work." *Child Care Information Exchange* (November): 57–60.

Daniel, Jerlean E. 1998. "A Modern Mother's Place Is Wherever Her Children Are: Facilitating Infant and Toddler Mothers' Transitions in Child Care." *Young Children* 53(6, November): 4–12

Evans, Judith, and Ellen Ilfeld. 1982. *Good Beginnings: Parenting in the Early Years.* Ypsilanti, MI: High/Scope Press.

Gonzalez-Mena, Janet, and Anne Stonehouse. 2000. "High-Maintenance Parents: Responding in the Spirit of Partnership." *Child Care Information Exchange* (January/February): 10–12.

Graves, Michelle. 2000. *The Essential Parent Workshop Resource: The Teacher's Idea Book 4.* Ypsilanti, MI: High/Scope Press.

Hohmann, Mary, and David P. Weikart. 1995. *Educating Young Children: Active Learning Practices for Preschool and Child Care Programs.* Chapters 3 and 4. Ypsilanti, MI: High/Scope Press.

Koch, Patricia, and Marsha McDonough. 1999. "Improving Parent-Teacher Conferences Through Collaborative Conversations." *Young Children* 54(2, March): 11–15.

Lambie, Dolores Z., James T. Bond, and David P. Weikart. 1974. *Home Teaching With Mothers and Infants.* Ypsilanti, MI: High/Scope Press.

Lane, Mary B., and Sheila Signer. 1990. *Infant and Toddler Caregiving: A Guide to Creating Partnerships With Parents.* Sacramento CA: California Department of Education.

Mangione, Peter, ed. 1995. *Infant and Toddler Caregiving: A Guide to Culturally Sensitive Care.* Sacramento, CA: California Department of Education.

Sturm, Connie. 1997. "Creating Parent-Teacher Dialogue: Intercultural Communication in Child Care." *Young Children* 52(4, July): 34–38.

Workman, Susan H., and Jim A. Gage. 1997. "Family-School Partnerships: A Family Strengths Approach." *Young Children* 52(4, May): 10–14.

With the support of caregiver teams and caregiver-parent partnerships, very young children can experience both tender care and early learning. Having the opportunity for safe, secure active learning puts this little boy in the driver's seat!

Index

A

Art

B

C

Early Childhood Resources from High/Scope®

The High/Scope® Approach for Under Threes, U.S. Edition

This video shows caregivers interacting with infants and toddlers to support and extend their active learning explorations and discoveries. Filmed in the UK, the video illustrates the adaptability of the High/Scope® approach to any setting in which caregivers wish to support very young children at their level of development.

BK-F1045 $50.95

High/Scope® UK. Color video, 68 minutes. 1-57379-088-5

Good Beginnings: Parenting in the Early Years

Encourages parents and caregivers to develop effective parenting styles as they care for and enjoy their children. Contains a wealth of information about seven stages of development up to age 3. The authors' relaxed, easy-to-read style complements the book's charming photographs and attractive format.

BK-F1000 $15.95

J. Evans and E. Ilfeld. Soft cover, 200 pages. 0-931114-15-2

Community Self-Help: The Parent-to-Parent Program

Describes the impact of an actual peer-to-peer program on its target community. Warm vignettes of program participants.

BK-F1023 $4.95

Soft cover, 32 pages. 1-57379-061-3

A Guide to Developing Community-Based Family Support Programs

This guide will help those who design, implement, and evaluate family support programs. Presents readers with a thoughtful discussion of the options available and encourages them to base their choice on their community's situation, their clients' needs, and their program's resources. Amply illustrated with case studies and examples drawn from a wide variety of family support programs operated throughout the country over the past 15 years.

BK-F1044 $29.95

A. Epstein, M. Larner, and R. Halpern. Soft cover, 312 pages. 0-929816-92-7

The Ypsilanti-Carnegie Infant Education Project: Longitudinal Follow-Up

Focuses on the long-term impact of the parent-infant program on mother-child interactions, children's development as learners, and the relations between interaction and development.

BK-R1026 $12.95

A. S. Epstein and D. P. Weikart. Soft cover, 80 pages. 0-931114-06-3

Guides to Rhythmically Moving 1–4

These guides are the first in the *Rhythmically Moving* 1–9 series. Each guide lists the title, band, length, and origin for each *Rhythmically Moving* musical selection. Each guide also indicates whether the selection is vocal or instrumental, the major instruments played, and the number of repetitions of the selection. Guides include suggested activities for each selection.

Guide to Rhythmically Moving 1
BK-M1009 $9.95

E. B. Carlton and P. S. Weikart. Soft cover, 60 pages. 1-57379-004-4

Guide to Rhythmically Moving 2
BK-M1011 $9.95

E. B. Carlton and P. S. Weikart. Soft cover, 72 pages. 1-57379-015-X

Guide to Rhythmically Moving 3
BK-M1014 $9.95

E. B. Carlton and P. S. Weikart. Soft cover, 76 pages. 1-57379-028-1

Guide to Rhythmically Moving 4
BK-M1015 $9.95

E. B. Carlton and P. S. Weikart. Soft cover, 72 pages. 1-57379-049-4

Round the Circle: Key Experiences in Movement for Children

Offers age-appropriate movement activities. Use with music from the *Rhythmically Moving* series.

BK-M1000 $19.95

P. S. Weikart. Soft cover, 125 pages. 0-931114-39-X

High/Scope® Block Sets & Accessories

Blocks have long been part of the basic tools used in High/Scope® programs. Now, we are offering block sets and accessories that are specifically designed to complement the High/Scope® active learning approach to education. **Please see our Web site or color catalog for the list of blocks and prices.**

High/Scope® Board Book Collection

Favorite infant-toddler storybook collection selected by High/Scope® consultants. **Please see our Web site for the list of these and other recommended books and prices.**

Early Childhood Resources from High/Scope®

Educating Young Children: Active Learning Practices for Preschool and Child Care Programs

Written for early childhood practitioners and college students, this manual presents essential strategies adults can use to make active learning a reality in their programs. Describes key components of the adult's role: planning the physical setting and establishing a consistent daily routine; creating a positive social climate; and using High/Scope's 58 preschool key experiences to understand and support young children. Other topics include family involvement, daily team planning, creating interest areas, choosing appropriate materials, supporting the plan-do-review process, and arranging small- and large-group times. Offers numerous anecdotes, photographs, illustrations, real-life scenarios, checklists, and practical suggestions for adults. Reflects High/Scope's current research findings and over 30 years of experience.

BK-P1111 $39.95. Now available in Spanish **BK-L1016**
M. Hohmann & D. P. Weikart. Soft cover, Lavishly illustrated, 560 pages. 0-929816-91-9

Supporting Children in Resolving Conflicts

This important new video will teach you six problem-solving steps you can use to help children in conflict situations. The problem-solving process is demonstrated with real scenes of successful conflict resolution from a New York City Head Start Center and from the High/Scope® Demonstration Preschool.

BK-P1130 rental $10, purchase $49.95
Video guide included. Color video, 30 minutes. 1-57379-042-7

The Essential Parent Workshop Resource: The Teacher's Idea Book 4

If you are interested in presenting workshops for parents of preschoolers, you will be delighted with this collection of 30 original workshops. Packed with handouts and charts, presenters will find it easy to follow the workshop format, which includes intended goals, a list of necessary materials, an introduction and interactive opening activity, central ideas for discussion, scenarios for reflection and application of ideas, and follow-up plans that encourage parents to apply the information at home. It's all you need for practical, dynamic parent workshops.

BK-P1137 $25.95
M. Graves. Soft cover, photos, 180 pages. 1-57379-018-4

Supporting Young Learners 1: Ideas for Preschool and Day Care Providers

Provides practical answers to the day-to-day questions that arise in early childhood programs. The updated selections, which originally appeared in *Extensions*, deal with these and other timely issues in developmentally appropriate education.

BK-P1083 $25.95
N. Brickman & L. Taylor, Eds. Soft cover, 314 pages. 0-929816-34-X

Supporting Young Learners 2: Ideas for Child Care Providers and Teachers

Like its popular predecessor, this new book is packed with practical strategies and tips for making an active learning program the best it can be. Contains over 50 *Extensions*

articles that have been updated to reflect the latest thinking on the High/Scope® Curriculum. A must-have for early childhood professionals!

BK-P1105 $25.95
N. Brickman, Ed. Soft cover, photos, 328 pages. 1-57379-006-0

High/Scope® Extensions

Learn about the High/Scope® early childhood approach from High/Scope® consultants and trainers. Practical tips, suggestions, and updates for understanding and implementing the High/Scope® Curriculum and for training others to do so. Special features include **Classroom Hints, Ask Us, Network News, Trainer-to-Trainer, Computer Learning**.

BK-P1000 $30.95/year, overseas $33.95
N. Brickman, Ed. Newsletter of the High/Scope® Curriculum, 8 pages/issue, 6 issues/year. ISSN 0892-5135

High/Scope® ReSource: A Magazine for Educators

ReSource is a guide to High/Scope's activities, products, and services. Sign up for this *free* publication by calling 1-800-40-PRESS or using our Web sign up at *www.highscope.org.*

Let's Go Outside! Designing the Early Childhood Playground

This book contains all the information you need to design, equip, and maintain safe yet challenging playgrounds for young children. Use this book to help children capture the wonder and challenge of outdoor play.

BK-P1141 $19.95
T. Theemes, soft cover, 144 pages. 1-57379-082-6

**To order these or any other High/Scope® products, contact High/Scope® Press: phone (800)40-PRESS fax (800)442-4FAX
To see a full listing of High/Scope® products, visit our Web site: www.highscope.org**